INTERMEDIATE

MICROSOFT®

WINDOWS® 10

D0077385

CLEMENS

For Microsoft® Windows® updates, go to sam.cengage.com

CENGAGE
Learning®

Australia • Brazil • Mexico • Singapore • United Kingdom • United States

Illustrated Microsoft® Windows® 10—Intermediate
Barbara Clemens

SVP, GM Skills & Global Product Management:
  Dawn Gerrain

Product Director: Kathleen McMahon

Senior Product Team Manager: Lauren Murphy

Product Team Manager: Andrea Topping

Associate Product Manager: Melissa Stehler

Senior Director, Development: Marah Bellegarde

Product Development Manager: Leigh Hefferon

Senior Content Developer: Christina Kling-Garrett

Developmental Editor: MT Cozzola

Product Assistant: Erica Chapman

Marketing Director: Michele McTighe

Marketing Manager: Stephanie Albracht

Senior Production Director: Wendy Troeger

Production Director: Patty Stephan

Full Service Project Management:
  GEX Publishing Services

Art Director: Diana Graham

Text Designer: Joseph Lee, Black Fish Design

Cover Template Designer: Lisa Kuhn, Curio Press, LLC
  www.curiopress.com

Composition: GEX Publishing Services

For product information and technology assistance, contact us at
Cengage Learning Customer & Sales Support, 1-800-354-9706

For permission to use material from this text or product, submit all requests online at **www.cengage.com/permissions**
Further permissions questions can be emailed to
permissionrequest@cengage.com

Library of Congress Control Number: 2016932224
Soft-cover Edition ISBN: 978-1-305-65658-1
Loose-leaf Edition ISBN: 978-1-337-25181-5

Cengage Learning
20 Channel Center Street
Boston, MA 02210
USA

Cengage Learning is a leading provider of customized learning solutions with employees residing in nearly 40 different countries and sales in more than 125 countries around the world. Find your local representative at **www.cengage.com**

Cengage Learning products are represented in Canada by Nelson Education, Ltd.

For your course and learning solutions, visit **www.cengage.com**

Purchase any of our products at your local college store or at our preferred online store **www.cengagebrain.com**

Mac users: If you're working through this product using a Mac, some of the steps may vary. Additional information for Mac users is included with the Data Files for this product.

Disclaimer: Any fictional data related to persons or companies or URLs used throughout this text is intended for instructional purposes only. At the time this text was published, any such data was fictional and not belonging to any real persons or companies.

Disclaimer: The material in this text was written using Microsoft Windows 10 Professional and was Quality Assurance tested before the publication date. As Microsoft continually updates the Windows 10 operating system, your software experience may vary slightly from what is presented in the printed text.

Printed in the United States of America
Print Number: 01   Print Year: 2016

Brief Contents

Contents

Getting Started with Windows 10

CASE You are about to start a new job, and your employer has asked you to get familiar with Windows 10 to help boost your productivity. You'll need to start Windows 10 and Windows apps, work with on-screen windows and commands, get help, and exit Windows. *Note: With the release of Windows 10, Microsoft now provides ongoing updates to Windows instead of releasing new versions periodically. This means that Windows features might change over time, including how they look and how you interact with them. The information provided in this text was accurate at the time this book was published.*

Module Objectives

After completing this module, you will be able to:

- Start Windows 10
- Navigate the desktop and Start menu
- Point, click, and drag
- Start an app
- Work with a window

- Manage multiple windows
- Use buttons, menus, and dialog boxes
- Get help
- Exit Windows 10

Files You Will Need

No files needed.

Start Windows 10

Learning Outcomes
• Power on a computer
• Log into Windows 10

Windows 10 is an **operating system**, a type of program that runs your computer and lets you interact with it. A **program** is a set of instructions written for a computer. If your computer did not have an operating system, you wouldn't see anything on the screen after you turned it on. Windows 10 reserves a special area called a **Microsoft account** where each user can keep his or her files. In addition, a Microsoft account lets you use various devices and services such as a Windows Phone or Outlook.com. You may have more than one Microsoft account. When the computer and Windows 10 start, you need to **sign in**, or select your Microsoft account name and enter a password, also called **logging in**. If your computer has only one Microsoft account, you won't need to select an account name. But all users need to enter a **password**, a special sequence of numbers and letters. Users cannot see each other's account areas or services without the other person's password, so passwords help keep your computer information secure. After you sign in, you see the Windows 10 desktop, which you learn about in the next lesson. **CASE** ▶ *You're about to start a new job, so you decide to learn more about Windows 10, the operating system used at your new company.*

STEPS

1. Press your computer's power button, which might look like 🔘 or ▭▭▭, then if the monitor is not turned on, press its power button

On a desktop computer, the power button is probably on the front panel. On a laptop computer it's likely at the top of the keys on your keyboard. After a few moments, a **lock screen**, showing the date, time, and an image, appears. See **FIGURE 1-1**. The lock screen appears when you first start your computer and also if you leave it unattended for a period of time.

QUICK TIP
To temporarily see the password characters, move the pointer ⬚ over the eye icon 👁 next to the password box, then press and hold down the mouse button (or press and hold on a touch screen).

2. Press [Spacebar], or click once to display the sign-in screen

The **sign-in screen** shows your Windows account picture, name, and e-mail address, as well as a space to enter your Microsoft account password. The account may have your name assigned to it, or it might have a general name like "Student" or "Lab User."

3. Type your password, as shown in FIGURE 1-2, using uppercase and lowercase letters as necessary

If necessary, ask your instructor or technical support person what password you should use. Passwords are **case sensitive**, which means that if you type any letter using capital letters when lowercase letters are needed, or vice versa, Windows will not let you use your account. For example, if your password is "booklet43+", typing "Booklet43+" or "BOOKLET43+" will not let you enter your account. For security, Windows substitutes bullets for the password characters you type.

TROUBLE
If you see a message saying your password is incorrect, click OK to redisplay the password entry box. Type your password carefully, then click or tap →.

4. Click or tap the Submit button →

The Windows 10 desktop appears. See **FIGURE 1-3**.

Using a touch screen with Windows

Windows 10 was developed to work with touch-screen computers, including tablets and smartphones. See **FIGURE 1-4**. So if you have a touch-screen device, you'll find that you can accomplish many tasks with gestures instead of a mouse. A **gesture** is an action you take with your fingertip directly on the screen, such as tapping or swiping. For example, when you sign into Windows 10, you can tap the Submit button on the screen, instead of clicking it.

FIGURE 1-4: Touch-screen device

© vovan/Shutterstock.com

FIGURE 1-1: Lock screen with time and date

Your lock
screen contents
may differ

10:49
Friday, July 31

FIGURE 1-2: Typing your password

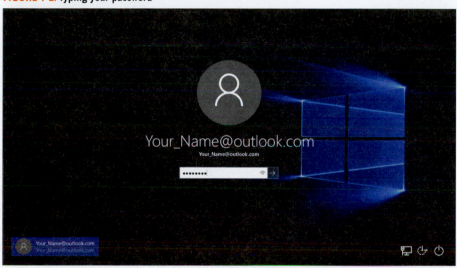

Your_Name@outlook.com
Your_Name@outlook.com

Your_Name@outlook.com
Your_Name@outlook.com

FIGURE 1-3: Windows 10 desktop

Recycle Bin

Ask me anything

3:03 PM
9/1/2017

Navigate the Desktop and Start Menu

Learning Outcomes
- Examine the desktop
- Open the Start menu
- View Start menu apps
- Close the Start menu

Every time you start your computer and sign in, the Windows 10 desktop appears. The **Windows 10 desktop** is an electronic work area that lets you organize and manage your information, much like your own physical desktop. The desktop contains controls that let you interact with the Windows 10 operating system. These controls are called its **user interface (UI)**. The Windows 10 user interface is called the **Windows 10 UI.** CASE ▶ *To become better acquainted with Windows 10, you decide to explore the desktop and Start menu.*

STEPS

TROUBLE

If you don't see the taskbar at the bottom of the screen, it may be set to automatically hide. Move the mouse pointer to the bottom edge of the screen to display it; on a touch screen, swipe up from the bottom of the screen.

1. **Examine the Windows 10 desktop**

   As shown in **FIGURE 1-5**, the desktop currently contains one item, an icon representing the **Recycle Bin**, an electronic wastepaper basket. You might see other icons, files, and folders placed there by previous users or by your school lab. The desktop lets you manage the files and folders on your computer. A **file** is a collection of stored information, such as a letter, video, or program. A **folder** is a container that helps you organize your files. A file, folder, or program opens in a window. You can open multiple windows on the desktop at once, and you can move them around so you can easily go back and forth between them. You work with windows later in this module. At the bottom of the screen is a bar called the **taskbar**, with buttons representing commonly used programs and tools. In a default Windows installation, the taskbar contains four buttons, described in **TABLE 1-1**. Also on the taskbar is the search box, which you can use to find an item on your computer or the Internet. On the right side of the status bar you see the **Notification area**, containing the time and date as well as icons that tell you the status of your computer. At the left side of the taskbar, you see the Start button. You click the **Start button** to display the **Start menu**, which lets you start the programs on your computer.

QUICK TIP

To add a button to the taskbar, right-click or tap and hold a Start menu item, then click or tap Pin to taskbar.

2. **Move the pointer to the left side of the taskbar, then click or tap the Start button** ⊞

   The Start menu appears, as shown in **FIGURE 1-6.** Your user account name and an optional picture appear at the top. The menu shows a list of often-used programs and other controls on the left, and variously-sized shaded rectangles called **tiles** on the right. Each tile represents an **app**, short for **application program**. Some tiles show updated content using a feature called **live tile**; for example, the Weather app can show the current weather for any city you choose. (Your screen color and tiles may differ from the figures shown here. Note that the screens in this book do not show live tiles.)

3. **Move the pointer near the bottom of the Start menu, then click or tap the All apps button**

   You see an alphabetical listing of all the apps on your computer. Only some of the apps are visible.

QUICK TIP

You can also click or tap any category letter to display a grid of clickable or tappable letters. Or just begin typing any program name, and it appears at the top of a list of choices.

4. **Move the pointer into the list, until the gray scroll bar appears on the right side of the list, place the pointer over the scroll box, press and hold down the mouse button, then drag to display the remaining programs; on a touch screen, swipe the list to scroll**

5. **Click or tap the Back button at the bottom of the Start menu**

   The previous listing reappears.

QUICK TIP

You can quickly open and close the Start menu by pressing ⊞ on your keyboard.

6. **Move the pointer back up over the desktop, then click or tap once to close the Start menu**

FIGURE 1-5: Windows 10 desktop

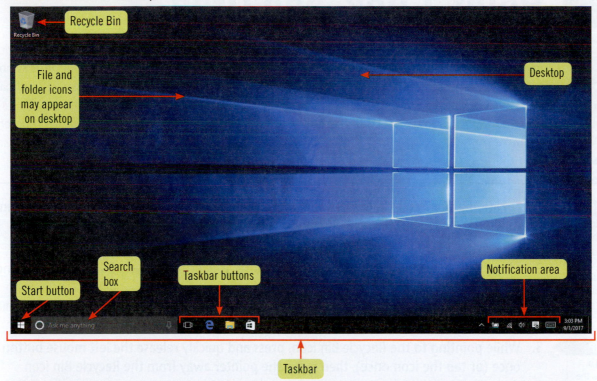

- Recycle Bin
- File and folder icons may appear on desktop
- Desktop
- Search box
- Taskbar buttons
- Notification area
- Start button
- Taskbar

FIGURE 1-6: Start menu

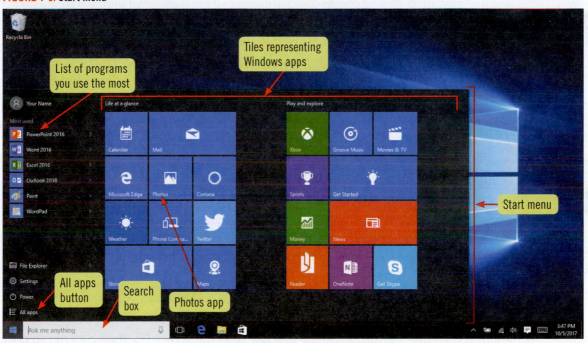

- List of programs you use the most
- Tiles representing Windows apps
- Start menu
- All apps button
- Search box
- Photos app

TABLE 1-1: Windows taskbar buttons

button	looks like	what it does
Task View		Shows miniatures of all open windows and lets you create multiple desktops, so you can switch from one to another
Microsoft Edge		Opens the Microsoft Edge web browser
File Explorer		Lets you explore the files in your storage locations
Store		Opens the Windows Store featuring downloadable apps, games, music, movies, and TV

Getting Started with Windows 10

Point, Click, and Drag

You communicate with Windows 10 using a variety of pointing devices (or, with a touch-screen device, your finger). A **pointing device** controls the movement of the **pointer**, a small arrow or other symbol that moves on the screen. Your pointing device could be a mouse, trackball, graphics tablet, or touchpad. There are five basic **pointing device actions** you use to communicate with your computer; see **TABLE 1-2**. Touch-screen users can tap, press, and tap and hold. **CASE** *You practice the basic pointing device actions.*

STEPS

1. **Locate the pointer ☐ on the desktop, then move your pointing device left, right, up, and down (or move your finger across a touch pad or screen)**

   The pointer shape ☐ is the **Select pointer**. The pointer moves in the same direction as your device.

2. **Move your pointing device so the Select pointer is over the Recycle Bin (if you are using a touch screen, skip this step)**

   You are **pointing to** the Recycle Bin icon. The icon becomes **highlighted**, looking as though it is framed in a box with a lighter color background. (Note that touch-screen users cannot point to items.)

3. **While pointing to the Recycle Bin icon, press and quickly release the left mouse button once (or tap the icon once), then move the pointer away from the Recycle Bin icon**

   You click or tap a desktop icon once to **select** it, which signals that you intend to perform an action. When an icon is selected, its background changes color and maintains the new color even when you point away from it.

4. **With a pointing device, point to (don't click) the Microsoft Edge button ☐ on the taskbar**

   The button becomes highlighted and an informational message called a **ScreenTip** identifies the program the button represents. ScreenTips are useful because they help you to learn about the tools available to you. **Microsoft Edge** is the new Microsoft web browser that lets you display and interact with webpages.

5. **If you are using a pointing device, move the pointer over the time and date in the notification area on the right side of the taskbar, read the ScreenTip, then click or tap once**

   A pop-up window appears, containing the current time and date and a calendar.

6. **Click or tap on the desktop, point to the Recycle Bin icon, then quickly click or tap twice**

   You **double-clicked** (or double-tapped) the icon. You need to double-click or double-tap quickly, without moving the pointer. A window opens, showing the contents of the Recycle Bin, as shown in **FIGURE 1-7**. The area at the top of the window is the title bar, which displays the name of the window. The area below the title bar is the **Ribbon**, which contains tabs, commands, and the Address bar. **Tabs** are groupings of **buttons** and other controls you use to interact with an object or a program.

7. **Click or tap the View tab**

   The buttons on that tab appear. Buttons act as **commands**, which instruct Windows to perform tasks. The **Address bar** shows the name and location of the item you have opened.

8. **Point to the Close button ☒ on the title bar, read the ScreenTip, then click or tap once**

9. **Point to the Recycle Bin icon, hold down the left mouse button, or press and hold the Recycle Bin image with your finger, move the mouse or drag so the object moves right as shown in FIGURE 1-8, release the mouse button or lift your finger, then drag the Recycle Bin back to its original location**

Getting Started with Windows 10

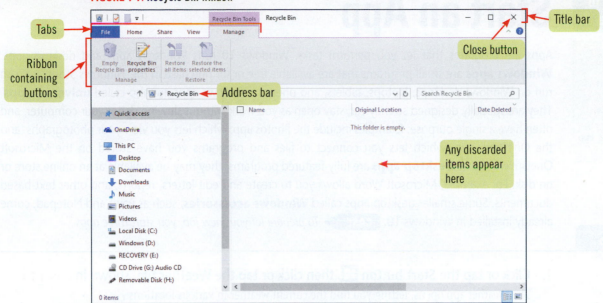

FIGURE 1-7: Recycle Bin window

Tabs

Ribbon containing buttons

Address bar

Title bar

Close button

Any discarded items appear here

FIGURE 1-8: Dragging the Recycle Bin icon

Releasing mouse button moves object to this location

TABLE 1-2: Basic pointing device actions

action	with a mouse	with a touch pad	use to
Point	Move mouse to position tip of pointer over an item	Move your finger over touch pad to position tip of pointer over an item	Highlight items or display small informational boxes called ScreenTips
Click	Press and release left mouse button once	Tap touch pad once	Select objects or commands, open menus or items on the taskbar
Double-click	Quickly press and release left mouse button twice	Tap touch pad twice in quick succession	Open programs, folders, or files represented by desktop icons
Drag	Point to an object, press and hold down left mouse button, move object to a new location, then release mouse button	Slide finger across touch pad to point to an object, press and hold left touch pad button, drag across touch pad to move object to new location, then release button	Move objects, such as icons, on the desktop
Right-click	Point to an object, then press and release right mouse button	Point to an object, then press and release right touchpad button	Display a shortcut menu containing options specific to the object

Selecting and moving items using touch-screen devices

If you use a touch-screen computer, a tablet, or a smartphone, you click desktop items by tapping them once on the screen. Tap an icon twice quickly to double-click and open its window. Press and hold an icon, then drag to move it. A touch-screen device does not let you point to an object without selecting it, however, as mice and touchpads do.

Start an App

Apps are programs that let you perform tasks. Windows 10 runs Windows apps and desktop apps. **Windows apps** are small programs that are available free or for purchase in the Windows Store, and can run on Windows desktops, laptops, tablets, and phones. Windows apps are also called **universal apps**. They are specially designed so they can stay open as you work without slowing down your computer, and often have a single purpose. Examples include the Photos app, which lets you view your photographs, and the OneDrive app, which lets you connect to files and programs you have stored on the Microsoft OneDrive website. **Desktop apps** are fully-featured programs; they may be available at an online store or on disk. For example, Microsoft Word allows you to create and edit letters, reports, and other text-based documents. Some smaller desktop apps called **Windows accessories**, such as Paint and Notepad, come already installed in Windows 10. **CASE** *To prepare for your new job, you start three apps.*

STEPS

1. Click or tap the Start button ⊞, then click or tap the Weather tile, shown in **FIGURE 1-9**
   The Weather app opens, letting you find the current weather in various locations.

2. If you are asked to choose a location, begin typing your city or town, then click the full name if it appears in the drop-down list
   The current weather for your selected city appears in Summary view. **FIGURE 1-10** shows a forecast for Boston, MA.

3. Click or tap the Weather app window's Close button ✕

4. Click or tap ⊞, then type onenote
   Typing an app name is another way to locate an app. At the top of the Start menu, you see the OneNote Trusted Windows Store app listed, as shown in **FIGURE 1-11**. OneNote is a popular app that lets you create tabbed notebooks where you can store text, images, files, and media such as audio and video.

5. Click or tap the OneNote Trusted Windows Store app name
   The OneNote app opens, showing a blank notebook (or a notebook you have previously created).

6. Click or tap the Close button ✕ in the upper right corner of the OneNote app window
   You have opened two Windows apps, Weather and OneNote.

7. Click or tap ⊞, then type paint
   The top of the Start menu lists the Paint Desktop app, shown in **FIGURE 1-12**. Paint is a simple accessory that comes installed with Windows and lets you create simple illustrations.

8. Click or tap the Paint Desktop app name at the top of the Start menu
   Other accessories besides Paint and Notepad include the Snipping Tool, which lets you capture an image of any screen area, and Sticky Notes, that let you create short notes.

Using the Windows Store

The Windows Store is an app that lets you find all kinds of apps for use on Windows personal computers, tablets, and phones. You can open it by clicking or tapping its tile on the Start menu or by clicking or tapping the Store button on the taskbar. To use the Windows Store, you need to be signed in to your Microsoft account. You can browse lists of popular apps, games, music, movies, and TV including new releases; you can browse the top paid or free apps. Browse app categories to find a specific type of app, such as Business or Entertainment. To locate a specific app, type its name in the Search box. If an app is free, you can go to its page and click the Free button to install it on your computer. If it's a paid app, you can click or tap the Free trial button to try it out, or click or tap its price button to purchase it. Any apps you've added recently appear in the Recently added category of the Start menu.

FIGURE 1-9: Weather tile on the Start menu

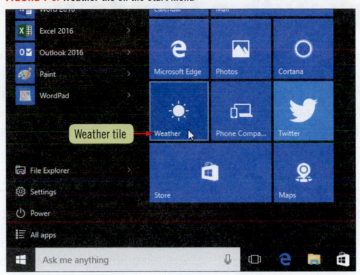

FIGURE 1-10: Weather app

FIGURE 1-11: OneNote Windows app name on Start menu

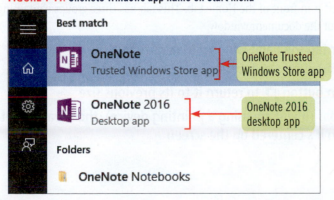

FIGURE 1-12: Paint Desktop app name on Start menu

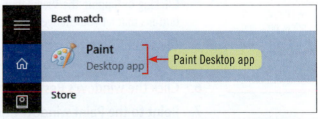

Work with a Window

When you start an app, its **window**, a frame displaying the app's tools, opens. In many apps, a blank file also opens so you can start creating a new document. For example, in Paint, a blank document opens so you can start drawing right away. All windows in the Windows 10 operating system have similar window elements. Once you can use a window in one app, you will know how to work with windows in many other apps. **CASE** ▶ *To become more familiar with the Windows 10 user interface, you explore elements in the Paint window.*

DETAILS

Many windows have the following common elements. Refer to FIGURE 1-13:

- At the top of the window, you see a **title bar**, a strip that contains the name of the document and app. This document has not been saved, so it has the temporary name "Untitled" and the app name is "Paint."

- On the right side of the title bar, the **Window control buttons** let you control the app window. The **Minimize button** — temporarily hides the window, making it a button on the taskbar. The app is still running, but its window is temporarily hidden until you click its taskbar button or its miniature window in Task view to reopen it. The **Maximize button** □ enlarges the window to fill the entire screen. If a window is already maximized, the Maximize button changes to the **Restore Down button** ⧉, which reduces it to the last non-maximized size. Clicking or tapping the **Close button** ✕ closes the app.

- Many windows have a **scroll bar** on the right side and/or the bottom of the window. You click (or press) and drag scroll bar elements to show additional parts of your document. See **TABLE 1-3**.

- Just below the title bar is the Ribbon, a bar containing tabs as well as a Help icon. The Paint window has three tabs: File, Home, and View. Tabs are divided into **groups** of buttons and tool palettes. The Home tab has five groups: Clipboard, Image, Tools, Shapes, and Colors. Many apps also include **menus** you click to show lists of commands, as well as **toolbars** containing buttons.

- The **Quick Access toolbar** lets you quickly perform common actions such as saving a file.

STEPS

1. **Click or tap the Paint window Minimize button** —
   The app is reduced to a taskbar button, as shown in **FIGURE 1-14**. The contrasting line indicates the app is still open.

2. **Click or tap the taskbar button representing the Paint app** 🎨 **to redisplay the app**

3. **Drag the gray scroll box down, notice the lower edge of the work area that appears, then click or tap the Up scroll arrow** ⌃ **until you see the top edge of the work area**

4. **Point to the View tab, then click or tap the View tab once**
   Clicking or tapping the View tab moved it in front of the Home tab. This tab has three groups containing buttons that let you change your view of the document window.

5. **Click the Home tab, then click or tap the Paint window Maximize button** □
   The window fills the screen, and the Maximize button becomes the Restore Down button ⧉.

6. **Click the window's Restore Down button** ⧉ **to return it to its previous size**

7. **Point to the Paint window title bar (if you are using a pointing device), then drag about an inch to the right to move it so it's centered on the screen**

FIGURE 1-13: Typical app window elements

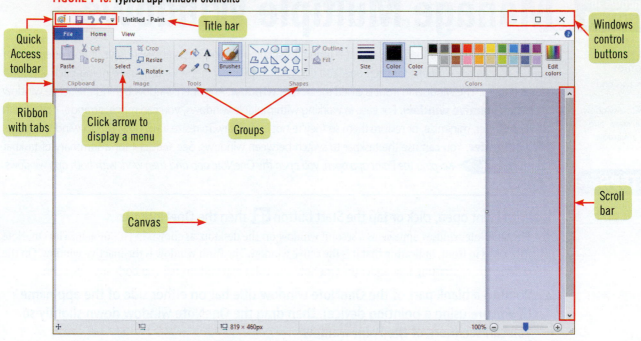

Quick Access toolbar

Ribbon with tabs

Click arrow to display a menu

Title bar

Groups

Windows control buttons

Scroll bar

Canvas

FIGURE 1-14: Taskbar with minimized Paint program button

Buttons without contrasting lines represent programs that are not open

Your buttons may differ

Paint program button with contrasting line indicating program is open

TABLE 1-3: Parts of a scroll bar

name	looks like	to use
Scroll box	☐ (Size may vary)	Drag to scroll quickly through a long document
Scroll arrows	⌃ ⌄	Click or tap to scroll up, down, left, or right in small amounts
Shaded area	(Above, below, or to either side of scroll box)	Click or tap to move up or down by one screen

Using the Quick Access toolbar

On the left side of the title bar, the Quick Access toolbar lets you perform common tasks with just one click. The Save button 💾 saves the changes you have made to a document. The Undo button ↩ lets you reverse (undo) the last action you performed.

The Redo button ↪ reinstates the change you just undid. Use the Customize Quick Access Toolbar button ⏷ to add other frequently used buttons to the toolbar, move the toolbar below the Ribbon, or minimize the Ribbon to show only tabs.

Manage Multiple Windows

Learning Outcomes
- Open a second app
- Activate a window
- Resize, snap, and close a window

You can work with more than one app at a time by switching among open app windows. If you open two or more apps, a window opens for each one. You can work with app windows individually, going back and forth between them. The window in front is called the **active window**. Any open window behind the active window is called an **inactive window**. For ease in working with multiple windows, you can move, arrange, make them smaller or larger, minimize, or restore them so they're not in the way. To resize a window, drag a window's edge, called its **border**. You can use the taskbar to switch between windows. See **TABLE 1-4** for a summary of taskbar actions. **CASE** ▶ *Keeping the Paint app open, you open the OneNote app and then work with both app windows.*

STEPS

1. **With Paint open, click or tap the Start button ⊞, then the OneNote tile**

   The OneNote window appears as a second window on the desktop, as shown in **FIGURE 1-15**. The OneNote window is in front, indicating that it is the active window. The Paint window is the inactive window. On the taskbar, the contrasting line under the OneNote and Paint app buttons tell you both apps are open.

2. **Point to a blank part of the OneNote window title bar on either side of the app name (if you are using a pointing device), then drag the OneNote window down slightly so you can see more of the Paint window**

3. **Click or tap once on the Paint window's title bar**

   The Paint window is now the active window and appears in front of the OneNote window. You can make any window active by clicking or tapping it, or by clicking or tapping an app's icon in the taskbar.

4. **Point to the taskbar if you are using a pointing device, then click or tap the OneNote window button**

   The OneNote window becomes active. When you open multiple windows on the desktop, you may need to resize windows so they don't get in the way of other open windows.

5. **Point to the lower-right corner of the OneNote window until the pointer changes to ⤢, if you are using a pointing device, or tap and press the corner, then drag down and to the right about an inch to make the window larger**

   You can also point to any edge of a window until you see the ⟷ or ↕ pointer, or tap and press any edge, then drag to make it larger or smaller in one direction only.

6. **Click or tap the Task View button ▢ on the taskbar, click or tap the Paint window, click or tap ▢ again, then click or tap the OneNote window**

   The **Task View button** is another convenient way to switch among open windows.

7. **Point to the OneNote window title bar if you are using a pointing device, drag the window to the left side of the screen until the pointer or your finger reaches the screen edge and you see a vertical line down the middle of the screen, then release the mouse button or lift your finger from the screen**

   The OneNote window instantly fills the left side of the screen, and any inactive windows appear on the right side of the screen. This is called the **Snap Assist** feature. You can also drag to any screen corner to snap open app windows to quarter-screen windows.

8. **Click or tap anywhere on the reduced-size version of the Paint window**

   The Paint window fills the right side of the screen. Snapping makes it easy to view the contents of two windows at the same time. See **FIGURE 1-16**.

9. **Click or tap the OneNote window Close button ✕, then click or tap the Maximize button ▢ in the Paint window's title bar**

   The OneNote app closes. The Paint app window remains open.

FIGURE 1-15: Working with multiple windows

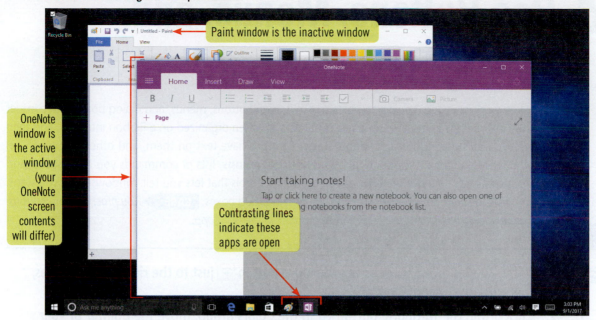

Paint window is the inactive window

OneNote window is the active window (your OneNote screen contents will differ)

Contrasting lines indicate these apps are open

FIGURE 1-16: OneNote and Paint windows snapped to each side of the screen

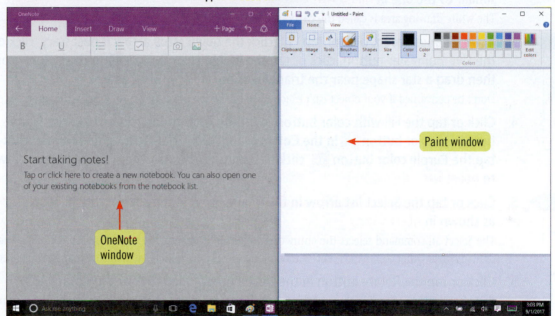

Paint window

OneNote window

TABLE 1-4: Using the taskbar

to	do this
Add buttons to taskbar	Open an app, right-click or press its icon on the taskbar, then click or tap Pin this program to taskbar
Change order of taskbar buttons	Drag any icon to a new taskbar location
See a list of recent documents opened	Right-click or press taskbar app button
Close a document using the taskbar	Point to taskbar button, point to document image, then click its Close button
Minimize/Redisplay all open windows	Click or press Show desktop button (the thin bar) to the right of taskbar date and time
See preview of documents in taskbar	With a pointing device, point to taskbar button for open app
Bring a minimized window to the front	Click or press the Task View button, then click or tap the window or desktop you want in front
Rearrange windows on the desktop	Right-click taskbar, click Cascade Windows, Show windows stacked, or Show windows side by side

Use Buttons, Menus, and Dialog Boxes

Learning Outcomes
- Use a button and a menu
- Work in a dialog box

When you work in an app, you communicate with it using buttons, menus, and dialog boxes. **Buttons** let you issue instructions to modify app objects. Buttons are often organized on a Ribbon into tabs, and then into groups like those in the Paint window. Some buttons have text on them, and others show only an icon that represents what they do. Other buttons reveal **menus**, lists of commands you can choose. And some buttons open up a **dialog box**, a window with controls that lets you tell Windows what you want. **TABLE 1-5** lists the common types of controls you find in dialog boxes. **CASE** *You practice using buttons, menus, and dialog boxes to create some simple graphics in the Paint app.*

STEPS

1. **In the Shapes group, click or tap the** More button ⏷ **just to the right of the shapes, then click the** Triangle button △

2. **Click or tap the** Turquoise button ▣ **in the Colors group, move the pointer or your finger over the white drawing area, then drag down and to the right, to draw a** triangle **similar to the one in FIGURE 1-17**

   The white drawing area is called the **canvas**.

3. **In the Shapes group, click or tap** ⏷, **click the** down scroll arrow **if necessary, click or tap the** Five-point star button, **click or tap the** Indigo color button ▣ **in the Colors group, then drag a star shape near the triangle, using FIGURE 1-17 as a guide**

   Don't be concerned if your object isn't exactly like the one in the figure, or in exactly the same place.

4. **Click or tap the** Fill with color button 🪣 **in the Tools group, click or tap the** Light turquoise color button ▣ **in the Colors group, click or tap inside the** triangle, **click or tap the** Purple color button ▣, **click or tap inside the** star, **then compare your drawing to FIGURE 1-17**

5. **Click or tap the** Select list arrow **in the Image group, then click or tap** Select all, **as shown in FIGURE 1-18**

   The Select all command selects the entire drawing, as indicated by the dotted line surrounding the white drawing area. Other commands on this menu let you select individual elements or change your selection.

6. **Click or tap the** Rotate button **in the Image group, then click or tap** Rotate 180°

   You often need to use multiple commands to perform an action—in this case, you used one command to select the items you wanted to work with, and another command to rotate them.

7. **Click or tap the** File tab, **then click or tap** Print

   The Print dialog box opens, as shown in **FIGURE 1-19**. This dialog box lets you choose a printer, specify which part of your document or drawing you want to print, and choose how many copies you want to print. The **default**, or automatically selected, number of copies is 1, which is what you want.

8. **Click or tap** Print, **or if you prefer not to print, click or tap** Cancel

   The drawing prints on your printer. You decide to close the app without saving your drawing.

9. **Click or tap the** File tab, **click or tap** Exit, **then click or tap** Don't Save

   You closed the file without saving your changes, then exited the app. Most apps include a command for closing a document without exiting the program. However, Paint allows you to open only one document at a time, so it does not include a Close command.

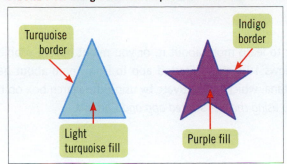
FIGURE 1-17: Triangle and star shapes filled with color

Turquoise border

Indigo border

Light turquoise fill

Purple fill

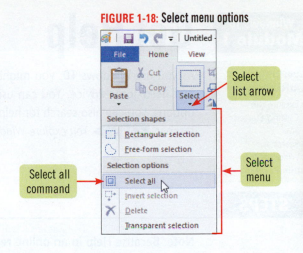
FIGURE 1-18: Select menu options

Select list arrow

Select all command

Select menu

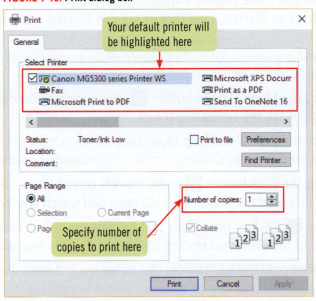
FIGURE 1-19: Print dialog box

Your default printer will be highlighted here

Specify number of copies to print here

TABLE 1-5: Common dialog box controls

element	example	description
Text box	1 - 27	A box in which you type text or numbers
Spin box	1	A box with up and down arrows; you can click or tap arrows or type to increase or decrease value
Option button		A small circle you click or tap to select the option; only one in a set can be selected at once
Check box		A small box that turns an option on when checked or off when unchecked; more than one in a set can be selected at once
List box		A box that lets you select from a list of options
Button	Save	A button you click or tap to issue a command

Getting Started with Windows 10

Get Help

As you use Windows 10, you might feel ready to learn more about it, or you might have a problem and need some advice. You can use the Windows 10 Getting Started app to learn more about help options. You can also search for help using Cortana, which you activate by using the search box on the taskbar. **CASE** ▶ *You explore Windows 10 help using the Get Started app and Cortana.*

STEPS

Note: Because Help in an online resource, topics and information are liable to change over time. If your screen choices do not match the steps below exactly, be flexible by exploring the options that are available to you and searching for the information you need.

1. Click or tap the Start button ⊞, then in the Explore Windows section click or tap the Get Started tile; if the Explore Windows section does not appear on your Start menu, begin typing Get Started, then click or tap Get Started Trusted Windows Store app in the list

    The Get Started app window opens. The window contains a menu expand button ☰ in the upper left and a bar containing buttons on the left side.

2. Click or tap the Menu Expand button ☰, move the pointer over the list of topics, then scroll down to see the remaining topics

3. Click or tap the Search and help topic, click the Search for anything, anywhere tile, then read the information, as shown in FIGURE 1-20, scrolling as necessary

4. Click or tap the Back button ← in the top-left corner of the window, click the Search for help tile, then read the Search for help topic and watch any available videos

5. Click or tap ☰, click or tap a topic that interests you, then read the information or click or tap one of the tiles representing a subtopic if one is available

6. After you have read the information, click or tap the Get started window's Close button ✕

    As the Help topic explained, you can also search the web for help with Windows using Cortana.

7. Click in the search box on the taskbar, then type windows help

    As you type, Cortana begins a search, and shows results on the Start menu. See FIGURE 1-21. Your results may also include topics from the Microsoft Store, the web, Store apps, and OneDrive, your online storage location.

8. Click any web option that interests you

9. When you are finished, click or tap the window's Close button ✕ to return to the desktop

FIGURE 1-20: Get Started Search and Help topic

Menu Expand button

FIGURE 1-21: Search results information

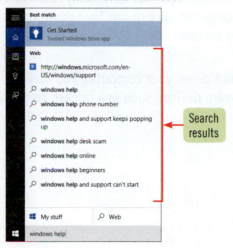

Search results

Cortana is the digital personal assistant that comes with Windows 10 and Windows phones. You can interact with Cortana typing or using your voice. Use Cortana to search the web, remind you of events or appointments, set alarms, change computer settings, get directions, get current news and weather, track airline flights, play, and even identify music. **FIGURE 1-22** shows Cortana's response to "What's the weather in New York?" which may also give a voice response. You call Cortana by saying, "Hey Cortana," or by clicking or tapping the microphone icon on the right side of the taskbar search box, and then asking a question or saying a command. Depending on your request, Cortana may reply out loud, display results in the Start menu, or display results in a Microsoft Edge web browser window. You may need to set up Cortana on your computer and answer security questions before you use it. The first time you use Cortana, you may be asked to answer questions to help the assistant recognize your voice or solve issues with your computer's microphone.

FIGURE 1-22: Using Cortana to check the weather

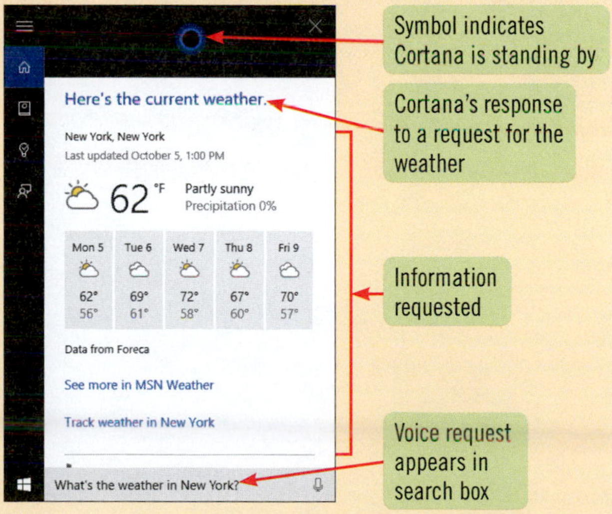

Symbol indicates Cortana is standing by

Cortana's response to a request for the weather

Information requested

Voice request appears in search box

Exit Windows 10

When you finish working on your computer, you should close any open files, exit any open apps, close any open windows, and exit (or **shut down**) Windows 10. **TABLE 1-6** shows options for ending your Windows 10 sessions. Whichever option you choose, it's important to shut down your computer in an orderly way. If you turn off or unplug the computer while Windows 10 is running, you could lose data or damage Windows 10 and your computer. If you are working in a computer lab, follow your instructor's directions and your lab's policies for ending your Windows 10 session. **CASE** *You have examined the basic ways you can use Windows 10, so you are ready to end your Windows 10 session.*

STEPS

1. **Click or tap the Start button ⊞, then click or tap Power**
   The Power button menu lists shut down options, as shown in **FIGURE 1-23**.

2. **If you are working in a computer lab, follow the instructions provided by your instructor or technical support person for ending your Windows 10 session; if you are working on your own computer, click or tap Shut down or the option you prefer for ending your Windows 10 session**

3. **After you shut down your computer, you may also need to turn off your monitor and other hardware devices, such as a printer, to conserve energy**

FIGURE 1-23: Shutting down your computer

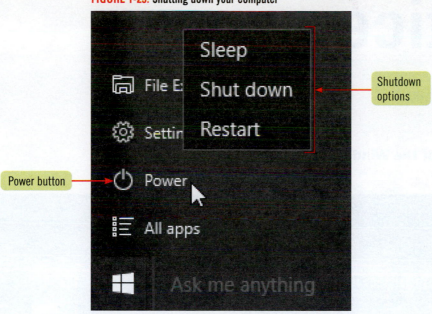

Shutdown options

Power button

TABLE 1-6: Power options

option	description
Sleep	Puts computer in a low-power state while keeping any open apps open so you can return immediately to where you left off
Shut down	Closes any open apps and completely turns off the computer
Restart	Closes any open apps, shuts down the computer, then restarts it

Installing updates when you exit Windows

Sometimes, after you shut down your machine, you might find that your machine does not shut down immediately. Instead, Windows might install software updates. If you see an option on your Power menu that lets you update, you can click or tap it to update your software. If you see a window indicating that updates are being installed, do not unplug or press the power switch to turn off your machine. Let the updates install completely. After the updates are installed, your computer will shut down, as you originally requested.

Practice

Concepts Review

Label the elements of the Windows 10 window shown in FIGURE 1-24.

FIGURE 1-24

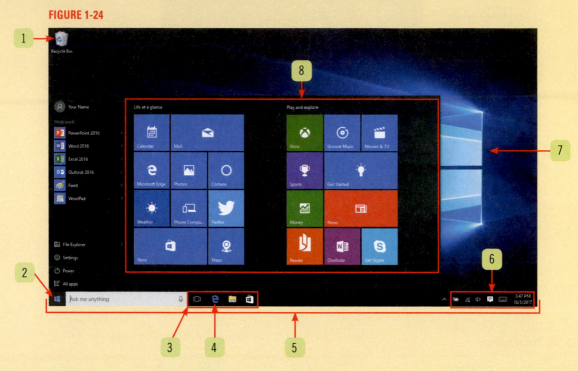

Match each term with the statement that best describes it.

9. Cortana	a. A special area of the operating system where your files and settings are stored
10. Snap Assist	b. Controls that let you interact with an operating system
11. Desktop app	c. The personal digital assistant in Windows 10
12. Microsoft account	d. Full-featured program that is installed on a personal computer
13. User interface	e. Feature that displays windows at full height next to each other on the screen
14. Operating system	f. Available from the Windows store, it runs on Windows laptops, tablets, and phones
15. Windows app	g. A program necessary to run your computer

Select the best answer from the list of choices.

16. The bar containing buttons and other elements at the bottom of the Windows 10 desktop is called the _____.

    a. title bar   **c.** scroll bar

    b. address bar   **d.** taskbar

17. Paint is an example of a(n) _____.

    a. group   **c.** active window

    b. accessory   **d.** operating system

18. **Which of the following is in the upper-left corner of a program window, and lets you perform common actions?**

   a. Application program   **c.** Operating system

   b. Quick Access toolbar   **d.** Accessory program

19. **The new Microsoft web browser is called Microsoft _____.**

   a. Paint   **c.** Edge

   b. WordPad   **d.** File Explorer

Skills Review

1. **Start Windows 10.**

   a. If your computer and monitor are not running, press your computer's and (if necessary) your monitor's power buttons.

   b. If necessary, select the user name that represents your user account.

   c. Enter your password, using correct uppercase and lowercase letters.

2. **Navigate the desktop and Start menu.**

   a. Examine the Windows 10 desktop.

   b. Open the Start menu.

   c. Display all the apps using a command on the Start menu, and scroll the list.

   d. Return to the Start menu.

   e. Close the Start menu.

3. **Point, click, and drag.**

   a. On the Windows 10 desktop, click or tap to select the Recycle Bin.

   b. Point to display the ScreenTip for Microsoft Edge in the taskbar, and then display the ScreenTip for each of the other icons on the taskbar.

   c. Double-click or double-tap to open the Recycle Bin window, then close it.

   d. Drag the Recycle Bin to a different corner of the screen, then drag it back to its original location.

   e. Click or tap the Date and Time area to display the calendar and clock, then click or tap it again to close it.

4. **Start an app.**

   a. Open the Start menu, then start the Maps app. (If asked to allow Windows to access your location, do so if you like.)

   b. Click or tap the icons on the left side of the Maps app window and observe the effect of each one.

   c. Close the Maps app.

   d. Reopen the Start menu, then type and click or tap to locate and open the Sticky Notes accessory.

   e. Click or tap the Sticky Notes Close button, clicking or tapping Yes to delete the note.

   f. Open the Weather Windows app.

5. **Work with a window.**

   a. Minimize the Weather window, then use its taskbar button to redisplay the window.

   b. Use the Weather app window's scroll bar or swiping to view the information in the lower part of the window, and then scroll or swipe up to display the top of it. (*Hint*: You need to move the pointer over the Weather app window, or swipe it, in order to display the scroll bar.)

   c. Click or tap the menu expand button, then click Historical Weather.

   d. Read the contents of the window, then click or tap two other menu buttons and read the contents.

   e. Maximize the Weather window, then restore it down.

6. **Manage multiple windows.**

   a. Leaving the Weather app open, go to the Start menu and type to locate the Paint app, open Paint, then restore down the Paint window if necessary.

   b. Click or tap to make the Weather app window the active window.

   c. Click or tap to make the Paint window the active window.

   d. Minimize the Paint window.

Skills Review (continued)

    e. Drag the Weather app window so it's in the middle of the screen.

    f. Redisplay the Paint window.

    g. Drag the Paint window so it automatically fills the right side of the screen.

    h. Click or tap the Weather app window image so it snaps to the left side of the screen.

    i. Close the Weather app window, maximize the Paint window, then restore down the Paint window.

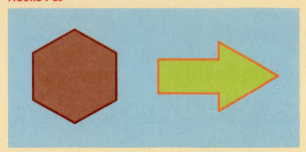

7. Use buttons, menus, and dialog boxes.

    a. In the Paint window, draw a Dark red Hexagon shape, similar to the one shown in **FIGURE 1-25**.

    b. Use the Fill with color button to fill the hexagon with a brown color.

    c. Draw an Orange right arrow to the right of the hexagon shape, using the figure as a guide.

    d. Use the Fill with color button to fill the orange arrow with a lime color.

    e. Fill the drawing background with Light turquoise color, as shown in the figure.

    f. Use the Select list arrow and menu to select the entire drawing, then use the Rotate command to rotate the drawing 180°.

    g. Open the Print dialog box, print a copy of the picture if you wish, then close the Paint app without saving the drawing.

8. Get help.

    a. Open the Get Started app, then use the menu expand button to display the available help topics.

    b. Use the Menu button to display help for Cortana.

    c. Click or tap a tile representing a Cortana help topic that interests you, read the help text, scrolling or swiping as necessary.

    d. Display the Search and Help topic, then close the Get Started window.

    e. In the search box on the taskbar, type Help Microsoft Account, then click the help Microsoft account result to search the web.

    f. In the Microsoft Edge browser window, select a help topic that interests you, read the information (ignore any commercial offers), then click or tap the Microsoft Edge window's Close button.

9. Exit Windows 10.

    a. Sign out of your account, or shut down your computer using the Shut down command in the Start menu's Power command or the preferred command for your work or school setting.

    b. Turn off your monitor if necessary.

Independent Challenge 1

You work for Chicago Instruments, a manufacturer of brass instruments. The company ships instruments and supplies to music stores and musicians in the United States and Canada. The owner, Emerson, wants to know an easy way for his employees to learn about the new features of Windows 10, and he has asked you to help.

    a. Start your computer if necessary, sign in to Windows 10, then use the search text box to search for **what's new in Windows 10**.

    b. Click or tap the Search the web link in the Best match section at the top of the Help menu, then in the Microsoft Edge browser window, click or tap a search result that interests you.

    c. Open the Getting Started app and review the new features listed there.

    d. Using pencil and paper, or the Notepad accessory if you wish, write a short memo to Emerson summarizing, in your own words, three important new features in Windows 10. If you use Notepad to write the memo, use the Print button to print the document, then use the Exit command on the File tab to close Notepad without saving your changes to the document.

Independent Challenge 1 (continued)

e. Close the browser window, then sign out of your account, or shut down your computer using the preferred command for your work or school setting. Turn off your monitor if necessary.

Independent Challenge 2

You are the new manager of Katharine Anne's Garden Supplies, a business that supplies garden tools to San Diego businesses. Some of their tools are from Europe and show metric sizes. For her American customers, Katharine Anne wants to do a simple calculation and then convert the result to inches.

a. Start your computer and log on to Windows 10 if necessary, then type to locate the Windows app called Calculator, and start it.

b. Click or tap to enter the number 96 on the Calculator.

c. Click or tap the division sign (÷) button.

d. Click or tap the number 4.

e. Click or tap the equals sign button (=), and write down the result shown in the Calculator window. (*Hint*: The result should be 24.)

f. Select the menu expand button in the Calculator window, then under CONVERTER, select Length.

g. Enter 24 centimeters, and observe the equivalent length in inches.

h. Start Notepad, write a short memo about how Calculator can help you convert metric measurements to inches and feet, print the document using the Print command on the File tab, then exit Notepad without saving.

i. Close the Calculator, then sign out of your account, or shut down your computer using the preferred command for your work or school setting. Turn off your monitor if necessary.

Independent Challenge 3

You are the office manager for Erica's Pet Shipping, a service business in Dallas, Texas, that specializes in air shipping of cats and dogs across the United States and Canada. It's important to know the temperature in the destination city, so the animals won't be in danger from extreme temperatures when they are unloaded from the aircraft. Erica has asked you to find a way to easily monitor temperatures in destination cities. You decide to use a Windows app so you can see current temperatures in Celsius on your desktop. (Note: To complete the steps below, your computer must be connected to the Internet.)

a. Start your computer and sign in to Windows 10 if necessary, then on the Start menu, click or tap the Weather tile.

b. Click or tap the Search icon in the location text box, then type **Toronto**.

c. Select Toronto, Ontario, Canada, in the drop-down list to view the weather for Toronto.

d. Search on and select another location that interests you.

e. Close the app.

f. Open Notepad, write Erica a memo outlining how you can use the Windows Weather app to help keep pets safe, print the memo if you wish, close Notepad, then sign out, or shut down your computer.

Independent Challenge 4: Explore

Cortana, the Windows 10 personal digital assistant, can help you with everyday tasks. In this Independent Challenge, you explore one of the ways you can use Cortana.

a. Click or tap the microphone icon, to the right of the search box in the Windows 10 taskbar, to activate Cortana and display its menu. (*Note*: If you have not used Cortana before, you will not see the microphone icon until you answer some preliminary questions and verify your user account; you may also need to first help Cortana to understand your speaking voice.) Cortana displays a pulsating circle, indicating that she is listening for speech, and then shows you a greeting and some general information.

Independent Challenge 4: Explore (continued)

FIGURE 1-26

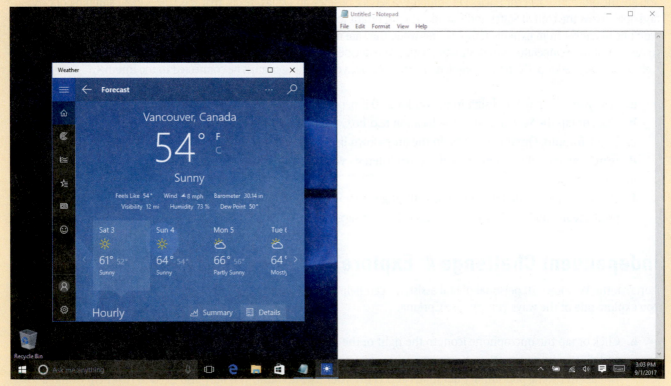

b. In the list of icons on the left side of the menu, click the menu expand button to show the names of each one, as shown in **FIGURE 1-26**.

c. Click or tap the Reminders button, then click the plus sign at the bottom of the menu. Click or tap Remember to…, then enter information for a to-do item, such as "Walk the dog." Click or tap the time box and use the spin boxes to set the time for one or two minutes from now. Click or tap the check mark, then click Remind to set the reminder. Click or tap the Reminders icon again to see your reminder listed, then click the desktop. When the reminder appears, click Complete.

d. Click or tap the microphone icon again, and when you see the pulsating circle, speak into your computer microphone and tell Cortana to remind you to do something in one minute. Click or tap Remind, then close the Cortana window. When the reminder appears, click or tap Complete.

e. Click or tap the Close button on the Cortana menu, then sign out of your account, or shut down your computer.

Visual Workshop

Using the skills you've learned in this module, open and arrange elements on your screen so it looks similar to **FIGURE 1-27**. Note the position of the Recycle Bin, and the size and location of the Notepad and Weather app windows, as well as the city shown. In Notepad, write a paragraph summarizing how you used pointing, clicking (or tapping), and dragging to make your screen look like the figure. Print your work if you wish, close Notepad and the Weather app without saving changes, then sign out or shut down your computer.

FIGURE 1-27

Understanding File Management

CASE ▶ Now that you are familiar with the Windows 10 operating system, your new employer has asked you to become familiar with **file management**, or how to create, save, locate and delete the files you create with Windows apps. You begin by reviewing how files are organized on your computer, and then begin working with files you create in the WordPad app. *Note: With the release of Windows 10, Microsoft now provides ongoing updates to Windows instead of releasing new versions periodically. This means that Windows features might change over time, including how they look and how you interact with them. The information provided in this text was accurate at the time this book was published.*

Module Objectives

After completing this module, you will be able to:

- Understand files and folders
- Create and save a file
- Explore the files and folders on your computer
- Change file and folder views

- Open, edit, and save files
- Copy files
- Move and rename files
- Search for files and folders
- Delete and restore files

Files You Will Need

No files needed.

Understand Files and Folders

As you work with apps, you create and save files, such as letters, drawings, or budgets. When you save files, you usually save them inside folders to help keep them organized. The files and folders on your computer are organized in a **file hierarchy**, a system that arranges files and folders in different levels, like the branches of a tree. **FIGURE 2-1** shows a sample file hierarchy. **CASE** *You decide to use folders and files to organize the information on your computer.*

DETAILS

Use the following guidelines as you organize files using your computer's file hierarchy:

• ### Use folders and subfolders to organize files

As you work with your computer, you can add folders to your hierarchy and name them to help you organize your work. As you've learned, folders are storage areas in which you can group related files. You should give folders unique names that help you easily identify them. You can also create **subfolders**, which are folders that are inside other folders. Windows 10 comes with several existing folders, such as Documents, Music, Pictures, and Videos, that you can use as a starting point.

• ### View and manage files in File Explorer

You can view and manage your computer contents using a built-in program called **File Explorer**, shown in **FIGURE 2-2**. A File Explorer window is divided into **panes**, or sections. The **Navigation pane** on the left side of the window shows the folder structure on your computer. When you click a folder in the Navigation pane, you see its contents in the **File list** on the right side of the window. To open File Explorer from the desktop, click the File Explorer button 📁 on the taskbar. To open it from the Start menu, click the File Explorer shortcut.

• ### Understand file addresses

A window also contains an **Address bar**, an area just below the Ribbon that shows the address, or location, of the files that appear in the File list. An **address** is a sequence of folder names, separated by the ❯ symbol, which describes a file's location in the file hierarchy. An address shows the folder with the highest hierarchy level on the left and steps through each hierarchy level toward the right; this is sometimes called a **path**. For example, the Documents folder might contain subfolders named Work and Personal. If you clicked the Personal folder in the File list, the Address bar would show Documents ❯ Personal. Each location between the ❯ symbols represents a level in the file hierarchy. If you see a file path written out, you'll most likely see it with backslashes. For example, in **FIGURE 2-1**, if you wanted to write the path to the Brochure file, you would write "Documents\Reason2Go\Marketing\Brochure.xlsx. File addresses might look complicated if they may have many levels, but they are helpful because they always describe the exact location of a file or folder in a file hierarchy.

• ### Navigate up and down using the Address bar and File list

You can use the Address bar and the File list to move up or down in the hierarchy one or more levels at a time. To **navigate up** in your computer's hierarchy, you can click a folder or subfolder name to the left of the current folder name in the Address bar. For example, in **FIGURE 2-2**, you can move up in the hierarchy three levels by clicking once on This PC in the Address bar. Then the File list would show the subfolders and files inside the This PC folder. To **navigate down** in the hierarchy, double-click a subfolder in the File list. The path in the Address bar then shows the path to that subfolder.

• ### Navigate up and down using the Navigation pane

You can also use the Navigation pane to navigate among folders. Move the mouse pointer over the Navigation pane, then click the small arrows to the left of a folder name to show ❯ or hide ⌄ the folder's contents under the folder name. Subfolders appear indented under the folders that contain them, showing that they are inside that folder.

FIGURE 2-1: Sample folder and file hierarchy

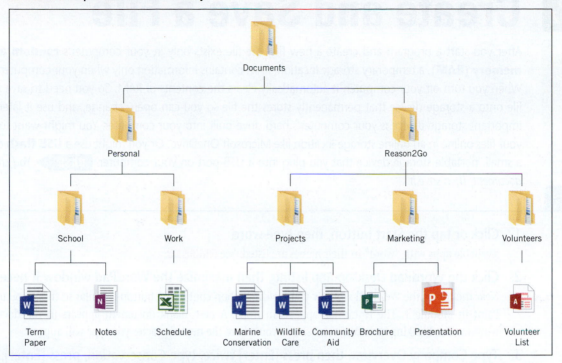

FIGURE 2-2: File Explorer window

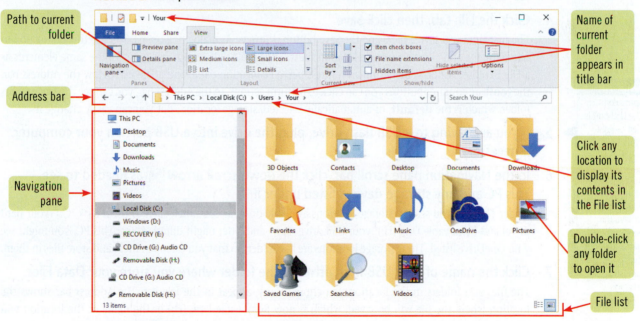

Path to current folder

Address bar

Navigation pane

Name of current folder appears in title bar

Click any location to display its contents in the File list

Double-click any folder to open it

File list

Plan your file organization

As you manage your files, you should plan how you want to organize them. First, identify the types of files you work with, such as images, music, and documents. Think about the content, such as personal, business, clients, or projects. Then think of a folder organization that will help you find them later. For example, you can use subfolders in the Pictures folder to separate family photos from business photos or to group them

by location or by month. In the Documents folder, you might group personal files in one subfolder and business files in another subfolder. Then create additional subfolders to further separate sets of files. You can always move files among folders and rename folders. You should periodically reevaluate your folder structure to make sure it continues to meet your needs.

Understanding File Management

Create and Save a File

**Learning
Outcomes**
• Start WordPad
• Create a file
• Save a file

After you start a program and create a new file, the file exists only in your computer's **random access memory (RAM)**, a temporary storage location. RAM contains information only when your computer is on. When you turn off your computer, it automatically clears the contents of RAM. So you need to save a new file onto a storage device that permanently stores the file so you can open, change, and use it later. One important storage device is your computer's hard drive built into your computer. You might want to store your files online in an online storage location like Microsoft OneDrive. Or you might use a **USB flash drive**, a small, portable storage device that you plug into a USB port on your computer. **CASE** *You create a document, then save it.*

STEPS

1. **Click or tap the Start button, then type word**
   Available apps with "word" in their names are listed. See **FIGURE 2-3**.

2. **Click the WordPad Desktop app listing, then maximize the WordPad window if necessary**
   Near the top of the WordPad window you see the Ribbon containing buttons, similar to those you used in Paint in Module 1. The Home tab appears in front. A new, blank document appears in the document window. The blinking insertion point shows you where the next character you type will appear.

3. **Type Company Overview, then press [Enter] twice, type Conservation, press [Enter], type Community Work, press [Enter], type Research, press [Enter] twice, then type your name**
   See **FIGURE 2-4**.

4. **Click the File tab, then click Save**
   The first time you save a file using the Save button, the Save As dialog box opens. You use this dialog box to name the file and choose a storage location for it. The Save As dialog box has many of the same elements as a File Explorer window, including an Address bar, a Navigation pane, and a File list. Below the Address bar, the **toolbar** contains buttons you can click to perform actions. In the Address bar, you can see the Documents folder, which is the **default**, or automatically selected, storage location. But you can easily change it.

5. **If you are saving to a USB flash drive, plug the drive into a USB port on your computer, if necessary**

6. **In the Navigation pane scroll bar, click the down scroll arrow ⌄ as needed to see This PC and any storage devices listed under it**
   Under This PC, you see the storage locations available on your computer, such as Local Disk (C:) (your hard drive) and Removable Disk (H:) (your USB drive name and letter might differ). Above This PC, you might see your OneDrive listed. These storage locations are like folders in that you can open them and store files in them.

7. **Click the name of your USB flash drive, or the folder where you store your Data Files**
   The files and folders in the location you chose, if any, appear in the File list. The Address bar shows the location where the file will be saved, which is now Removable Disk (H:) or the name of the location you clicked. You need to give your document a meaningful name so you can find it later.

8. **Click in the File name text box to select the default name Document.rtf, type Company Overview, compare your screen to FIGURE 2-5, then click Save**
   The document is saved as a file on your USB flash drive. The filename Company Overview.rtf appears in the title bar. The ".rtf" at the end of the filename is the file extension that Windows added automatically. A **file extension** is a three- or four-letter sequence, preceded by a period, which identifies a file to your computer, in this case **Rich Text Format**. The WordPad program creates files in RTF format.

9. **Click the Close button ✕ on the WordPad window**
   The WordPad program closes. Your Company Overview document is now saved in the location you specified.

Understanding File Management

FIGURE 2-3: Results at top of Start menu

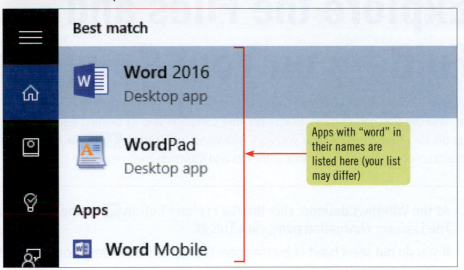

Apps with "word" in their names are listed here (your list may differ)

FIGURE 2-4: WordPad document

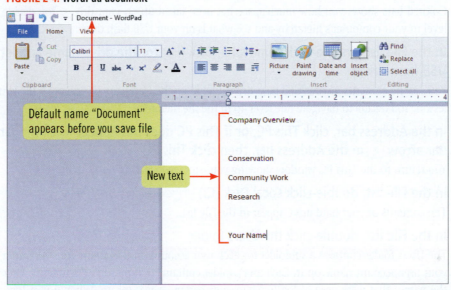

Default name "Document" appears before you save file

New text

FIGURE 2-5: Save As dialog box

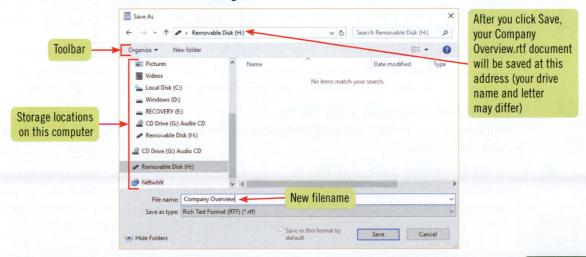

Toolbar

Storage locations on this computer

New filename

After you click Save, your Company Overview.rtf document will be saved at this address (your drive name and letter may differ)

Explore the Files and Folders on Your Computer

In a File Explorer window, you can navigate through your computer contents using the File list, the Address bar, and the Navigation pane. Examining your computer and its existing folder and file structure helps you decide where to save files as you work with Windows 10 apps. **CASE** *In preparation for organizing documents at your new job, you look at the files and folders on your computer.*

STEPS

1. **At the Windows desktop, click the File Explorer button** 📁 **on the taskbar, then in the File Explorer Navigation pane, click This PC**

2. **If you do not see a band of buttons near the top of the window, double-click the View tab**

   TROUBLE

   If you don't see the colored bars, click the View tab, click Tiles in the Layout group.

   The band containing buttons is called the **Ribbon**. Your computer's storage devices appear in a window, as shown in **FIGURE 2-6**. These include hard drives; devices with removable storage, such as CD and DVD drives or USB flash drives; portable devices such as smartphones or tablets; and any network storage locations. Colored bars shows you how much space has been taken up on your drives. You decide to move down a level in your computer's hierarchy and see what is on your USB flash drive.

3. **In the File list, double-click Removable Disk (H:) (or the drive name and letter for your USB flash drive)**

   You see the contents of your USB flash drive, including the Company Overview.rtf file you saved in the last lesson. You decide to navigate one level up in the file hierarchy.

   TROUBLE

   If you do not have a USB flash drive, click the Documents folder instead.

4. **In the Address bar, click This PC, or if This PC does not appear, click the far-left address bar arrow** ⯈ **in the Address bar, then click This PC**

   You return to the This PC window showing your storage locations.

5. **In the File list, double-click Local Disk (C:)**

   The contents of your hard drive appear in the File list.

6. **In the File list, double-click the Users folder**

   The Users folder contains a subfolder for each user account on this computer. You might see a folder with your user account name on it. Each user's folder contains that person's documents. User folder names are the names that were used to log in when your computer was set up. When a user logs in, the computer allows that user access to the folder with the same user name. If you are using a computer with more than one user, you might not have permission to view other users' folders. There is also a Public folder that any user can open.

7. **Double-click the folder with your user name on it**

   Depending on how your computer is set up, this folder might be labeled with your name; however, if you are using a computer in a lab or a public location, your folder might be called Student or Computer User or something similar. You see a list of folders, such as Documents, Music, and OneDrive. See **FIGURE 2-7**.

8. **Double-click Documents in the File list**

   QUICK TIP

   In the Address bar, you can click ⯈ to the right of a folder name to see a list of its subfolders; if the folder is open, its name appears in bold in the list.

   In the Address bar, the path to the Documents folder is This PC ⯈ Local Disk (C:) ⯈ Users ⯈ *Your User Name* ⯈ Documents.

9. **In the Navigation pane, click This PC**

   You once again see your computer's storage locations. You can also move up one level at a time in your file hierarchy by clicking the Up arrow ⬆ on the toolbar, or by pressing [Backspace] on your keyboard. See **TABLE 2-1** for a summary of techniques for navigating through your computer's file hierarchy.

Open, Edit, and Save Files

Learning Outcomes
- Open a file
- Edit a file
- Save a file

Once you have created a file and saved it with a name to a storage location, you can easily open it and **edit** (make changes to) it. For example, you might want to add or delete text or add a picture. Then you save the file again so the file contains your latest changes. Usually you save a file with the same filename and in the same location as the original, which replaces the existing file with the most up-to-date version. To save a file you have changed, you use the Save command. **CASE** *You need to complete the company overview list, so you need to open the new Company Overview file you created earlier.*

STEPS

QUICK TIP
When you double-click a file in a File Explorer window, the program currently associated with that file type opens the file; to change the program, right-click a file, click Open with, click Choose another app, click the program name, select the Always use this app to open [file type] files check box, then click OK.

1. **Click the Start button, begin typing wordpad, then click the WordPad program if it is not selected or, if it is, simply press [Enter]**
   The WordPad program opens on the desktop.

2. **Click the File tab, then click Open**
   The Open dialog box opens. It contains a Navigation pane and a File list like the Save As dialog box and the File Explorer window.

3. **Scroll down in the Navigation pane if necessary until you see This PC and the list of computer locations, then click Removable Disk (H:) (or the location where you store your Data Files)**
   The contents of your USB flash drive (or the file storage location you chose) appear in the File list, as shown in **FIGURE 2-12**.

QUICK TIP
You can also double-click a file in the File list to open it.

4. **Click Company Overview.rtf in the File list, then click Open**
   The document you created earlier opens.

5. **Click to the right of the "h" in Research, press [Enter], then type Outreach**
   The edited document includes the text you just typed. See **FIGURE 2-13**.

QUICK TIP
To save changes to a file, you can also click the Save button ⊟ on the Quick Access toolbar (on the left side of the title bar).

6. **Click the File tab, then click Save, as shown in FIGURE 2-14**
   WordPad saves the document with your most recent changes, using the filename and location you specified when you previously saved it. When you save changes to an existing file, the Save As dialog box does not open.

7. **Click the File tab, then click Exit**
   The Company Overview document and the WordPad program close.

Comparing Save and Save As

Many apps, including Wordpad, include two save command options—Save and Save As. The first time you save a file, the Save As dialog box opens (whether you choose Save or Save As). Here you can select the drive and folder where you want to save the file and enter its filename. If you edit a previously saved file, you can save the file to the same location with the same file-name using the Save command. The Save command updates the stored file using the same location and filename without opening the Save As dialog box. In some situations, you might want to save a copy of the existing document using a different filename or in a different storage location. To do this, open the document, click the Save As command on the File tab, navigate to the location where you want to save the copy if necessary, and/or edit the name of the file.

FIGURE 2-6: File Explorer window showing storage locations

Click this arrow if necessary to navigate to a different location

Storage locations on this PC

Colored bars show how full drives are

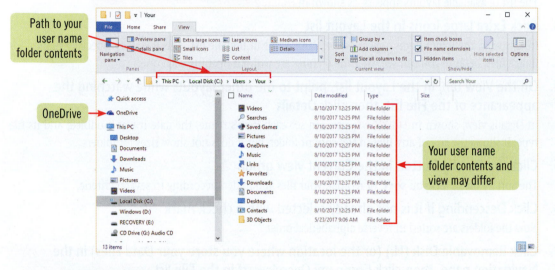

FIGURE 2-7: Your user name folder

Path to your user name folder contents

OneDrive

Your user name folder contents and view may differ

TABLE 2-1: Navigating your computer's file hierarchy

to do this	Navigation pane	Address bar	File list	keyboard
Move up in hierarchy	Click a drive or folder name	Click an item to the left of ➤ or Click the **Up to** button ↑		Press [Backspace]
Move down in hierarchy	Click a drive or folder name that is indented from the left	Click an item to the right of ➤	Double-click a folder	Press ↑ or ↓ to select a folder, then press [Enter] to open the selected folder
Return to previously viewed location		Click the **Back to** button ← or **Forward** button →		

Using and disabling Quick Access view

When you first open File Explorer, you see a list of frequently-used folders and recently used files, called Quick access view. Quick Access view can save you time by giving you one-click access to files and folders you use a lot. If you want File Explorer to open instead to This PC, you can disable Quick Access View. To do this, open a File Explorer window, click the View tab, click the Options button on the right side of the Ribbon, then click Change folder and search options. On the General tab of the Folder Options dialog box, click the Open File Explorer to list arrow, click This PC, then click OK.

Change File and Folder Views

Learning Outcomes
- View files as large icons
- Sort files
- Preview files

As you view your folders and files, you can customize your **view**, which is a set of appearance choices for files and folders. Changing your view does not affect the content of your files or folders, only the way they appear. You can choose from eight different **layouts** to display your folders and files as different sized icons, or as a list. You can change the order in which the folders and files appear, and you can also show a preview of a file in the window. **CASE** ▶ *You experiment with different views of your folders and files.*

STEPS

QUICK TIP
To expand your view of a location in the Navigation pane, click the Expand button ▶ next to that location.

1. **In the File Explorer window's Navigation pane, click Local Disk (C:); in the File list double-click Users, then double-click the folder with your user name**
   You opened your user name folder, which is inside the Users folder.

2. **Click the View tab on the Ribbon if necessary, then if you don't see eight icons in the Layout list, click the More button ▼ in the Layout group**
   The list of available layouts appears, as shown in **FIGURE 2-8**.

3. **Click Extra large icons in the Layout list**
   In this view, the folder items appear as very large icons in the File list. This layout is especially helpful for image files, because you can see what the pictures are without opening each one.

QUICK TIP
You can scroll up and down in the Layout group to see views that are not currently visible.

4. **On the View tab, in the Layout list, point to the other layouts while watching the appearance of the File list, then click Details**
   In Details view, shown in **FIGURE 2-9**, you can see each item's name, the date it was modified, and its file type. It shows the size of any files in the current folder, but it does not show sizes for folders.

5. **Click the Sort by button in the Current view group**
   The Sort by menu lets you **sort**, or reorder, your files and folders according to several criteria.

6. **Click Descending if it is not already selected with a check mark**
   Now the folders are sorted in reverse alphabetical order.

QUICK TIP
Clicking Quick Access in the Navigation pane displays folders you use frequently; to add a folder or location to Quick Access, display it in the File list, then drag it to the Quick Access list.

7. **Click Removable Disk (H:) (or the location where you store your Data Files) in the Navigation pane, then click Company Overview.rtf in the File list**

8. **Click the Preview pane button in the Panes group on the View tab if necessary**
   A preview of the selected Company Overview.rtf file you created earlier appears in the Preview pane on the right side of the screen. The WordPad file is not open, but you can still see the file's contents. See **FIGURE 2-10**.

9. **Click the Preview pane button again to close the pane, then click the window's Close button ☒**

Using the Windows Action Center

The Windows Action Center lets you quickly view system notifications and selected computer settings. To open the Action Center, click the Notifications button on the right side of the taskbar. The Action Center pane opens on the right side of the screen. Any new notifications appear in the upper part of the pane, including messages about apps, Windows tips, and any reminders you may have set. In the lower part of the pane, you see Quick Action buttons, shown in **FIGURE 2-11**, for some commonly-used Windows settings. For example, click Note to open the OneNote app; click the Brightness button repeatedly to cycle though four brightness settings; click the Airplane mode button to place your computer in airplane mode,

which turns off your computer's wireless transmission; click Quiet hours to silence your computer's notification sounds. Clicking the All settings button opens the Settings windows, where you can access all Windows settings categories. Note that the buttons available will vary depending on your hardware and software configuration.

FIGURE 2-11: Quick Action buttons

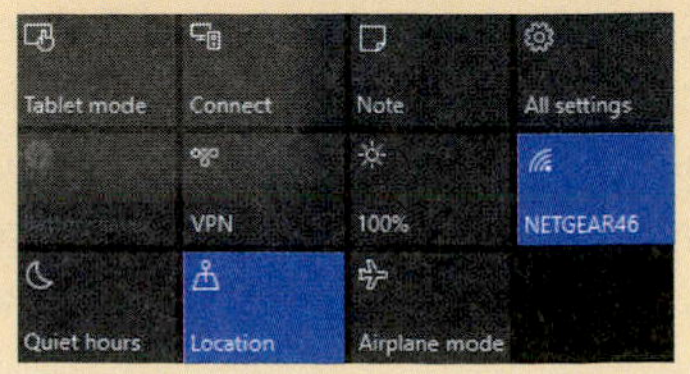

FIGURE 2-8: Layout options for viewing folders and files

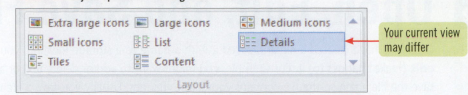

Your current view may differ

FIGURE 2-9: Your user name folder contents in Details view

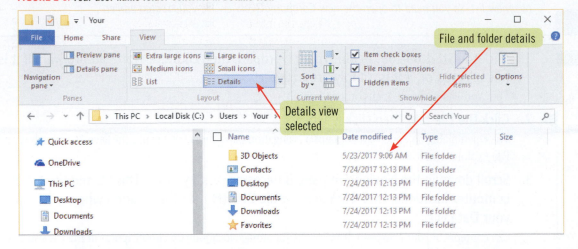

File and folder details

Details view selected

FIGURE 2-10: Preview of selected Company Overview.rtf file

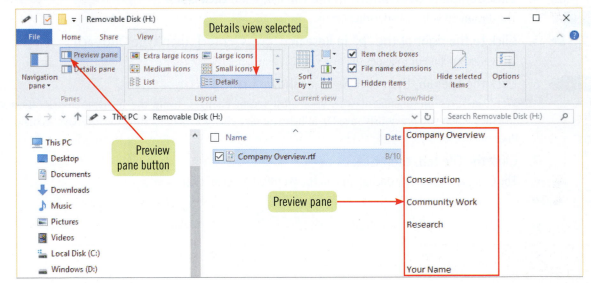

Details view selected

Preview pane button

Preview pane

Customizing Details view

When you use File Explorer to view your computer contents in Details view, you see a list of the files and folders in that location. At the top of the list you see each item's Name, Size, Type, and Date Modified. If the list of file and folder details doesn't show what you need, you can customize it. To change a column's location, drag a column heading to move it quickly to a new position. To change the order of, or **sort**, your files and folders, click any column header to sort the list by that detail; click it a second time

to reverse the order. To show only a selected group of, or **filter**, files, click the ⌄ icon to the right of the Name, Size, Type, or Date Modified, column headers, and select the check boxes for the type of items you want to include. To change the kind of details you see, right-click or tap-hold a column heading in Details view, then click or tap the detail you want to show or hide. To see more details or to change the list order, right-click or tap-hold a column title, then click or tap More.

FIGURE 2-12: Navigating in the Open dialog box

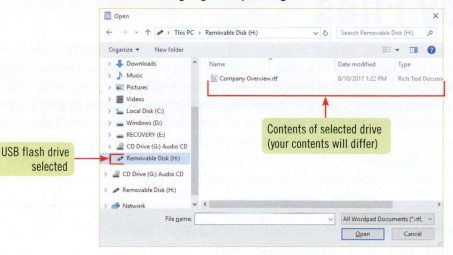

USB flash drive selected

Contents of selected drive (your contents will differ)

FIGURE 2-13: Edited document

Added text

FIGURE 2-14: Saving the updated document

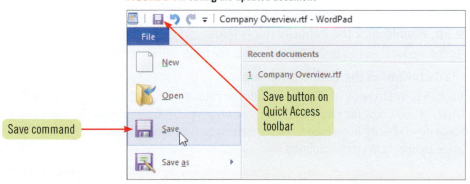

Save command

Save button on Quick Access toolbar

Using Microsoft OneDrive

Microsoft OneDrive is a location on the World Wide Web where you can store your files. Because OneDrive is an online location instead of a disk or USB device, it's often called a **cloud storage location**. When you store your files on OneDrive, you can access them from different devices, including laptops, tablets, and smartphones. Any changes you make to a file stored "in the cloud" are automatically made on OneDrive; this is known as **file syncing**. For example, if you make changes to a file from your laptop, and then open it on your tablet, you will see the changes. You can share OneDrive folders with others so they can view or edit files using a web browser such as Microsoft Edge or Internet Explorer. You can even have multiple users edit a document simultaneously. In Windows 10, OneDrive appears as a storage location in the navigation bar in File Explorer, and in the Open and Save As dialog boxes in Windows apps, so you can easily open, modify, and save files stored there. You can also download the free OneDrive Windows app from the Windows Store to help manage your OneDrive files from all your devices.

Copy Files

Sometimes you need to make a copy of an existing file. For example, you might want to put a copy on a USB flash drive so you can open the file on another machine or share it with a friend or colleague. Or you might want to create a copy as a **backup**, or replacement, in case something happens to your original file. You can copy files and folders using the Copy command and then place the copy in another location using the Paste command. You cannot have two copies of a file with the same name in the same folder. If you try to do this, Windows asks you if you want to replace the first one, and then gives you a chance to give the second copy a different name. **CASE** ▶ *You want to create a backup copy of the Company Overview document that you can store in a folder for company publicity items. First you need to create the folder, then you can copy the file.*

STEPS

1. **On the desktop, click the File Explorer button 📁 on the taskbar**

2. **In the Navigation pane, click Removable Disk (H:) (or the location where you store your Data Files)**

   First you create the new folder you plan to use for storing publicity-related files.

▶ 3. **In the New group on the Home tab, click the New folder button**

   A new folder appears in the File list, with its default name, New folder, selected.

4. **Type Publicity Items, then press [Enter]**

   Because the folder name was selected, the text you typed, Publicity Items, replaced it. Pressing [Enter] confirmed your entry, and the folder is now named Publicity Items.

▶ 5. **In the File list, click the Company Overview.rtf document you saved earlier, then click the Copy button in the Clipboard group, as shown in FIGURE 2-15**

   After you select the file, its check box becomes selected (the check box appears only if the Item check boxes option in the Show/Hide group on the View tab is selected). When you use the Copy command, Windows places a duplicate copy of the file in an area of your computer's random access memory called the **clipboard**, ready to paste, or place, in a new location. Copying and pasting a file leaves the file in its original location.

6. **In the File list, double-click the Publicity Items folder**

   The folder opens. Nothing appears in the File list because the folder currently is empty.

▶ 7. **Click the Paste button in the Clipboard group**

   A copy of the Company Overview.rtf file is pasted into the Publicity Items folder. See **FIGURE 2-16**. You now have two copies of the Company Overview.rtf file: one on your USB flash drive in the main folder, and another in your new Publicity Items folder. The file remains on the clipboard until you end your Windows session or place another item on the clipboard.

Copying files using Send to

You can also copy and paste a file using the Send to command. In File Explorer, right-click the file you want to copy, point to Send to, then in the shortcut menu, click the name of the device you want to send a copy of the file to. This leaves the original file on your hard drive and creates a copy in that location. You can send a file to a compressed file, the desktop, your Documents folder, a mail recipient, or a drive on your computer. See **TABLE 2-2**.

FIGURE 2-15: Copying a file

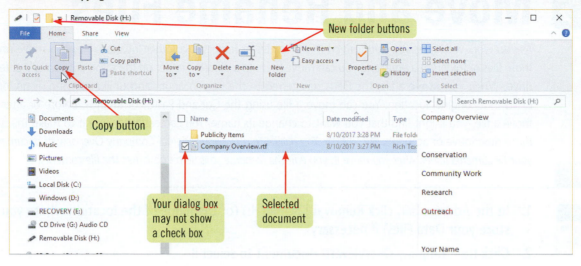

FIGURE 2-16: Duplicate file pasted into Publicity items folder

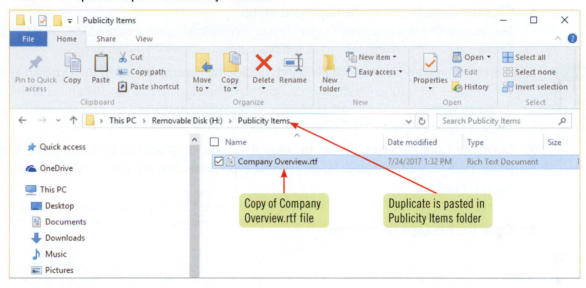

TABLE 2-2: Selected Send to menu commands

menu option	use to
Compressed (zipped) folder	Create a new, compressed (smaller) file with a .zip file extension
Desktop (create shortcut)	Create a shortcut (link) for the file on the desktop
Documents	Copy the file to the Documents library
Fax recipient	Send a file to a fax recipient
Mail recipient	Create an e-mail with the file attached to it (only if you have an e-mail program on your computer)
DVD RW Drive (D:)	Copy the file to your computer's DVD drive (your drive letter may differ)
CD Drive (G:) audio CD	Copy the file to your computer's CD drive (your drive letter may differ)
Removable Disk (H:)	Copy the file to a removable disk drive (your drive letter may differ)

Move and Rename Files

Learning Outcomes
• Cut and paste a file
• Rename a file

As you work with files, you might need to move files or folders to another location. You can move one or more files or folders at a time, and you can move them to a different folder on the same drive or to a different drive. When you **move** a file, the file is transferred to the new location, and unlike copying, it no longer exists in its original location. You can move a file using the Cut and Paste commands. Before or after you move a file, you might find that you want to change its name. You can easily rename it to make the name more descriptive or accurate. **CASE** ▶ *You decide to move your original Company Overview.rtf document to your Documents folder. After you move it, you edit the filename so it better describes the file contents.*

STEPS

1. In the Address bar, click Removable Disk (H:) (or the name of the location where you store your Data Files) if necessary

2. Click the Company Overview.rtf document to select it

3. Click the Cut button in the Clipboard group on the Ribbon, as shown in **FIGURE 2-17**

4. In the Navigation Pane, under This PC, click Documents
   You navigated to your Documents folder.

5. Click the Paste button in the Clipboard group
   The Company Overview.rtf document appears in your Documents folder and remains selected. See **FIGURE 2-18**. The filename could be clearer, to help you remember that it contains a list of company goals.

6. With the Company Overview.rtf file selected, click the Rename button in the Organize group
   The filename is highlighted. The file extension isn't highlighted because that part of the filename identifies the file to WordPad and should not be changed. If you deleted or changed the file extension, WordPad would be unable to open the file. You decide to change the word "Overview" to "Goals."

7. Move the I pointer after the "w" in "Overview", click to place the insertion point, press [Backspace] eight times to delete Overview, type Goals as shown in **FIGURE 2-19**, then press [Enter]
   You changed the name of the pasted file in the Documents folder. The filename now reads Company Goals.rtf.

8. Close the File Explorer window

Using Task View to create multiple desktops

As you have learned in Module 1, you can have multiple app windows open on your desktop, such as WordPad, Paint, and OneNote. But you might need to have a different set of apps available for a different project. Instead of closing all the apps and opening different ones, you can use Task View to work with multiple desktops, each containing its own set of apps. Then, when you need to work on another project, you can switch to another desktop to quickly access those apps. To open Task View, click the **Task View** button 🖳 on the taskbar. The current desktop becomes smaller and a New desktop button appears in the lower-right corner of the screen. Click the New desktop button. A new desktop appears in a bar at the bottom of the screen, which you can click to activate and work with its apps. See **FIGURE 2-20**. To switch to another desktop, click the Task View button and click its icon.

FIGURE 2-20: Working with multiple desktops in Task view

Desktops

Desktop #2 is displayed

New Desktop button

FIGURE 2-17: Cutting a file

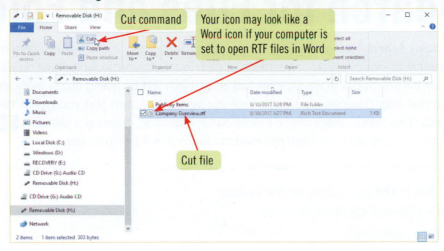

FIGURE 2-18: Pasted file in Documents folder

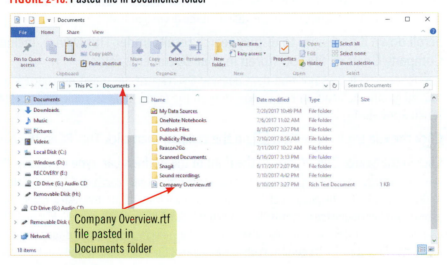

FIGURE 2-19: Renaming a file

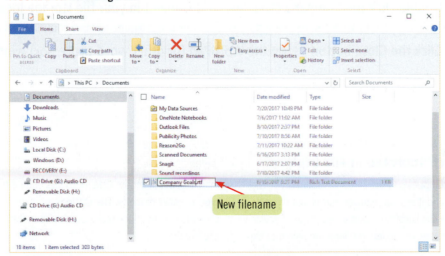

Search for Files and Folders

Learning Outcomes
• Search for a file
• Open a found file

Windows Search helps you quickly find any app, folder, or file. You can search from the Search box on the taskbar to locate applications, settings, or files. To search a particular location on your computer, you can use the Search box in File Explorer. You enter search text by typing one or more letter sequences or words that help Windows identify the item you want. The search text you type is called your **search criteria**. Your search criteria can be a folder name, a filename, or part of a filename. **CASE** *You want to locate the Company Overview.rtf document so you can print it for a colleague.*

STEPS

1. **Click in the search box on the taskbar**

   The Cortana menu opens.

2. **Type company**

   The Search menu opens with a possible match for your search at the top, and some other possible matches below it. You may see results from The Windows Store, the Internet, or your computer settings.

3. **Click My stuff, near the bottom of the menu**

   This limits your search to the files and folders in your storage locations on this device. It includes documents with the text "company" in the title or in the document text.

4. **Scroll down if necessary to display search results under This Device, including the Company Goals.rtf file you stored in your Documents folder**

   See **FIGURE 2-21**. It does not find the Company Overview.rtf file stored on your Flash drive because it's searching only the items on this device. To open the found file, you could click its listing. You can also search using File Explorer.

   > **QUICK TIP**
   > If you navigate to a specific folder in your file hierarchy, Windows searches that folder and any subfolders below it.

5. **Click the File Explorer button 📁 on the taskbar, then click This PC in the Navigation pane**

6. **Click in the Search This PC box to the right of the Address bar, type company, then press [Enter]**

   > **QUICK TIP**
   > Windows search is not case-sensitive, so you can type upper- or lowercase letters, and obtain the same results.

   Windows searches your computer for files that contain the word "company" in their title. A green bar in the Address bar indicates the progress of your search. After a few moments, the search results, shown in **FIGURE 2-22**, appear. Windows found the renamed file, Company Goals.rtf, in your Documents folder, and the original Company Overview.rtf document on your removable drive, in the Publicity Items folder. It may also locate shortcuts to the file in your Recent folder. It's good to verify the location of the found files, so you can select the right one.

7. **Click the View tab, click Details in the Layout group then look in the Folder column to view the path to each file, dragging the edge of the Folder column header with the ⟷ pointer to widen it if necessary**

   > **TROUBLE**
   > If you see a message asking how you want to open the file, click WordPad.

8. **Double-click the Company Overview.rtf document in your file storage location**

   The file opens in WordPad or in another word-processing program on your computer that reads RTF files.

9. **Click the Close button ⊠ on the WordPad (or other word-processor) window**

Using the Search Tools tab in File Explorer

The **Search Tools tab** appears in the Ribbon as soon as you click the Search text box, and it lets you narrow your search criteria. Use the commands in the Location group to specify a particular search location. The Refine group lets you limit the search to files modified after a certain date, or to files of a particular kind, size, type, or other property. The Options group lets you repeat previous searches, save searches, and open the folder containing a found file.

FIGURE 2-21: Found file

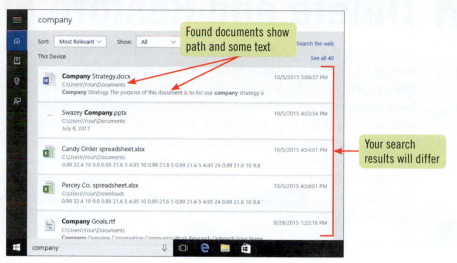

Found documents show path and some text

Your search results will differ

FIGURE 2-22: Apps screen and Search pane

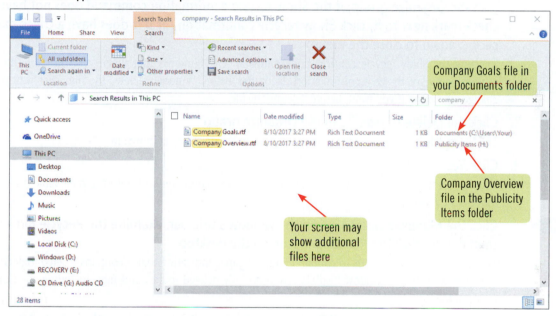

Company Goals file in your Documents folder

Company Overview file in the Publicity Items folder

Your screen may show additional files here

Using Microsoft Edge

When you search for files using the search box on the Windows taskbar and click Web, the new web browser called **Microsoft Edge** opens. You can also open Edge by clicking its icon  on the taskbar. Created to replace the older Internet Explorer browser, Edge is a Windows app that runs on personal computers, tablets, and smartphones. Edge features a reading mode that lets you read a webpage without ads. It also lets you annotate pages with markup tools such as a pen or highlighter, and add typed notes, as shown in **FIGURE 2-23**. You can also add pages to a Reading list or share them with OneNote or a social networking site.

FIGURE 2-23: Web page annotated in Microsoft Edge

Understanding File Management

Delete and Restore Files

Learning Outcomes
• Delete a file
• Restore a file
• Empty the Recycle Bin

If you no longer need a folder or file, you can delete (or remove) it from the storage device. By regularly deleting files and folders you no longer need and emptying the Recycle Bin, you free up valuable storage space on your computer. Windows places folders and files you delete from your hard drive in the Recycle Bin. If you delete a folder, Windows removes the folder as well as all files and subfolders stored in it. If you later discover that you need a deleted file or folder, you can restore it to its original location, as long as you have not yet emptied the Recycle Bin. Emptying the Recycle Bin permanently removes deleted folders and files from your computer. However, files and folders you delete from a removable drive, such as a USB flash drive, do not go to the Recycle Bin. They are immediately and permanently deleted and cannot be restored. **CASE** ▷ *You decide to delete the Company Goals document that you stored in your Documents folder.*

STEPS

1. **Click the Documents folder in the File Explorer Navigation pane**
   Your Documents folder opens.

2. **Click Company Goals.rtf to select it, click the Home tab, then click the Delete list arrow ✗ in the Organize group; if the Show recycle confirmation command does not have a check mark next to it, click Show recycle confirmation (or if it does have a check mark, click ✗ again to close the menu)**
   Selecting the Show recycle confirmation command tells Windows that whenever you click the Delete button, you want to see a confirmation dialog box before Windows deletes the file. That way you can change your mind if you want, before deleting the file.

3. **Click the Delete button ✗ in the Organize group**
   The Delete File dialog box opens so you can confirm the deletion, as shown in **FIGURE 2-24**.

4. **Click Yes**
   You deleted the file. Because the file was stored on your computer and not on a removable drive, it was moved to the Recycle Bin.

QUICK TIP
If the Recycle Bin icon does not contain crumpled paper, then it is empty.

5. **Click the Minimize button ▬ on the window's title bar, examine the Recycle Bin icon, then double-click the Recycle Bin icon on the desktop**
   The Recycle Bin icon appears to contain crumpled paper, indicating that it contains deleted folders and/or files. The Recycle Bin window displays any previously deleted folders and files, including the Company Goals.rtf file.

QUICK TIP
Another way to delete a file completely is to select the file, press and hold [Shift], then press [Delete]; if you click Yes in the message box that opens, Windows deletes the file without sending it to the Recycle Bin. Use caution, because you cannot restore the file.

6. **Click the Company Goals.rtf file to select it, then click the Restore the selected items button in the Restore group on the Recycle Bin Tools Manage tab, as shown in FIGURE 2-25**
   The file returns to its original location and no longer appears in the Recycle Bin window.

7. **In the Navigation pane, click the Documents folder**
   The Documents folder window contains the restored file. You decide to permanently delete this file after all.

8. **Click the file Company Goals.rtf, click ✗ in the Organize group on the Home tab, click Permanently delete, then click Yes in the Delete File dialog box**

9. **Minimize the window, double-click the Recycle Bin, notice that the Company Goals.rtf file is no longer there, then close all open windows**

FIGURE 2-24: Delete File dialog box

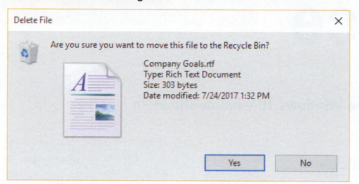

FIGURE 2-25: Restoring a file from the Recycle Bin

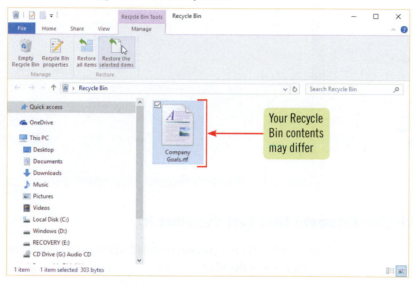

More techniques for selecting and moving files

To select a group of items that are next to each other in a window, click the first item in the group, press and hold [Shift], then click the last item in the group. Both items you click and all the items between them become selected. To select files that are not next to each other, click the first file, press and hold [Ctrl], then click the other items you want to select as a group. Then you can copy, cut, or delete the group of files or folders you selected. **Drag and drop** is a technique in which you use your pointing device to drag a file or folder into a different folder and then drop it, or let go of the mouse button, to place it in that folder. Using drag and drop does not copy your file to the clipboard. If you drag and drop a file to a folder on a different drive, Windows *copies* the file. However, if you drag and drop a file to a folder on the same drive, Windows *moves* the file into that folder

instead. See **FIGURE 2-26**. If you want to move a file to another drive, hold down [Shift] while you drag and drop. If you want to copy a file to another folder on the same drive, hold down [Ctrl] while you drag and drop.

FIGURE 2-26: Moving a file using drag and drop

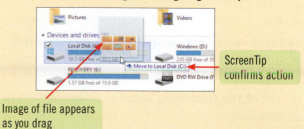

Image of file appears as you drag

ScreenTip confirms action

Understanding File Management

Practice

Concepts Review

Label the elements of the Windows 10 window shown in FIGURE 2-27.

FIGURE 2-27

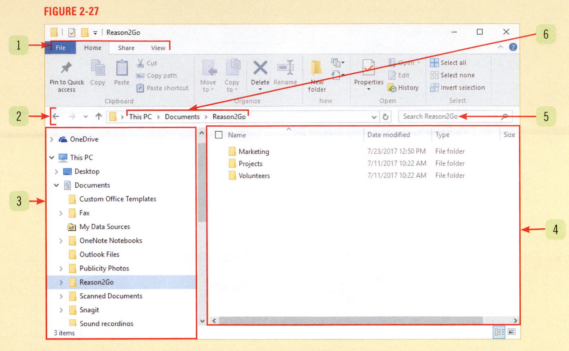

Match each term with the statement that best describes it.

7. **View**
8. **File extension**
9. **Address bar**
10. **Path**
11. **Clipboard**
12. **Snap Assist**

a. A series of locations separated by small triangles or backslashes that describes a file's location in the file hierarchy

b. A feature that helps you arrange windows on the screen

c. An area above the Files list that contains a path

d. A three- or four-letter sequence, preceded by a period, that identifies the type of file

e. A set of appearance choices for files and folders

f. An area of a computer's RAM used for temporary storage

Select the best answer from the list of choices.

13. **Which part of a window lets you see a file's contents without opening the file?**
    a. File list
    b. Address bar
    c. Navigation pane
    d. Preview pane

14. **The new Microsoft web browser is called Microsoft _____.**
    a. View
    b. Task
    c. Edge
    d. Desktop

15. **The text you type in a Search text box is called:**
    a. Sorting.
    b. RAM.
    c. Search criteria.
    d. Clipboard.

16. **Which of the following is not a visible section in a File Explorer window?**
    a. Clipboard
    b. Navigation pane
    c. File list
    d. Address bar

Skills Review

1. Understand files and folders.

   a. Create a file hierarchy for an ice cream manufacturing business, using a name that you create. The business has departments for Product Development, Manufacturing, and Personnel. Product development activities include research and testing; manufacturing has facilities for ice cream and frozen yogurt; and Personnel handles hiring and payroll. How would you organize your folders and files using a file hierarchy of three levels? How would you use folders and subfolders to keep the documents related to these activities distinct and easy to navigate? Draw a diagram and write a short paragraph explaining your answer.

   b. Use tools in the File Explorer window to create the folder hierarchy in the Documents folder on your computer.

   c. Open NotePad and write the path of the Hiring folder, using backslashes to indicate levels in the hierarchy. Do the same for the Testing folder.

2. Create and save a file.

   a. Connect your USB flash drive to a USB port on your computer, then open WordPad from the Start menu.

   b. Type **Advertising Campaign** as the title, then start a new line.

   c. Type your name, press [Enter] twice, then create the following list:

     Menu ads

     Email customers

     Web page specials

     Local TV spots

   d. Save the WordPad file with the filename **Advertising Campaign.rtf** in the location where you store your Data Files, view the filename in the WordPad title bar, then close WordPad.

3. Explore the files and folders on your computer.

   a. Open a File Explorer window.

   b. Use the Navigation pane to navigate to your USB flash drive or the location where you store your Data Files.

   c. Use the Address bar to navigate to This PC.

   d. Use the File list to navigate to your local hard drive (C:).

   e. Use the File list to open the Users folder, and then open the folder that represents your user name.

   f. Open the Documents folder. (*Hint*: The path is This PC\Local Disk (C:) \Users\Your User Name\Documents.)

   g. Use the Navigation pane to navigate back to This PC.

4. Change file and folder views.

   a. Navigate to your Documents folder or the location of your Data Files using the method of your choice.

   b. Use the View tab to view its contents as large icons.

   c. View the folder's contents in the seven other views.

   d. Sort the items in this location by date modified in ascending order.

   e. Open the Preview pane, view a selected item's preview, then close the Preview pane.

5. Open, edit, and save files.

   a. Start WordPad, then use the Open dialog box to open the Advertising Campaign.rtf document you created.

   b. After the text "Local TV spots," add a line with the text **Social media**.

   c. Save the document and close WordPad.

6. Copy files.

   a. In the File Explorer window, navigate to the location where you store your Data Files if necessary.

   b. Copy the Advertising Campaign.rtf document.

   c. Create a new folder named **Advertising** on your USB flash drive or the location where you store your Data Files (*Hint*: Use the Home tab), then open the folder.

   d. Paste the document copy in the new folder.

7. Move and rename files.

   a. Navigate to your USB flash drive or the location where you store your Data Files.

   b. Select the Advertising Campaign.rtf document located there, then cut it.

    c. Navigate to your Documents folder, then paste the file there.

    d. Rename the file **Advertising Campaign - Backup.rtf**.

8. Search for files and folders.

    a. Use the search box on the taskbar to search for a file using the search text **backup**. (*Hint*: Remember to select My stuff.)

    b. If necessary, scroll to the found file, and notice its path.

    c. Open the Advertising Campaign - Backup document from the search results, then close WordPad. (*Hint*: Closing the program automatically closes any open documents.)

    d. Open a File Explorer window, click in the search box, search your USB flash drive using the search text **overview**.

    e. Open the found document from the File list, then close WordPad.

9. Delete and restore files.

    a. Navigate to your Documents folder.

    b. Verify that your Delete preference is Show recycle confirmation, then delete the Advertising Campaign - Backup.rtf file.

    c. Open the Recycle Bin, and restore the document to its original location.

    d. Navigate to your Documents folder, then move the Advertising Campaign - Backup.rtf file to the Advertising folder on your USB flash drive (or the location where you store your Data Files).

Independent Challenge 1

To meet the needs of gardeners in your town, you have opened a vacation garden care business named GreenerInc. Customers hire you to care for their gardens when they go on vacation. To promote your new business, your website designer asks you to give her selling points to include in a web ad.

    a. Connect your USB flash drive to your computer, if necessary.

    b. Create a new folder named **GreenerInc** on your USB flash drive or the location where you store your Data Files.

    c. In the GreenerInc folder, create two subfolders named **Handouts** and **Website**.

    d. Use WordPad to create a short paragraph or list that describes three advantages of your business. Use **GreenerInc Selling Points** as the first line, followed by the paragraph or list. Include your name and email address after the text.

    e. Save the WordPad document with the filename **Selling Points.rtf** in the Website folder, then close the document and exit WordPad.

    f. Open a File Explorer window, then navigate to the Website folder.

    g. View the contents in at least three different views, then choose the view option that you prefer.

    h. Copy the Selling Points.rtf file, then paste a copy in the Documents folder.

    i. Rename the copied file **Selling Points Backup.rtf**.

    j. Cut the Selling Points Backup.rtf file from the Documents folder, and paste it in the GreenerInc\Website folder in the location where you store your Data Files, then close the File Explorer window.

Independent Challenge 2

As a freelance webpage designer for nonprofit businesses, you depend on your computer to meet critical deadlines. Whenever you encounter a computer problem, you contact a computer consultant who helps you resolve the problem. This consultant has asked you to document, or keep records of, your computer's available drives.

    a. Connect your USB flash drive to your computer, if necessary.

    b. Open File Explorer and go to This PC so you can view information on your drives and other installed hardware.

    c. View the window contents using three different views, then choose the one you prefer.

    d. Open WordPad and create a document with the text **My Drives** and your name on separate lines. Save the document as **My Drives.rtf**.

Independent Challenge 2 (continued)

e. Use Snap Assist to view the WordPad and File Explorer windows next to each other on the screen. (*Hint*: Drag the title bar of one of the windows to the left side of the screen.)

f. In WordPad, list the names of the hard drive (or drives), devices with removable storage, and any other hardware devices installed on the computer as shown in the Devices and Drives section of the window.

g. Switch to a view that displays the total size and amount of free space on your hard drive(s) and removable storage drive(s), and edit each WordPad list item to include the amount of free space for each one (for example, 22.1 GB free of 95.5 GB).

h. Save the WordPad document with the filename **My Drives** on your USB flash drive or the location where you store your Data Files.

i. Close WordPad, then maximize the File Explorer window. Navigate to your file storage location, then preview your document in the Preview pane, and close the window.

Independent Challenge 3

You are an attorney at Garcia and Chu, a large accounting firm. You participate in the company's community outreach program by speaking at career days in area schools. You teach students about career opportunities available in the field of accounting. You want to create a folder structure to store the files for each session.

a. Connect your USB flash drive to your computer (if necessary), then open the window for your USB flash drive or the location where you store your Data Files.

b. Create a folder named **Career Days**.

c. In the Career Days folder, create a subfolder named **Valley Intermediate**. Open this folder, then close it.

d. Use WordPad to create a document with the title **Accounting Jobs** at the top of the page and your name on separate lines, and the following list of items:

Current Opportunities:
Bookkeeper
Accounting Clerk
Accountant
Certified Public Accountant (CPA)

e. Save the WordPad document with the filename **Accounting Jobs.rtf** in the Valley Intermediate folder. (*Hint*: After you switch to your USB flash drive in the Save As dialog box, open the Career Days folder, then open the Valley Intermediate folder before saving the file.) Close WordPad.

f. Open WordPad and the Accounting Jobs document again, add **Senior Accountant** after Accountant, then save the file and close WordPad.

g. Store a copy of the file using the Save As command to your Documents folder, renaming it **Accounting Jobs - Copy.rtf**, then close WordPad.

h. In File Explorer, delete the document copy in your Documents folder so it is placed in the Recycle Bin, then restore it.

i. Open the Recycle Bin window, snap the File Explorer to the left side of the screen and the Recycle in to the right side, then verify that the file has been restored to the correct location.

j. Cut the file from the Documents folder and paste it in the Career Days\Valley Intermediate folder in your Data File storage location, then close all windows.

Independent Challenge 4: Explore

Think of a hobby or volunteer activity that you do now, or one that you would like to start. You will use your computer to help you manage your plans or ideas for this activity.

a. Using paper and pencil, sketch a folder structure with at least two subfolders to contain your documents for this activity.

b. Connect your USB flash drive to your computer, then open the window for your USB flash drive.

Independent Challenge 4: Explore (continued)

c. In File Explorer, create the folder structure for your activity, using your sketch as a reference.

d. Think of at least three tasks that you can do to further your work in your chosen activity.

e. Start a new WordPad document. Add the title **Next Steps** at the top of the page and your name on the next line.

f. Below your name, list the three tasks. Save the file in one of the folders created on your USB flash drive, with the title **To Do.rtf**.

g. Close WordPad, then open a File Explorer window and navigate to the folder where you stored the document.

h. Create a copy of the file, place the copied file in your Documents folder, then rename this file with a name you choose.

i. Delete the copied file from your Documents folder, restore it, then cut and paste the file into the folder that contains your To Do.rtf file, ensuring that the filename of the copy is different so it doesn't overwirte the To Do.rtf file.

j. Open Microsoft Edge using its button on the taskbar, click in the search text box, then search for information about others doing your desired hobby or volunteer activity.

k. Click the Make a Web Note button at the top of the window, click the Highlighter tool, then highlight an item that interests you.

l. Click the Share button , click Mail, choose your desired email account, then send the annotated page to yourself. You will receive an email with an attachment showing the annotated page.

m. Close Edge, your email program, and any open windows.

Visual Workshop

Create the folder structure shown in FIGURE 2-28 on your USB flash drive (or in the location where you store your Data Files). Create a WordPad document containing your name and today's date, type the path to the Midsize folder, and save it with the filename **Midsize.rtf** in a Midsize folder on your USB Flash drive or the location where you store your Data Files.

FIGURE 2-28

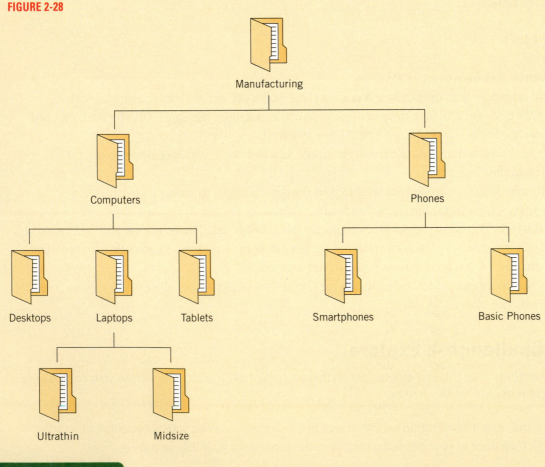

Display Apps

Learning Outcomes
- Display all apps on a device
- Display app folder contents

When you open the Windows 10 Start menu, you see tiles that represent apps installed on your computer. As you learned in Module 1, an app is software you use to accomplish tasks, such as writing a report in Microsoft Word, setting an appointment in Calendar, or checking the latest news stories with News. The apps available on the Start menu are not all the apps installed on your computer or mobile device. The Start menu contains an All apps command that shows you all the apps you have installed, which may include desktop apps like Microsoft Office, Windows Store apps like Calculator or Camera, and Windows Accessories. **CASE** ➤ *You display the apps on your computer or mobile device to see what is available for you to use.*

STEPS

QUICK TIP

If you are using a Windows device without a keyboard, such as a Windows tablet or a Windows phone, the device will start in **tablet mode**, in which the tiles fill the screen.

1. **If necessary, start Windows 10, then sign in with your username and password**
   The Windows 10 desktop appears.

2. **Click or tap the Start button ⊞ on the Windows taskbar**
   The shaded rectangles on the right represent a selection of the apps available. If your computer has been used by others, the grid might include many different apps in a customized arrangement.

3. **Click or tap the All apps button ▤ on the Start menu**
   The Apps list appears, displaying all the available apps installed on your device.

QUICK TIP

In addition to using the scroll bar to navigate the All apps menu, you can use the keyboard arrow keys or the [PgUp], [PgDn], [Home], and [End] keys.

4. **Point to or swipe the Apps list to display the scroll bar to the right of the list, then scroll down**
   The Apps list displays all the apps on your computer in alphabetical sections, as shown in **FIGURE 3-1**. Some of the listings show icons representing apps. Other listings show a folder icon with a small downward-pointing arrow ▾, which means that there are items inside the folder.

5. **Scroll up if necessary, then click or tap A near the top of the list**
   A grid of letters, numbers, and symbols appears, so that you can quickly jump to any section, such as all apps starting with A.

QUICK TIP

If you highlight an app on the All apps menu using the keyboard arrow keys, you can press the [Enter] key to start the app.

6. **Click or tap W in the grid, as shown in FIGURE 3-2, then click or tap the expand arrow ▾ next to Windows Accessories**
   The Windows accessories folder opens to display the Windows Accessories apps, which are apps that come with Windows 10. See **FIGURE 3-3**. You learned about the Paint, NotePad, WordPad, Snipping Tool, and Sticky Notes Windows accessories in previous modules. **TABLE 3-1** describes several other Windows Accessory programs that can help you accomplish tasks.

7. **Click or tap the Back button to return to the Start menu, then click or tap ⊞ to close the Start menu**

TABLE 3-1: Additional windows accessories

Windows accessory	lets you
Character Map	Locate and copy special characters such as symbols and small images in different fonts
Remote Desktop Connection	Connect to another Windows computer on the same network or on the Internet
Steps Recorder	Record computer actions to document a task; can be useful for technical support
Windows Fax and Scan	Send and receive faxed document without having a fax machine
Windows Journal	Handwrite notes and drawings with a graphics tablet or a tablet PC

Working with Windows Apps

CASE   Now that you are familiar with Windows 10, you want to learn how to use apps, specifically how to install new ones from the online Windows Store, and how to organize them on the Start menu. *Note: With the release of Windows 10, Microsoft now provides ongoing updates to Windows instead of releasing new versions periodically. This means that Windows features might change over time, including how they look and how you interact with them. The information provided in this text was accurate at the time this book was published.*

Module Objectives

After completing this module, you will be able to:

- Display apps
- Search for apps
- Install apps from the Windows Store
- Uninstall apps
- Manage apps using multiple desktops
- Customize the Start menu
- Group apps on the Start menu

Files You Will Need

No files needed.

FIGURE 3-1: All apps alphabetical groupings

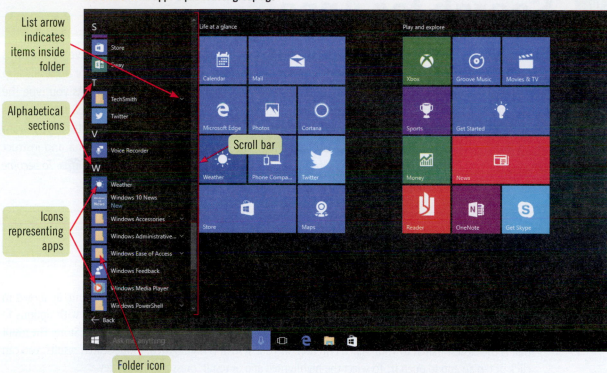

List arrow indicates items inside folder

Alphabetical sections

Icons representing apps

Folder icon

Scroll bar

FIGURE 3-2: Section groupings

FIGURE 3-3: Contents of the Windows Accessories folder

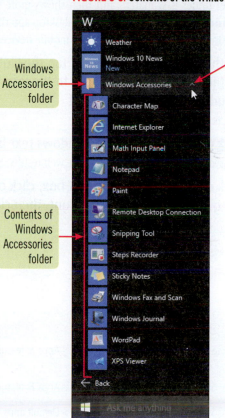

Windows Accessories folder

Expand arrow becomes Collapse arrow while folder contents are displayed

Contents of Windows Accessories folder

Search for Apps

Learning Outcomes
• Enter search text
• Examine search results
• Search without Cortana

A common way to look for a specific app is to use the All apps menu. However, when you have a lot of apps installed on your device, this method can be time consuming. A more direct way to search for a specific app is through the search box on the Start menu, just as you would search for files or folders. As you type the search criteria in the Search box, Windows narrows down and displays the search results. If Cortana is activated, Windows searches your computer and makes suggestions based on web results. If you want Windows to search only your computer and not show web results, you can turn off Cortana and instruct Windows not to search the web. To manage the apps on your computer, see **TABLE 3-2.** **CASE** ▶ *To become familiar with the search capabilities of Windows 10, you search for apps.*

STEPS

TROUBLE
If your search box says "Search Windows," Cortana is off. To activate Cortana, click or tap the search box, click or tap the Settings button ⚙, drag the slider under "Cortana can give you suggestions…" to the right, then click or tap Use Cortana.

1. **Verify that your search box says "Ask me anything"**
   This verifies that the digital assistant, Cortana, is on.

2. **Click or tap in the search box, then type windows**
   As you type, Windows narrows down the search results and displays them in the Start menu, as shown in **FIGURE 3-4**. The results are divided into categories: Best match, Apps, Settings, and Folders, with options to search My stuff or Web at the bottom. Your list may show other categories, such as Photos and Store. The result that is the closest match to your search criterion on your system is highlighted. In the search results, you can click or tap an app to open it. To select the highlighted app or result, press the [Enter] key.

3. **Press [Spacebar], then type media**
   The search criterion is now "windows media." The results list now displays the desktop app Windows Media Player under Best match, and then shows more possibilities in Web and Store groupings. See **FIGURE 3-5**. **Windows Media Player** is a free desktop app that lets you play audio and video files and view images on Windows computers and Windows mobile devices.

QUICK TIP
To quickly start a search at any time, you can press the [⊞] key on your keyboard and start typing.

4. **On the Cortana menu click or tap the Notebook button 🔳, click or tap Settings, drag the Cortana can give you… slider to the left, then, if necessary, drag the Search online and include web results to the left**
   Cortana is no longer active.

5. **Click or tap in the Search Windows text box, then type windows media**
   The search results no longer include web results. See **FIGURE 3-6**.

6. **Click or tap in the Search text box, click or tap the Settings button, drag the Cortana can give you… slider to the right, then click or tap Use Cortana to turn Cortana back on**

TABLE 3-2: Managing your apps

to	go to
View app sizes and storage locations	Start button > Settings > System > Apps & features
Move or uninstall an app	Start button > Settings > System > Apps & features > click or tap an app > click Move or Uninstall
Choose which app starts when you double-click a file	Start button > Settings > System > Default apps
Show/hide most used or recently added apps on Start menu	Start button > Settings > Personalization > Start

FIGURE 3-4: Cortana menu showing search results for "windows"

Best matches on your system appear here

Search results divided into categories

Search criterion "windows"

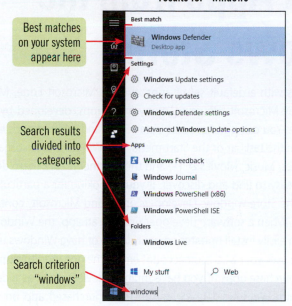

FIGURE 3-5: Results for search text "windows media"

Window Media Player is now the best match

Search results show Web results

Cortana menu

Search criterion "windows media"

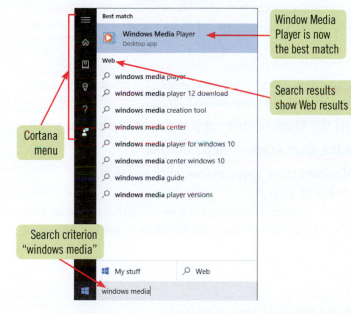

FIGURE 3-6: Search results with Cortana not activated

With Cortana off, menu displays fewer options

Search results no longer show Web results

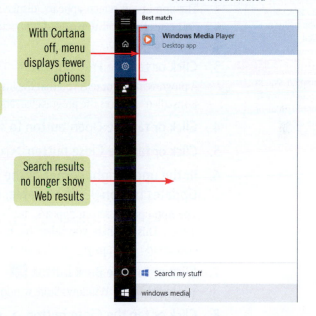

Working with Windows Apps

Install Apps from the Windows Store

Windows 10 comes with a default set of apps, such as Microsoft Edge, Mail, Photos, Movies & TV, and News, developed by Microsoft. However, many more apps, developed by third parties, are available for almost any purpose. You can purchase and install Store and desktop apps from the Windows Store, which you can access from the taskbar or the Start menu. The Windows Store organizes apps by main categories, such as Apps, Games, Music, Movies & TV, and then further breaks them down into more specific categories, to make apps easy to find and discover. If you're looking for a particular app, you can use the search box at the top of the Store window. Developers, including Microsoft, continually update apps to provide additional features. When a software developer updates an app, the Windows Store shows that an update is available. You can easily install updates on your device or have Windows update your apps automatically. The Windows Store uses your Microsoft account email (the one used to sign in to Windows 10) as the basis for an account to purchase apps. If you have multiple devices, such as a desktop computer and a mobile tablet or phone, with Windows 10, you can install a purchased app on up to ten of them using your Microsoft account. **CASE** ▶ *To learn more about a variety of subjects, you decide to install the Khan Academy app.*

STEPS

1. **Click or tap the Store button 🗔 on the taskbar, in the Store window click or tap in the Search box, type khan, then press [Enter]**
   The Windows Store app opens and the search results appear, as shown in **FIGURE 3-7**.

2. **Click or tap the Khan Academy tile**
   The app install screen appears, displaying overview information about the app, as shown in **FIGURE 3-8**. You can also scroll down to display customer reviews, a complete list of features, and detailed requirements for the app.

3. **Click or tap the Free button**
   A progress indicator tells you that the installation is underway. When it is complete, the message "The product is installed" replaces the progress bar, and the Free button becomes an Open button.

4. **Click or tap the Open button to start the Khan Academy app and examine its categories**

5. **Click or tap the Close button ✕ on the Khan Academy app's title bar**

6. **In the upper-right corner of the Windows store app window, click or tap the Updates button ↓₁, if available, or skip to Step 7**
   The App updates screen appears, displaying the updates available for the apps currently installed on your device. This is where you select (with a checkmark) the apps you want to update or deselect (without a checkmark) the apps you don't want to update.

7. **Click or tap the Back button ←**
   You return to the Windows Store window.

8. **Click or tap the Close button ✕ on the Windows Store window**
   The Windows Store app closes.

9. **Click or tap the Start button ⊞, verify that Khan Academy appears under Recently added, then press [Esc] to close the menu**

FIGURE 3-7: Search results in the Windows Store

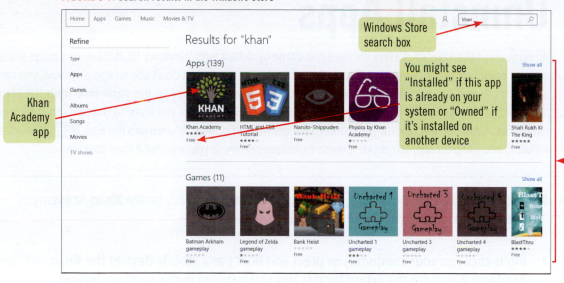

Windows Store search box

You might see "Installed" if this app is already on your system or "Owned" if it's installed on another device

Khan Academy app

Search results for "khan"; your results may differ

FIGURE 3-8: Khan Academy app install screen in the Windows Store

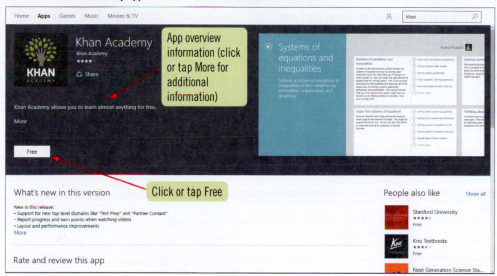

App overview information (click or tap More for additional information)

Click or tap Free

Updating apps

Developers, including Microsoft, continually update apps to provide additional features. If a new version of an app you have installed is available, Windows automatically generates an update link for you in the Windows Store. To access the App updates screen, click or tap the Store button on the taskbar, then click or tap the Updates link in the upper-right corner of the Windows Store screen. If the Updates link is not available, then all of the apps you have installed on your device are up to date with the latest version. After you click or tap the Updates button, Windows displays a list of apps with an available update. You can also manually check for updates; click or tap your profile picture on the Windows Store screen, click or tap Downloads and Updates, then click or tap Check for updates. To have updates installed automatically, click or tap your profile picture, click or tap Settings, then drag the Update apps automatically slider to On. Note that the Home version of Windows 10 may not have the Update apps automatically option.

Uninstall Apps

When you install an app, including the ones that come by default with Windows 10, it takes up storage space on your computer or mobile device. If space becomes limited or you just don't use an app anymore, you can uninstall it to free up storage space. You can uninstall one or more apps at the same time from the Start menu or the All apps listing. Simply right-click or press and hold the app you want to uninstall, then click or tap Uninstall. After an alert message to confirm the uninstall, Windows 10 uninstalls the app. **CASE** *After installing and using an app, you decide it doesn't meet your needs, so you uninstall it from your device.*

STEPS

1. **Click or tap the Start button ⊞, then under Recently added, locate Khan Academy or the app you installed in the previous lesson**
   See **FIGURE 3-9**.

2. **Right-click (on your computer) or press and hold (on a mobile device) the Khan Academy listing (or the listing for the app you installed in the previous lesson)**
   The pop-up menu includes an option for uninstalling the app.

3. **Click or tap Uninstall on the pop-up menu**
   An alert message box appears, asking you to confirm the uninstall, as shown in **FIGURE 3-10**.

4. **Click or tap Uninstall in the alert message box**
   The app is removed from the Start menu and Windows uninstalls the app from your device.

5. **Press [Esc]**
   The Start menu closes.

Viewing all your apps

If you're not sure what Windows Store apps you own, you can display a list of them in the Windows Store. Click or tap the Store button on the taskbar. At the top of the Store screen, click or tap your account picture, then click or tap My Library. To display all the apps you own for your Microsoft account, including apps, games, music, movies, and TV shows, click or tap Show all next to each category. The list appears in two parts: those that work on the current device, and those that don't. For example, there may be apps that work only on your Windows phone. If there is an arrow to the right of an app name that works on the current device, click or tap it to install the app on your current device. You can install a purchased app on up to ten different devices using the same Microsoft account. To see all the apps you own, including Store and nonstore apps, click or tap the Start button, click or tap Settings, click or tap System, then click or tap Apps & features. The apps listing that appears doesn't include any Windows 10 apps installed along with the operating system, such as Windows accessories. The list is sorted by size. To locate a particular app, click or tap the Sort list arrow, then click or tap Sort by name and scroll down the list.

FIGURE 3-9: Newly installed app on Start menu

App newly installed on this device

FIGURE 3-10: Uninstalling the Khan Academy app

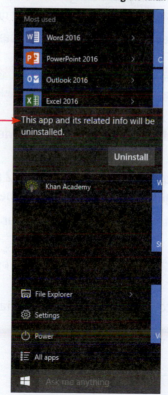

Message asks you to confirm the uninstall

Learning
Outcomes
• Create a new
desktop
• Open apps on a
second desktop
• Close a second
desktop

Manage Apps using Multiple Desktops

When you work with many apps at once, they can be difficult to manage as your taskbar fills up with app icons. And, in today's multitasking world, you may find you use different groups of apps for different purposes. For example, you might use Microsoft Word and Excel for your everyday work and then use the News, Weather, and Sports apps during your lunch break. Instead of having all the apps available on the taskbar at once, you can place your work apps on one desktop and your lunchbreak apps on a second one, sometimes called a **virtual desktop**, with its own taskbar. Then you can quickly switch between the two desktops and their respective taskbars so that only the apps you need are readily available. You create and manage multiple desktops in Task View. If you close a desktop that contains an open app, that app moves to the other desktop automatically. **CASE** *You are researching current events using the News and Money apps, but you are also planning a trip using the Maps and Calendar apps. You decide to set up separate desktops for each task.*

STEPS

TROUBLE

If the News and
Money apps do not
appear as tiles on
your Start menu,
click or tap All apps
and locate them; if
they do not appear
there, download
them from the
Windows Store.

1. Click or tap the Start button ⊞, click or tap the News app tile, click or tap ⊞, then click or tap the Money app tile

2. Drag the title bar of the Money app to the left side of the screen, then release it when a rectangle fills the left side of the screen

   Snap Assist displays the News app, as well as any other open apps, as thumbnails on the right half of the screen.

3. Click or tap the thumbnail representing the News app

   The Money and News apps are now snapped to the left and right sides of the screen.

QUICK TIP

To display Task View
using the keyboard,
press [⊞][Tab]

4. Click or tap the Task View button ▦ on the taskbar, then click or tap the New desktop button

   A second desktop appears in the lower part of the screen, as shown in **FIGURE 3-11**. Your original desktop, containing any apps you had open previously, becomes Desktop 1, and the new, empty desktop becomes Desktop 2.

5. Click or tap Desktop 2, then click or tap ⊞ as needed to open the Maps and Calendar apps

QUICK TIP

To quickly switch
between multiple
desktops, press
[Ctrl][⊞][→]

6. Using the same technique you followed in Steps 2 and 3, snap the Maps and Calendar apps to the left and right sides of the screen, respectively

7. Click or tap ▦ , point to Desktop 1, compare your screen to **FIGURE 3-12**, then click Desktop 1

QUICK TIP

To move a window
from one desktop to
another, click or tap
the Task View button,
then drag any win-
dow into another
desktop in Task View.

8. Close the News and Money apps, switch to Desktop 2, then close the Maps and Calendar apps

9. Click or tap ▦ , point to Desktop 2, then click or tap its Close button ✕, as shown in **FIGURE 3-13**

   The Close button turns red when you point to it.

FIGURE 3-11: Second desktop added in Task View

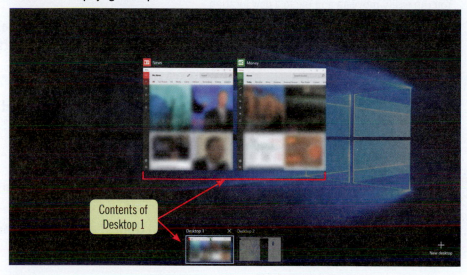

New desktop

New desktop
button

Original desktop
becomes Desktop 1

Task view

FIGURE 3-12: Displaying Desktop 1

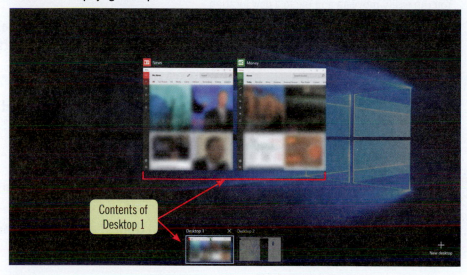

Contents of
Desktop 1

FIGURE 3-13: Closing Desktop 2

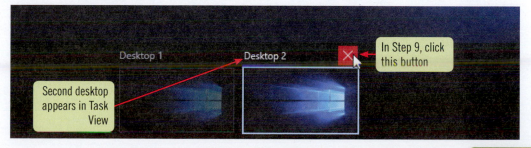

In Step 9, click
this button

Second desktop
appears in Task
View

Working with Windows Apps

Customize the Start Menu

The Start menu is the beginning point for accessing apps and features in Windows 10. The Start menu tiles represent pinned items from the Apps list. **Pinned items** are shortcuts that let you open an app or accessory with one click or tap. The Start menu comes with a default set of pinned items when you install Windows 10. You can make it easier to find the apps or accessories you use most often by adding, removing, resizing, and rearranging tiles to suit your preference. You can pin desktop apps, Windows Store apps, or Windows accessories to the Start menu, and also customize the way the Start menu looks and functions. The pinned items remain on the Start menu like pushpins hold paper on a bulletin board, until you unpin them. When you unpin an item, Windows removes the shortcut from the Start menu. However, it doesn't remove the app or accessory from the App list or your system. **CASE** *Because you frequently create sound files using the Voice Recorder program, you decide to pin it to the Start menu for easy access.*

STEPS

1. **Click or tap the** Start button ⊞, **then click or tap** All apps

2. **Go to the** V **category, then locate the** Voice Recorder **app**

3. **Right-click or press and hold** Voice Recorder, **then click or tap** Pin to Start, **as shown in** FIGURE 3-14

   A tile representing the Voice Recorder app appears in a blank area of the Start menu. See FIGURE 3-15. You can easily move an app tile to a new location.

4. **Drag the** Voice Recorder tile **to a different location on the Start menu, releasing the mouse button (or removing your finger from the screen) when the tile reaches the new location**

   As you drag, other tiles move to make room for the tile.

5. **Right-click the** Voice Recorder tile, **click** Resize; **on a touch screen, press and hold, tap the** More button ⊙, **then tap** Resize

   The four available size options appear in a pop-up menu. See FIGURE 3-16.

6. **Click or tap** Wide

   The Voice Recorder tile widens. Different apps have different sizes available. You decide to remove the tile from the Start menu.

7. **Right-click the** Voice Recorder tile, **then click** Unpin from Start; **on a touch screen, press and hold the tile, then tap the** Unpin button ⊗

Working with Windows Apps

FIGURE 3-14: Pinning the Voice Recorder app to the Start menu

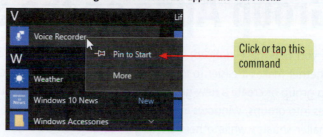

Click or tap this command

FIGURE 3-15: Voice Recorder tile added to Start menu

Voice Recorder remains on All apps list

Voice Recorder tile added to Start menu

FIGURE 3-16: Resizing an app tile on the Start menu

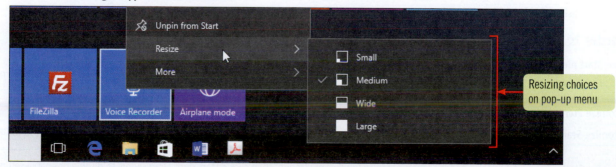

Resizing choices on pop-up menu

Working with Windows Apps

Windows 10

Group Apps on the Start Menu

Learning Outcomes
- Create a group of app tiles
- Name a group of app tiles
- Remove a group from the Start menu

As you may have noticed, the app tiles on the Start menu are arranged in groups. Grouping apps together makes it easier to locate and use them individually. You can arrange app items within an existing group or create a new group simply by repositioning them on the Start menu. When you move app tiles into groups, Windows arranges them by default within the group. Because tile sizes vary—some are smaller squares while others are larger rectangles—they don't always fit seamlessly into place. If you want the tile groups to appear more precisely, you can resize them at any time. **TABLE 3-3** shows additional ways to customize Start menu elements. After you organize your apps into a group, you can name each group for easy identification. If the name you originally chose for a group no longer fits, or you want to delete it, you can edit or remove the group name. **CASE** *Because you use your device for both work and personal tasks, you decide to group your apps on the Start menu for better organization.*

STEPS

1. **With the Start menu still open, drag the News tile to the bottom of the menu, as shown in FIGURE 3-17, then release the mouse button or lift your finger from the screen**

    As you drag to the bottom of the Start menu, a horizontal bar appears indicating a new group. The News tile appears in a new group.

QUICK TIP
You can also use the Name box to edit or remove a group name.

2. **Drag the Weather tile to the new group**

    The Weather tile appears in the new group.

3. **Point to the area above the News and Weather apps, then click or tap Name group; on a touch screen, tap the area above the two apps**

    The Name box appears, so that you can enter a name for the group, as shown in **FIGURE 3-18**.

QUICK TIP
To move an entire group, click or press and hold a group name, then drag the group to a new location.

4. **Type Current Events in the Name box, then press [Enter]**

    The group name appears above the newly created group.

5. **Drag the News app back to its original location**

6. **Drag the Weather app back to its original location**

    The group name no longer appears below the tiles.

TABLE 3-3: Customizing Start menu elements

in order to	do this
Resize Start menu	Move pointer over the right or top edge, until the pointer shape becomes ⟷ or ↕, then drag left, right, up, or down; you cannot drag the corner; app tiles remain the same sizes, but Start menu takes up more or less room on the screen
Customize Start menu entries	Right-click or press and hold an item, tap More if necessary, then click or tap Don't show in this list
Customize Start menu tiles	Right-click a tile, then click Turn live tile off; on a touch screen, press and hold a tile, tap the ellipses button, tap More if necessary, then tap Turn live tile off
Customize Start menu settings	Click or tap Settings, click or tap Personalization, then click or tap Start. Drag sliders to disable or enable settings

FIGURE 3-17: Dragging an app tile to a new group

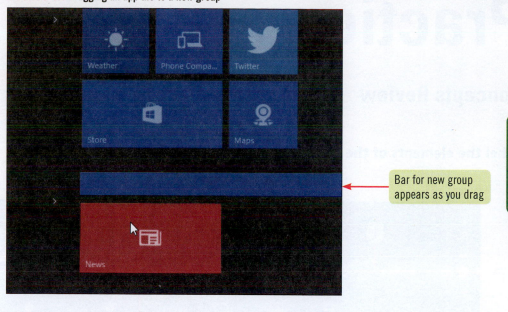

Bar for new group appears as you drag

FIGURE 3-18: Naming a new group

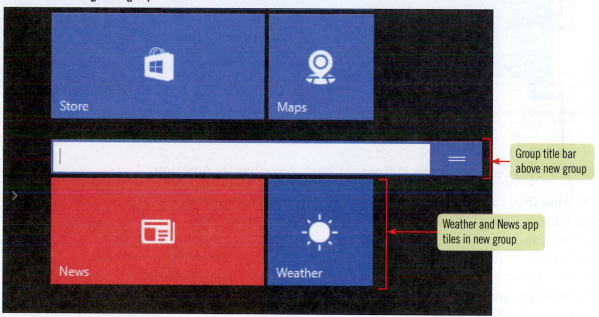

Group title bar above new group

Weather and News app tiles in new group

Practice

Concepts Review

Label the elements of the Windows 10 screen shown in FIGURE 3-19.

FIGURE 3-19

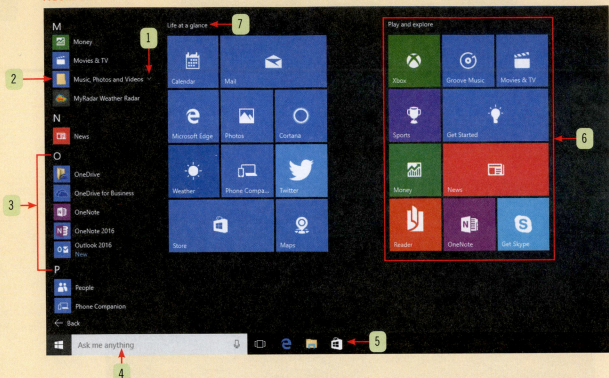

Match each term with the statement that describes its function.

8. Apps list
9. Windows Media Player
10. Start menu
11. Virtual desktop
12. My Library
13. Windows Store

a. Can be customized and resized
b. Lets you install or update apps
c. Shows desktop apps, Store apps, and accessories
d. Lets you play audio and video files and view images
e. A location where you can have a separate set of apps open
f. A place in the Windows Store that lists your apps

Select the best answers from the following lists of choices.

14. Which task is *not* accomplished in the Windows Store?
    a. Install an app.
    b. Update an app.
    c. Uninstall an app.
    d. Unpin from Start.

15. From which of the following can you uninstall an app?
    a. Start menu
    b. Desktop
    c. File Explorer window
    d. Virtual desktop

16. Which feature lets you have two or more sets of apps running simultaneously that you can switch between?
    a. Windows Store
    b. Task view
    c. Windows Media Player
    d. Start menu group

17. Which Windows 10 area allows you to create a group?
    a. Start menu
    b. Personalization settings
    c. My Library
    d. Windows Store

18. Where would you go to update an app?
    a. Virtual desktop
    b. Start menu
    c. Desktop
    d. Windows Store

19. When searching for an app on your computer using the Start menu, which of the following is not a category that might appear in the results?
    a. Best match
    b. Settings
    c. Cortana
    d. Apps

20. Where can you see all the apps installed on your computer?
    a. Desktop
    b. Windows Journal
    c. Windows Store
    d. All apps list

21. Which Windows accessory would you use to handwrite notes and drawings on a graphics tablet?
    a. Steps Recorder
    b. Character Map
    c. Windows Journal
    d. Remote Desktop Connection

22. Which of the following indicates when a Windows Store app has an update available?
    a. A message on the Start menu
    b. An update link in the Windows Store
    c. A live tile
    d. An update link on a virtual desktop

23. Which of the following would you create on the Start menu to help organize your apps?
    a. Live tiles
    b. Character Map
    c. Group
    d. Steps Recorder

24. For ease of access, you can _____ apps to the Start menu.
    a. uninstall
    b. customize
    c. pin
    d. update

Skills Review

1. Display apps.

    a. Start Windows and sign in, if necessary.

    b. Use the All apps button on the Start menu to show all apps.

    c. Scroll the apps list to view all the alphabetical categories.

    d. Navigate to a different alphabetical category using a category letter.

    e. Open the Windows Accessories folder in the apps list, then observe the apps it contains.

    f. Return to the Start menu, then close it.

2. Search for apps.

    a. In the Search box, type **character** and observe the results on the Start menu.

    b. After "character," press [Spacebar], continue typing **map** and observe the results.

    c. In the Best match category, click or tap the Character Map app to open it.

    d. Close the app.

3. Install apps from the Windows Store.

    a. Use a button on the taskbar to open the Windows Store app.

    b. Explore the categories of available apps.

    c. Use the Store search box to locate the Duolingo app. (If this app is not available, search for a different app of your choosing.)

    d. Examine the Duolingo information screen, its ratings and reviews, and its additional information.

    e. Install the Duolingo app (or another app that interests you).

    f. Locate the newly installed app on the Start menu and in the All apps list.

    g. Open the new app.

    h. Close the app.

4. Uninstall apps.

    a. Select the app you installed in Step 4e.

    b. Uninstall the app.

    c. If prompted, follow app-specific instructions to complete the uninstall.

    d. Verify the app no longer appears on the Start menu or in the All apps list.

5. Manage apps using multiple desktops.

    a. Open the Weather app, then open the Calendar app.

    b. Arrange the apps so each one fills half of the screen.

    c. Use the Task View button to create a second desktop.

    d. Display the second desktop.

    e. Open WordPad, then then open the Windows Store app.

    f. Arrange the two apps so each one fills half of the screen.

    g. Display Desktop 1, then close the Calendar and Weather apps.

    h. Display Desktop 2, then close the WordPad and Windows Store apps.

    i. Close Desktop 2.

6. Customize the Start menu.

    a. On the All apps list, locate the People app, then pin it to the Start menu.

    b. Use the Back button to return to the Start menu.

    c. Drag the People app tile to a different location on the Start menu.

    d. Resize the People app tile to Wide.

    e. Unpin the People app from the Start menu.

Skills Review (continued)

7. **Group apps on the Start menu.**
   a. Drag the Groove Music app to the bottom of the Start menu to create a new group.
   b. Drag the Movies & TV app into the new group.
   c. Name the new group **Entertainment**. See **FIGURE 3-20**; note that your tile sizes may differ.
   d. Drag the new group to a new location on the Start menu.
   e. Drag the Groove Music and Movies & TV apps back to their original locations.

FIGURE 3-20

Independent Challenge 1

You are working with a tutorial service that provides after-school study help to local high school students. In your next tutoring session, you plan to show your student useful note taking and word processing apps. In this Independent Challenge, you'll review your existing word processing apps and explore the Windows Store for note taking apps. Then you'll organize word processing and note taking apps on the Start menu for easy access.

a. Display the Start menu and the All apps list. Review which word processing apps you currently have.
b. Pin your existing word processing apps (including Windows accessories) to the Start menu.
c. If necessary, drag the tiles representing each word processing app into a new group.
d. Name the group **Word processing and note taking**.
e. Open the Windows Store and search for note taking apps, using the Search box.
f. Open the information screen for several of the free note taking apps. Read each one's description, ratings, and additional information.
g. Choose one free note taking app that interests you and install it.
h. Search for the new app using the Search text box on the taskbar to verify that it was installed.
i. Pin the newly installed app to the Start menu, then if necessary, add it to your Word processing and note taking group.

Independent Challenge 1 (continued)

j. Verify that all the apps in your group are Medium-sized. See **FIGURE 3-21** for an example; your apps and group placement will differ.
k. Drag the group to a new location on your Start menu.
l. Uninstall the note taking app that you installed in Step g.
m. Unpin the word processing apps from the Start menu, then verify that the group and its name are no longer visible.

FIGURE 3-21

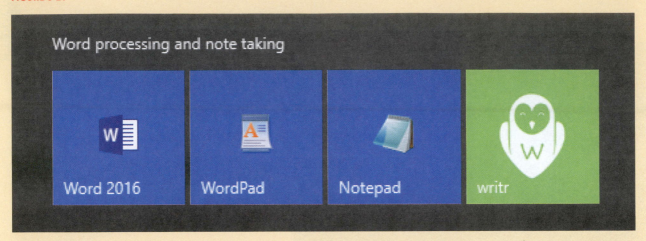

Independent Challenge 2

You are a marketing analyst for a company that is developing a new free app that helps students prepare for the SAT exam. You want to learn more about competing apps in this area and share your findings with your co-workers.

a. Open the Windows Store app, then search for apps using the search text **SAT**.
b. Examine the results for the most highly rated free SAT preparation apps.
c. Search for the WordPad accessory, open it, then use Snap Assist to arrange the Store app and the WordPad app next to each other on the screen.
d. In WordPad, list three of the most highly rated apps. Note the app name, the number of ratings, and any notable benefits or drawbacks noted in user comments. Write a short paragraph about each one, noting the number and quality of reviews, and some benefits or drawbacks of the five apps you have selected. Include your evaluation of the reviews: Do you think all the reviews are authentic?
e. Add your name to the end of the document, then save the document as **Free SAT apps.rtf** in the location where you store your Data Files.

Independent Challenge 3

You have just updated your work and home computers to Windows 10. You want to explore some of the more highly recommended Windows 10 apps for possible use.

a. Start Microsoft Edge, then search the web using search text such as "best free Windows 10 apps" to locate apps that technical publications or sites recommend.

Independent Challenge 3 (continued)

    b. Choose three free apps that you would like to try out. Open WordPad, create a new document, save it as **Best Free Windows 10 apps.rtf** in the location where you store your Data Files, and note the following for each app:

- App name
- Category (Games, Education, Home and Office, Photos and Graphics, and so forth)
- The total number of reviews
- What the app does
- Why you would like to try it

       Add your name to the end of the document, then save your work.

    c. Search your system to see if it already has any of your chosen apps installed.

    d. Install one free app from your list, open it, and examine its features.

    e. Create a new tile for the app on your Start menu, and display a live tile if available.

    f. Move the app to a new group called **Apps to Try**.

    g. Remove the app from the Start menu, then uninstall it.

Independent Challenge 4: Explore

In this Independent Challenge, you will apply the skills you learned in this module to the Start menu and apps on your own computer. The object is to organize the apps on your computer in an arrangement that makes them logically organized and easy to find. (*Note*: Before you start, if you are working in a school lab or at a public computer, verify that you have permission to make permanent changes to the Start menu.)

    a. Display the Start menu, and make a sketch and/or notes on the location of all app tiles and groups, so you can restore it later. (If you can use your PrintScreen key, take a screenshot of the Start menu by pressing the PrintScreen or Prt Sc key to copy it to the clipboard, open WordPad, then paste the screenshot into a new document, using the Paste command in the Clipboard group on the Home tab. Add your name to the end of the document, then save the document as **Original Start menu.rtf** in the location where you store your Data Files.)

    b. Explore your All apps list and your Start menu, and evaluate how well the current organization of your tiles reflects your personal and professional needs. If you use your computer for both personal and professional purposes, consider which apps relate to each area.

    c. On the Start menu, unpin any apps that you are unlikely to use frequently. As you unpin each one, check your All apps list to verify that the app is still installed on your computer.

    d. Open the All apps list, then pin each app you use frequently to the Start menu. (*Hint*: Refer to the Most used section of the Start menu to verify the apps you use most.)

    c. On the Start menu, drag your apps into groupings that will meet your needs. Name each group appropriately, and drag each group so the arrangement is pleasing and is convenient for the way you work.

    f. Search the Windows Store for any additional apps that you think would be useful in your work or personal life, evaluate their reviews, install them, pin them to the Start menu, and add them to the groups you created. Add additional groups as necessary.

    g. Create a sketch of your new Start menu tile layout, including group and app names. (If you can use your PrintScreen key, take a screenshot of the Start menu by pressing the PrintScreen (or Prt Sc) key to copy it to the clipboard, open WordPad, then paste the screenshot into a new document, using the Paste command in the Clipboard group on the Home tab. Add your name to the end of the document, then save it as **My Start menu.rtf** in the location where you store your Data Files).

    h. Restore your Start menu to its original state, using the sketch or screen shot you created in Step a. Uninstall any new apps you don't think you will need.

Visual Workshop

Use pinning to create a group on your desktop that shows the app tiles shown in **FIGURE 3-22**. Note the apps included, their arrangement, and the relative sizes of the tiles. If you can use your computer's PrintScreen key, take a screenshot, paste it into a WordPad document using the Paste command in the Clipboard group on the Home tab, add your name to the end of the document, then save it as **Windows Accessories.rtf** in the location where you store your Data Files.

FIGURE 3-22

Using Apps to Get and Share Information

> **CASE** ▶ Windows 10 includes apps that help you find information and communicate with others on the Internet. You want to learn how to use apps to browse and search the web, send and receive email and instant messages, manage calendar events, and store files online. *Note: With the release of Windows 10, Microsoft now provides ongoing updates to Windows instead of releasing new versions periodically. This means that Windows features might change over time, including how they look and how you interact with them. The information provided in this text was accurate at the time this book was published.*

Module Objectives

After completing this module, you will be able to:

- Browse the web with Edge
- Search the web
- Manage web results
- Add contacts to People
- Send messages with Mail
- Receive and respond to messages
- Use instant messaging
- Manage events with Calendar
- Store information on OneDrive

Files You Will Need

Jesse.jpg   Lighthouse.jpg
Melissa.jpg   Fog.jpg

Browse the Web with Edge

The **Internet** is a global collection of millions of computers linked together to share information. The **web** (also known as the **World Wide Web** or **WWW**) is a part of the Internet that consists of websites located on different computers around the world. A **website** contains webpages linked together to make searching for information on the Internet easier. **Webpages** are specially formatted electronic documents containing text and graphics. **Web browsers** are software applications that you use to "surf the web," or display, navigate, and interact with webpages. As you open websites, you can display each site in a separate tab, so you can view multiple websites in a single window. A **web address**, also called a **URL** (which stands for **Uniform Resource Locator**), is a unique place on the Internet where a webpage resides. When you enter the URL for a webpage, Microsoft Edge **loads** and displays the page from the Internet. **CASE** ▸ *You open the Microsoft Edge web browser and browse two websites.*

STEPS

1. **Click or tap the Microsoft Edge button** 🅴 **on the taskbar**

   The Microsoft Edge app opens, displaying the default home page in the browser screen. The **home page**, the main webpage around which a website is built, appears when you start Microsoft Edge. The default home page in Edge shows "Where to next?" with a search box below it. See **FIGURE 4-1**.

2. **With the insertion point in the search box, type www.loc.gov, then click or tap the Go button** ➡ **or press [Enter]**

   As you type, a feature called **AutoComplete** displays a drop-down menu with possible matches from addresses you've typed previously, as well as search suggestions. The Library of Congress website appears in the Edge window, and an **address bar** showing the page's URL, loc.gov, appears at the top of the screen. See **FIGURE 4-2**.

3. **With a pointing device, move the pointer over the Sound Recordings link on the webpage**

   The pointer becomes the hand pointer 🖑, indicating that you are pointing to a **hyperlink** (or simply a **link**), a highlighted word, phrase, and graphic that you click or tap to open another webpage.

4. **Click or tap the link once; (on a mobile device, tap the link), then scroll down**

   A webpage about the Library of Congress audio recording collection opens.

5. **Click or tap the Back button** ⬅ **on the left side of the address bar, or tap your mobile device's Back button**

   The webpage you previously viewed—the Library of Congress home page—reloads in the browser window.

6. **Click or tap the New tab button** ➕ **above the address bar to open a new tab**

7. **Type www.nasa.gov, then press [Enter] or tap your device's Go button**

   The NASA webpage, shown in **FIGURE 4-3**, appears on a second tab, and contains information about the NASA space program. A complete Internet address begins with http://www, which stands for Hypertext Transfer Protocol and World Wide Web. But you don't need to type these characters because Edge automatically "assumes" that information.

8. **Click or tap the International Space Station link, click or tap the Back button** ⬅ **twice to return to the new tab, then click or tap the Forward button** ➡ **to return to the NASA home page**

9. **Click or tap the Library of Congress tab, point to the NASA tab, click or tap its Close button** ✕ **, then click or tap the Back button** ⬅

   Pointing to the tab with a pointing device displays a thumbnail of the page before you click or tap it. You closed the NASA tab while the Library of Congress tab was active; the Where to next? page now appears.

FIGURE 4-1: Microsoft Edge Where to next? page

Search box

Where to next?

Your page may show a news feed here

Windows 10

FIGURE 4-2: Library of Congress website open in Edge

URL for Library of Congress website in address box

Option buttons

Address bar

Navigation arrows

To change Homepage, click this button, then click Settings.

Sound Recordings link (yours may be in a different location)

FIGURE 4-3: NASA site open in a second tab

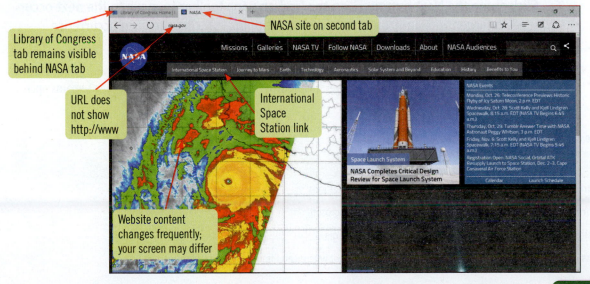

Library of Congress tab remains visible behind NASA tab

NASA site on second tab

URL does not show http://www

International Space Station link

Website content changes frequently; your screen may differ

Search the Web

You can search the web by typing text into a search engine. A **search engine** is a program provided by a **search provider** to search through a collection of Internet information to find what you want. When you use the Where to next? page to search the web, Edge automatically uses the Microsoft Bing search engine. In addition to Bing, other search engines are available on the web, such as Google or Yahoo!. To use a search engine from any browser, you go to its website, such as bing.com, google.com, or yahoo.com. When you perform a search, you type words or phrases, known as **keywords** (also called **search criteria**), that best describe what you want to find. After you press [Enter], the search engine displays the information it found for you, called search results. The results are links to websites related to your search, known as **hits**. The search results of different search engines vary. If you're looking for specific information on a page, you can use the Find on page toolbar to highlight the text you want to locate. **CASE** *As part of a research project, you decide to search the web for information on cattle ranching.*

STEPS

1. **On the Where to next? page, click or tap in the search box if necessary, type ranching, then press [Enter]**

    The search results for "ranching" appear on the Bing search results page, in order of decreasing relevance. See **FIGURE 4-4**. You can narrow the search by adding more keywords. As you add keywords, the search engine finds more specific webpages that contain all of those words. See **TABLE 4-1** for tips on narrowing your search results.

2. **Click or tap after "ranching" in the search box, press [Spacebar], type cattle, then press [Enter]**

    The search results become more specific, showing sites related to cattle ranching.

3. **Locate and click or tap a search result that contains Wikipedia in its name (scrolling if necessary to locate one)**

    A Wikipedia page opens.

4. **Click or tap the More button ⋯ on the right side of the Address bar, then click or tap Find on page**

    The Find on page toolbar appears under the address bar, where you can search for occurrences of specific text on the current page.

5. **In the "Enter text to search" text box on the Find on page toolbar, type argentina**

    The number of occurrences appears on the toolbar, and all occurrences on the page become highlighted.

6. **Click or tap the Next button ▷ on the Find on page toolbar to move to the next occurrence of argentina, and continue clicking or tapping ▷ to locate each occurrence**

    See **FIGURE 4-5**.

7. **Click or tap the Close button ✕ on the Find on page toolbar to close it**

    The occurrences of Argentina are no longer highlighted in yellow, and the Wikipedia page remains open.

TABLE 4-1: Ways to narrow search results

method	example
Use quotation marks to locate exact phrases	"high-paying computer jobs"
Add specific information	Smartphone small Microsoft
Use AND to find sites including all search words	Centerville AND Georgia
Eliminate unnecessary words	Nearby bookstores (*not* where can I find a nearby bookstore)

FIGURE 4-4: Bing Search results for keyword "ranching"

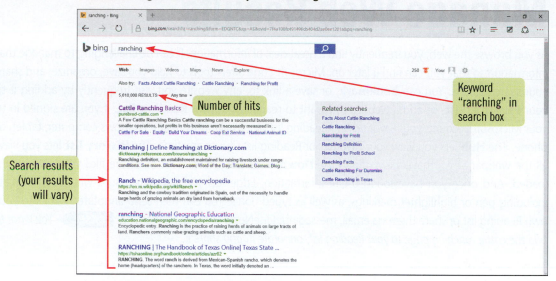

Keyword "ranching" in search box

Number of hits

Search results (your results will vary)

FIGURE 4-5: Using Find on page to locate occurrences of "argentina"

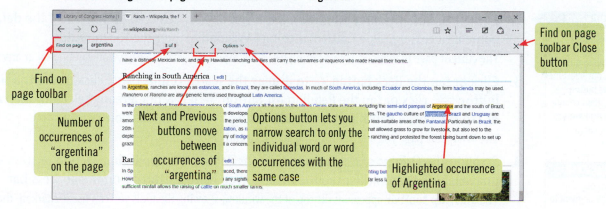

Find on page toolbar Close button

Find on page toolbar

Number of occurrences of "argentina" on the page

Next and Previous buttons move between occurrences of "argentina"

Options button lets you narrow search to only the individual word or word occurrences with the same case

Highlighted occurrence of Argentina

Using Cortana with Edge

If you have the Cortana digital assistant enabled, you can use it to learn more as you use Edge to browse the web. Simply highlight any website text, such as a person, location, or an unfamiliar word, right-click or press and hold it, then click or tap Ask Cortana, as shown in **FIGURE 4-6**. A panel opens on the right side of the screen, showing more information, images, and related links, if available. In addition, you can often type text in the address bar or on a Where to next? page, and Cortana will display results personalized for you, right on the drop-down menu. For example, if you type "weather," Cortana displays weather for your location. Type a sports team name to see recent scores.

FIGURE 4-6: Getting more information on selected text

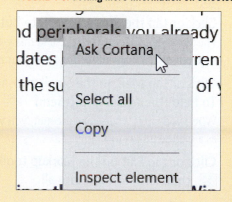

Using Apps to Get and Share Information

Manage Web Results

Learning
Outcomes
• Add a webpage to
  the Reading list
• Navigate to a
  page using the
  Reading list
• Annotate and
  email a webpage

As you browse the web, you frequently find a great deal of information. It can be challenging to manage that information so that you can find it later on. Microsoft Edge offers tools to help you save, organize, and share your search results. You can **bookmark**, or save a link to, any website you visit frequently by adding it to your **Favorites list**, or add a website you want to read later to your **Reading list**. If you are signed in to your Microsoft account, your Favorites and Reading lists are available from any Windows computer, tablet, or phone. The **Hub** lets you view your Favorites or Reading list sites at any time. The **History list** lets you view all the webpages you have viewed, and the **Downloads list** shows a list of all the files you have downloaded. And once you have found useful information, Edge lets you annotate pages with **Web Notes**, including pen or highlighter markings, as well as typed notes. You can then send annotated pages to your own Reading list or share them via email, messaging, OneNote, or social networking. **CASE** ▸ *You want to add the cattle ranching page to your Reading list, annotate it, and share it.*

STEPS

1. **With the cattle ranching page open, click or tap the Add to favorites or reading list button ☆ on the address bar**

   A drop-down window opens, as shown in **FIGURE 4-7**, displaying a Favorites button and a Reading list button at the top of the window. The currently selected button is blue. You want to add the current page to your Reading list.

2. **Click or tap the Reading list button if it is not already selected (blue), select the default name if necessary, type Cattle Ranching - Wikipedia, then click or tap Add**

   The current page is added to your Reading list. Now, after you leave the page, you can open it at any time.

3. **Click or tap the Back button ← to display the search results page, click or tap the Hub button ≡, click or tap the Reading list button ≣ if it is not already selected, then click or tap the Cattle Ranching - Wikipedia listing in the Today section**

   The Wikipedia page you added to your Reading list earlier reopens.

4. **Scroll to the Origins of ranching section (or another section if that section is unavailable), then click or tap the Make a Web Note button ✎ on the address bar**

   The **Markup toolbar** appears at the top of the window, showing the tools you can use to mark up the page.

5. **Click or tap the Highlighter tool 🖍, then drag to highlight the text Origins of ranching (or the name of the section you displayed in Step 4)**

   You can "scrub" back and forth with the highlighter tool to get good coverage, if you like.

6. **Click or tap the Add a typed note tool 🗨, click or tap near the highlighted heading, then type Interesting history here!**

   See **FIGURE 4-8**.

7. **Click or tap the Share Web Note button 🔗 on the Markup toolbar**

   The Share pane opens. You will send this segment to yourself. When you send a page with Web Notes, Edge includes a JPG image of the page and your markings, rather than the webpage itself.

8. **Click or tap Mail, in the email message that opens enter your email address in the To field, then click or tap Send**

   When you check your email account, you will find a message with the entire annotated webpage attached as a picture in JPG format.

9. **Click or tap Exit on the Markup toolbar, click or tap the Edge Window Close button ✕, then click or tap Close all**

Using Apps to Get and Share Information

FIGURE 4-7: Adding a site to your Favorites or Reading list

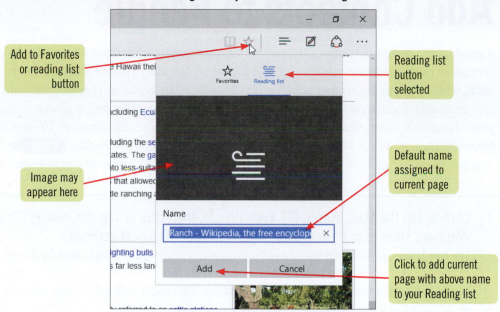

FIGURE 4-8: Annotated webpage

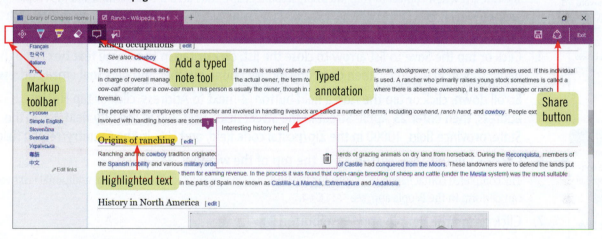

Viewing webpages in Reading view

Reading view lets you view webpages without advertisements or unnecessary content in an easy-to-read format. It shows only the page text, without toolbars or sidebars, but does include images that are part of the text. To use Reading view, open a webpage in Edge, then click or tap the Reading view button on the right side of the address bar. The Reading view button is available if its color is black. If the button is gray, Reading view is not available for the current site. If it is blue, the page is already in Reading view. Reading view lets you select and annotate text. To change the appearance of Reading view, click or tap the More button on the right side of the address bar, click or tap Settings, then scroll down. Choose a Reading view style (Light, Medium, or Dark) or a Reading view font size (Small, Medium, Large, or Extra Large).

Windows 10

Add Contacts to People

Learning
Outcomes
• View all your
  contacts
• Create a contact

A **contact** is a person or company with whom you communicate. Windows 10 uses the People app as a centralized place to add and manage contact information, including a person's name, address, phone, and email, which you can use in other apps, including Mail and Messaging, to communicate with others. You can create and manage contacts in People and add contacts from other online service accounts, such as your Microsoft account, Outlook, Twitter, and Skype. When you set up Windows 10, you also set up a Microsoft account, which becomes your default account and profile in People. **CASE** ▸ *You want to maintain an up-to-date list of colleagues, so you create a new contact for a recently hired employee.*

STEPS

1. **Click or tap the Start button ⊞, type People, then click or tap the People - Trusted Windows Store app; if prompted, sign in to your Microsoft account**

   The People app opens, displaying a list of your contacts on the left, and information for the selected contact on the right. See **FIGURE 4-9**. The search box lets you locate contacts. Below the search box, the app indicates which group of contacts currently appears in your list. Yours might read "all," "some accounts," or "none."

2. **Click or tap the New button ⊞ near the top of the window**

   The New Microsoft account contact screen opens, displaying fields that let you assign the contact to an account and enter contact information.

3. **Click or tap the Save to list arrow, then view the accounts to which you can save the new contact**

   You can save a new contact to your Microsoft account or any other account that is linked to the People app, such as Outlook. When you select an account, the account name appears at the top of the screen, such as New Outlook contact.

4. **Click or tap the Save to list arrow to close the list, click or tap in the Name text box, type the name shown in FIGURE 4-10, then enter the mobile phone number and personal email address**

5. **Scroll down, click or tap the Add a field button ⊞ next to Address, click or tap Home address, then enter 23 Apple Street in the Street field, Anytown in the City field, NY in the State/province field, 10000 in the Zip/postal code field, and U.S. in the Country/region field**

6. **Click or tap the Save button 💾 at the top of the window**

   The completed contact appears, displaying the information you entered. To learn about additional tasks you can perform in the People app, see **TABLE 4-2**.

7. **Click or tap the People app Close button ✕**

TABLE 4-2: Additional People app tasks

to	do this
Add a photo to a contact	Click or tap ✎, click or tap Add photo, select photo, drag edges to crop, then click or tap ✓
Change sort or display order; filter contacts	Click or tap ••• in left pane, click Settings, then select the desired sort, display or filter options
Pin a contact as a tile on the Start menu	Click or tap 📌 above contact information
Link or unlink multiple occurrences of same contact	Click or tap ∞ above contact information, then click Yes
Share a contact	Click or tap ••• in the blue area, click or tap Share contact, click or tap the checkmark ✓, then click or tap the email or messaging account with which you want to share the information

Using Apps to Get and Share Information

FIGURE 4-9: People app with highlighted contact

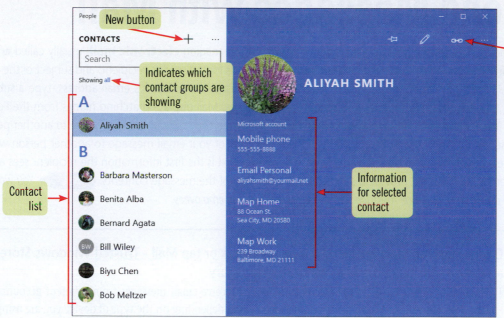

FIGURE 4-10: Adding a new contact

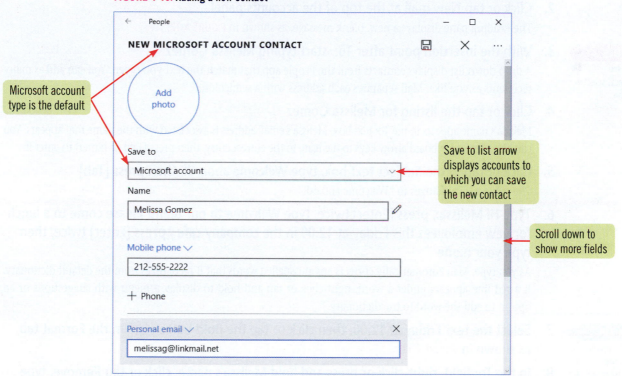

Adding and using other accounts

In addition to using the default Microsoft account, you can add contacts from other online service accounts, such as Outlook, Apple iCloud, Gmail, and Exchange. To add an online service account, click or tap the See more button in the white area of the Contacts screen, click or tap Settings, click or tap Add an account, click or tap an account type, then follow the on-screen instructions to connect to the account. Enter your username and password to authorize the account, and sign in if prompted. When your contacts update their information or send notifications, you automatically receive them in the People app.

Windows 10

Send Messages with Mail

Windows includes the Mail app, a powerful program for managing **electronic mail**, usually called **email**. Email messages follow a standard memo format, with fields for the sender, recipient, and subject of the message. To send an email message, you need to enter or select the recipient's email address, type a subject, then type the message itself. As you enter recipient names, Mail displays matching names from the People app. You can also use the Cc (carbon copy) button to send a copy of your email message to another person or use the Bcc (blind carbon copy) button to send a copy of your email message to another person whose name will not appear in the email message. The subject text is the first information the recipient sees about the email, so it should provide a short, concise summary of the message contents. **CASE** *You want to send a colleague an email message about a luncheon for new employees.*

STEPS

1. **Click or tap the Start button ⊞, type mail, click or tap Mail - Trusted Windows Store app, then maximize the Mail window if necessary**

   The Mail app opens, displaying options to send and receive email messages from different accounts. See **FIGURE 4-11**. The size and layout of the Mail screen varies depending on the type of device you are using. On a laptop, you see panels for accounts, the Inbox (a list of messages you have received), and a Reading pane showing the contents of the selected message.

2. **Click or tap New mail at the top of the accounts panel**

   The Reading pane displays a new, blank message, as shown in **FIGURE 4-12**.

3. **With the insertion point after To:, start typing Melissa Gomez**

   A drop-down list displays contacts from the People app that match the text you typed. You can add as many recipients as you like. Mail separates each address with a semicolon.

4. **Click or tap the listing for Melissa Gomez**

   Melissa's name appears in the To: text box. Melissa's email address is associated with the name that appears. You can also use the keyboard arrow keys to navigate to the correct entry, then press [Tab] or [Enter] to enter it.

5. **Click or tap in the Subject text box, type Welcome aboard!, then press [Tab]**

   The subject text changes to "Welcome aboard!".

6. **Type Hi Melissa:, press [Enter] twice, type Welcome to our team! Please come to a lunch for new employees this Friday at 12:00 in the company cafe., press [Enter] twice, then type your name**

   As you type, Mail automatically corrects any misspelled words that it recognizes from the default dictionary. If a red line appears under a word, right-click or tap and hold to display a menu with suggestions or an option to add the word to the dictionary.

7. **Select the text Friday at 12:00, then click or tap the Bold button B on the Format tab, as shown in FIGURE 4-13**

8. **In the To: field, right-click or press and hold Melissa's name, click or tap Remove, type your own email address, then click or tap Send**

   The email message is sent to your email account. After a moment, the message arrives in your Inbox.

FIGURE 4-11: Mail app

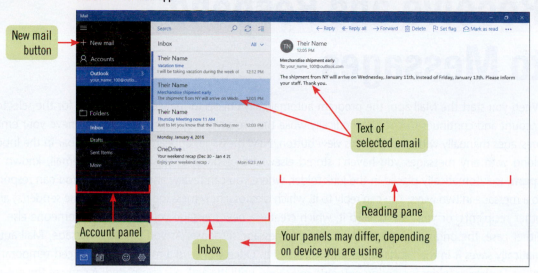

New mail button

Text of selected email

Reading pane

Account panel

Inbox

Your panels may differ, depending on device you are using

FIGURE 4-12: Blank mail message in Reading pane

Your email address is automatically entered as the sender

Click or tap to include courtesy copies

Blank message

FIGURE 4-13: Completed message with formatting

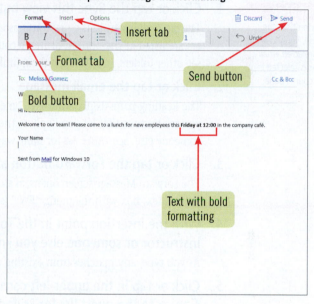

Insert tab

Format tab

Send button

Bold button

Text with bold formatting

Setting up your email accounts

When you first start Mail, you are asked to add your email account. On the Welcome screen, click or tap Get Started, and on the Accounts screen, click or tap Add Account. On the Choose an account screen, choose an account type, such as Outlook.com, Google, or Yahoo! Mail. Add your email address and email password. On the next screen, enter the name that you want to appear in the From: line of your emails. Then click or tap Done. When you're finished, click or tap Ready to go. Your accounts will appear under Accounts on the Mail startup screen. To edit your account settings, click or tap Accounts on the Mail screen, then click or tap an account in the Accounts pane that appears. To add an account later, click or tap Add account in the Accounts pane.

Receive and Respond to Messages

Learning Outcomes
• View email accounts
• Receive email messages
• Respond to email messages

When you start the Mail app, the program automatically checks for new email messages for the selected account and continues to check periodically while the program is open. You can also retrieve your email messages manually with the Sync this view button. New messages appear with a shaded bar in the Inbox along with any messages you haven't stored elsewhere or deleted. Unsolicited mass email, known as **spam**, is automatically placed in the Junk folder, where you can review and delete later. You can respond to a message in two ways: You can reply to it, which creates a new message addressed to the sender(s) and other recipients, or you can forward it, which creates a new message you can send to someone else. In either case, the original message appears in the message response. As you create a message, Mail automatically saves it in the Drafts folder until you send it. Once you send a message, it is placed temporarily in the Outbox, a folder for storing outgoing messages, until the action is completed. A copy of the outgoing message is also placed in the Sent Items folder. **CASE** ▶ *To prepare for the new-employee luncheon, you want to forward a relevant email message you received.*

STEPS

1. **Click or tap the Sync this view button 🔄 at the top of the Inbox**
   The email you sent in the previous lesson appears, showing the subject line "Welcome aboard!" Email folders are listed at the bottom of the Accounts pane, including Inbox, Drafts, and Sent. Click or tap More to see other folders, including Outbox, Junk, and Trash.

2. **Click or tap the email message**
   The Reading pane displays the Welcome aboard! message. See **FIGURE 4-14**. At the top of the Reading pane, you see buttons that let you Reply to the sender, Reply to all message recipients, or Forward the message to someone else. See **TABLE 4-3** for more ways to manage your messages.

3. **Click or tap the Forward button at the top of the Reading pane**
   The Forward Message screen opens, as shown in **FIGURE 4-15**, displaying the original email subject title in the Subject text box with the prefix "FW:" (short for Forward) and the original message in the message box.

4. **With the insertion point in the To text box, begin typing the email address of your instructor or someone else you know, then select the contact if available**
   As you type, any matches from existing contacts appear in a drop-down list.

5. **Click or tap in the upper-left corner of the Message text box, type Please add Melissa Gomez to the guest list for Friday's lunch., then click or tap the Send button**
   The Forward Message screen closes, and the Mail screen reappears. The email message is automatically sent.

6. **Click or tap the Mail window Close button ✖**

Attaching a file to an email message

You can easily share a file, such as a photo, using email by attaching it to an email message. The recipient can open the file in a compatible program or save it. For example, suppose that you are working on a report with a colleague in another part of the country. After you finish the report, you can attach the report file to an email message and send the message to your colleague, who can then open, edit, and print the report. To attach a file to an email, create the message (using New, Reply, Reply all, or Forward options), click or tap the Insert tab at the top of the Reading pane, then click or tap Attach. In the Open dialog box, browse to and select a file, then click or tap Open. When you reply to a message that has an attachment, the attachment isn't returned to the original sender. However, when you forward an attachment, it is included along with the message.

FIGURE 4-14: Received message in Reading pane

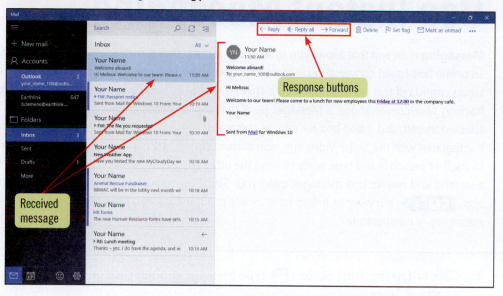

FIGURE 4-15: Forwarding a message

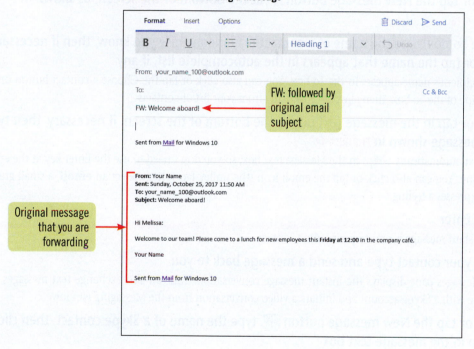

TABLE 4-3: Mail response actions

to	do this
Delete a message	Point to message in the Inbox, then click or tap the Delete button; in Reading pane, click or tap Delete
File a message	Select the message in the Inbox, click or tap the Actions button [•••] in the Reading pane, click or tap Move. In the Move to panel, click or tap the folder; or drag a message to a folder in the Accounts panel
Flag a message	Point to a message in the Inbox, then click or tap the Set Flag on item icon [⚑]
Mark a message as unread	Right-click or press and hold the message in the Inbox, then click or tap Mark as unread
Find a message	Click or tap in the search box at the top of the Inbox, type search text, then press or tap Enter

Use Instant Messaging

Learning Outcomes
• View instant message threads
• Create an instant message
• Send and respond to instant messages

Messaging is an app that allows you to send and receive instant messages. An **instant message (IM)** is an online text-based conversation in real time between two or more contacts. An instant message conversation consists of text exchanges, called a **thread**. The Messaging app screen includes a Threads pane for tracking your conversations, a Messages pane that contains each conversation you have in the currently selected thread, and a text box for adding comments to that thread. The Windows Store Messaging app is integrated with the Skype Video app, also available from the Windows Store. **Skype Video** lets you talk to another person in real time while viewing the other party using your computer's video camera. You can also send and receive text messages using your Skype account and start video calls from the Messaging app. **CASE** *You want to talk to an associate about an upcoming meeting, so you decide to use instant messaging to communicate.*

STEPS

1. **Click or tap the Start button ⊞, type Messaging, then click or tap Messaging - Trusted Windows Store app**

   The Messaging app opens, displaying options to send and receive instant messages.

2. **Click or tap the New message button ⊞ at the bottom of the screen, as shown in FIGURE 4-16**

3. **In the To box, type the name of a contact or someone else you know, then if necessary, click or tap the name that appears in the autocomplete list, if any**

   The recipient's name appears in the To box. You can also click or tap the Choose a contact button on the right side of the To box, then click or tap a name from your list of contacts.

4. **Click or tap in the message text box at the bottom of the screen, if necessary, then type the message shown in FIGURE 4-17**

   The text automatically wraps in the Message text box, so you don't need to use the Enter key at the end of each line. You can also click or tap the emoji icon (the smiley face), then select an **emoji**, a small graphic that expresses a feeling.

5. **Press Enter**

   The instant message is sent to your online contact.

6. **Have your contact type and send a message back to you**

   The Messages pane displays the instant message conversation. You can also exchange text messages with anyone with a Skype account and initiate a video conversation from the Messaging window.

7. **Click or tap the New message button ⊞, type the name of a Skype contact, then click or tap in the message text box**

   If you do not have a Skype account, skip steps 7 and 8.

8. **Type a message to your Skype contact, then click or tap Send**

   You will see Send on: Skype under the contact's name. Once the messaging exchange has begun, you can click the Audio 📞 or Video 📷 icons in the bottom right corner of the Messaging window to initiate a Skype video or audio call.

9. **Close the Messaging app window and, if necessary, the Skype app window**

FIGURE 4-16: Messaging app

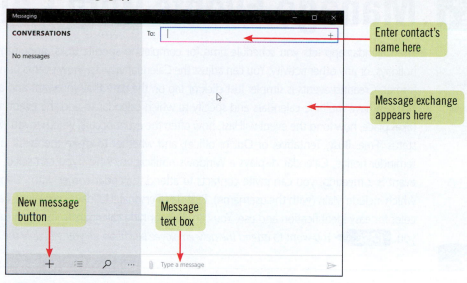

Enter contact's name here

Message exchange appears here

New message button

Message text box

FIGURE 4-17: Conversation in Messaging app

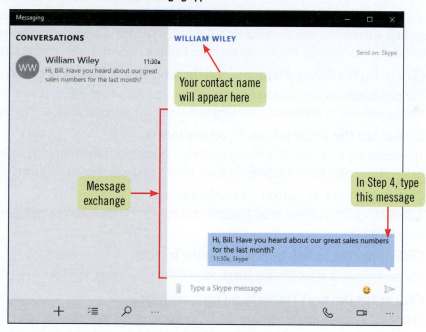

Your contact name will appear here

Message exchange

In Step 4, type this message

Creating a Skype account

To create a Skype account, go to www.skype.com, then click or tap the Sign in link. If you don't have a Skype account, click the Join us link. Enter your name, email address, and whatever profile information you wish to share with others, such as your birthday, location, and mobile phone number. (*Remember that this information will be visible to anyone on Skype, so think carefully about how much information you are comfortable sharing.*) Choose and enter a Skype Name, which is a unique username you want to use with Skype, as well as a password. Choose any other options you want, type in a verification code, agree to the terms of use, then click or tap Get Account. You will then be able to search for other people with Skype accounts and request that they accept you as a contact. Once they accept, you can exchange messages and video calls with them when they are online.

Using Apps to Get and Share Information

Manage Events with Calendar

Learning
Outcomes
• View a calendar of
  events
• Create a calendar
  event

The Calendar app lets you schedule time for completing specific tasks, appointments, meetings, vacations, holidays, or any other activity. You can adjust the Calendar view to show events using the Day, Week, or Month format. Creating events is simple: Just click or tap on the date that you want and add your new event details. You can have multiple calendars and specify to which calendar to add the event, where and when the event takes place, how long the event will last, how often the event occurs, whether you want a reminder notice, your status (Free, Busy, Tentative, or Out of office), and whether to make the event private. When you specify a reminder notice, Calendar displays a Windows notification, which you can select to display the event. If the event is a meeting, you can invite contacts to attend. Calendar comes with calendars for different purposes, which include Main (with the username), Birthday, Personal, Holidays, and Work. Each calendar uses a different color for easy identification and use. You can show or hide calendars to focus on the events most important to you. **CASE** ▶ *You want to attend the new-employee luncheon, so you schedule the event in your calendar.*

STEPS

TROUBLE
If you don't see a cal-
endar listing on the
left side of your
screen, click the
Expand button ▤
to expand the pane.

1. **Click or tap the Start button ⊞, type Calendar, click or tap Calendar - Trusted Windows Store app, then maximize the Calendar window if necessary**

   The Calendar app opens, displaying your calendar in Month format, as shown in **FIGURE 4-18**. On the left side of the screen, you see an overview of the month, as well as a listing of existing online calendars from which the app is showing events, such as Outlook.com, Gmail, iCloud, or your company's Exchange calendar. You can uncheck any calendar item check box in the left pane if you don't want to include its appointments. If you see birthdays on the calendar that you did not enter, Calendar is showing them from a social media account.

2. **Click or tap the Forward button ⌄ on the toolbar near the top of the window**

   The next month on the calendar appears. You can also navigate to different days, weeks, and months by swiping vertically or horizontally, scrolling with the mouse wheel, or using the keyboard arrow keys.

3. **Click or tap the Today button ▤ on the toolbar**

   The current day appears in dark blue in the Month format. Notice that after you click or tap the Today button, a brief weather forecast appears for today and the next four days on the calendar.

QUICK TIP
If you want to display
more than one day in
Day view, point to
the Day button, click
or tap the list arrow
that appears, then
choose how many
days to display at
once, up to six.

4. **Click or tap the Day button ▢ on the toolbar**

   A detailed schedule appears in an hourly format for today, where you can click or tap to add or edit the information.

5. **Click or tap the Month button ▦ on the toolbar**

   The current month appears in the Month format with today's date highlighted in a dark blue.

6. **Click or tap the next Thursday on your calendar**

   The New Calendar Event screen appears. Here you can specify to which calendar to add the event, where and when the event takes place, and how long it will last. You can add more specific information, such as how often the event occurs, whether you want a reminder notice, your status, and whether to make the event private, in the details screen.

QUICK TIP
Click or tap the pad-
lock icon to make it
private, so that oth-
ers sharing your cal-
endar cannot see it.

7. **Click or tap More details, then enter the information and specify the settings shown in FIGURE 4-19; use Thursday's date instead of the one shown**

   The New Calendar Event screen shows the completed event information.

8. **Click or tap Save and close on the toolbar, then point to the appointment**

   The appointment details appear in a pop-up window.

9. **Right-click or press and hold the event, click or tap Delete, then click or tap the Calendar app window's Close button ✕**

   The Calendar app closes, and the desktop appears.

Using Apps to Get and Share Information

FIGURE 4-18: Calendar app showing Month format

- Forward button
- Month overview
- Checkmarks indicate that information from all existing calendars is included
- Today button
- Calendar appears in Month format

FIGURE 4-19: New Calendar Event screen

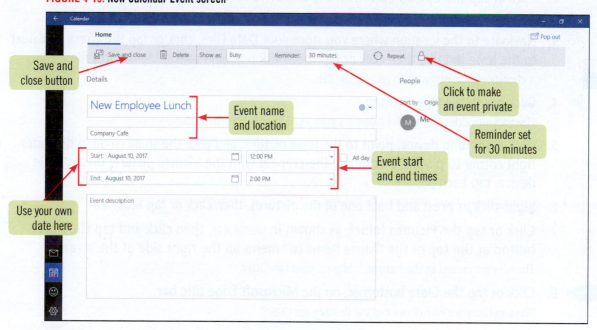

- Save and close button
- Use your own date here
- Event name and location
- Event start and end times
- Click to make an event private
- Reminder set for 30 minutes

Working with existing events

After you create an event, you can edit or delete it. You can edit or delete a single occurrence of an event or all occurrences. In any of the format views, click or tap the event, then click or tap Edit Series, if necessary. To edit the event, make changes to event details, then click or tap Save and close. If the event is a meeting to which others have been invited, click or tap Send update to send an update to attendees. To delete the event, right-click or press and hold the event, then click or tap Delete.

Windows 10

Store Information on OneDrive

Learning Outcomes
- View files on your OneDrive
- Add files to your OneDrive

OneDrive is an online file-hosting service that allows you to upload and sync files to and access them from the OneDrive app in Windows 10, a web browser, or a mobile device, including a Windows phone, Apple iPhone or iPad, or Android. OneDrive allows you to organize your files so that you can share them with contacts, make them public, or keep them private. The online service offers limited free storage for new users; however, additional storage is available for purchase or for Office 365 subscribers. OneDrive comes with a default set of folders—Documents, Favorites, Pictures, and Public (Shared)—you can use to store your files. Depending on your OneDrive setup, your folders might differ. When you store files on OneDrive, it automatically makes them available on your other devices without having to sync them. The files you store in your Public (Shared) folder are available for anyone to view and edit. You can view a file on OneDrive by clicking or tapping it. **CASE** *You have some recent employee photos that you want to store and share with other departments, so you add them on your OneDrive.*

STEPS

1. **Click or tap the Edge button** e **in the taskbar, click or tap the search box, then type www.onedrive.live.com**
   You see the onedrive.live.com website, showing the files and folder you have stored there. See **FIGURE 4-20**.

2. **Click or tap the Upload button on the OneDrive toolbar, then click or tap Files**
   The Open dialog box opens, where you can select the files you want to store on your OneDrive.

3. **Navigate to the location where you store your Data Files, click or tap the check box next to the Jesse.jpg file, then click or tap the check box next to the Melissa.jpg file**
   A checkmark appears next to each of the files.

4. **Click or tap the Open button**
   The files are added to the Files folder on your OneDrive, below the folders.

5. **With a pointing device, point to the Jesse picture, and click the small circle in its upper-right corner to place a checkmark, then repeat with the Melissa picture; on a mobile device, tap each picture**

6. **Right-click or press and hold one of the pictures, then click or tap Move to**

7. **Click or tap the Pictures folder, as shown in FIGURE 4-21, then click and tap the Move button at the top of the "Move items to" menu on the right side of the screen**
   The files are moved to the Pictures folder on your OneDrive.

8. **Click or tap the Close button** ☒ **on the Microsoft Edge title bar**
   The OneDrive website closes and the desktop appears.

FIGURE 4-20: Your OneDrive website

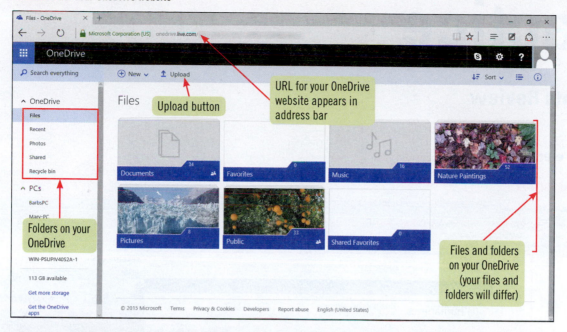

Upload button

URL for your OneDrive website appears in address bar

Folders on your OneDrive

Files and folders on your OneDrive (your files and folders will differ)

FIGURE 4-21: Moving uploaded pictures to the Pictures folder

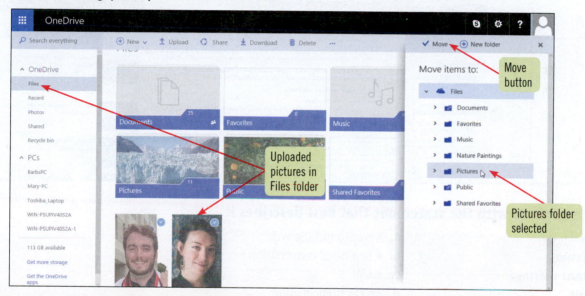

Move button

Uploaded pictures in Files folder

Pictures folder selected

Creating and editing files using Office Online

OneDrive provides more than a location for storing your files in the cloud. You can create and edit files using small, online versions of Microsoft Office products, including Word, Excel, PowerPoint, and OneNote, that you can access through OneDrive. Click or tap the New button on the OneDrive toolbar, then click or tap Word document, Excel workbook, PowerPoint presentation, OneNote notebook, Excel survey, or Plain text document. The Office Online apps contain many, though not all, of the features of the full Office programs. If you click or tap an Office file on OneDrive, it automatically opens in an Office online product, in a separate Edge tab. **FIGURE 4-22** shows a document open in Word Online.

FIGURE 4-22: Word document open in Word Online

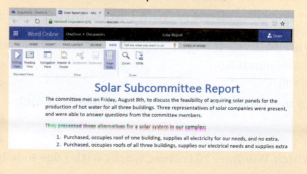

Practice

Concepts Review

Label the elements shown in FIGURE 4-23.

FIGURE 4-23

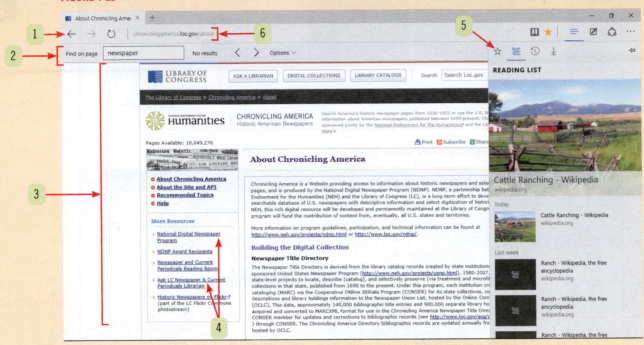

Match each term with the statement that best describes it.

7. **Web**

8. **Internet**

9. **Instant message**

10. **Email**

11. **Web address**

12. **Web browser**

a. A way to surf the Web

b. A text-based conversation

c. A URL

d. An electronic message

e. Global collection of linked webpages

f. Global collection of linked computers

Select the best answers from the following lists of choices.

13. **Which Microsoft Edge feature lets you annotate webpages?**

   a. Downloads list

   b. URL

   c. Address bar

   d. Web Notes

14. **An instant message conversation consists of a(n):**

   a. thread

   b. notification

   c. calendar

   d. email

15. **Which Windows 10 feature works with Edge to help you learn more?**

   a. Web Notes

   b. Calendar

   c. People

   d. Cortana

Skills Review

1. Browse the web with Edge.
   a. Open the Microsoft Edge app.
   b. Type **www.data.gov** in the Search or enter web address box, then press [Enter].
   c. Use at least two hyperlinks to find data about education.
   d. Use the Back button to return to the www.data.gov home page, then use the Forward button to display the previous page.
   e. Open a new tab, enter **www.epa.gov** in the Search or enter web address box.
   f. Follow at least two links to investigate a topic that interests you.
   g. Use the Back button to return to epa.gov, then close the epa.gov tab.

2. Search the web.
   a. Open a new tab, and in the Search or enter web address box, enter **computer jobs**, then notice the number of hits.
   b. Click or tap a hyperlink that interests you.
   c. Return to the list of hits, then edit your search text to **computer jobs training**, and search again. Compare the number of hits to your previous search.
   d. Click or tap a hyperlink that interests you.
   e. Open the Find on page toolbar, and search the page for **software** or another computer job training term.
   f. Use the Next and Previous buttons to navigate among the highlighted terms. (If no terms are highlighted, search the page using another relevant term.)
   g. Close the Find on page toolbar.

3. Manage web results.
   a. Navigate to any of the sites you visited in Step 2 above, and click or tap a link for a position that interests you.
   b. Use the Add to favorites or reading list button to add the page to your Reading list, using the default page name.
   c. Use Web Notes to add highlighting to a section of interest.
   d. Circle another item of interest using the Pen tool.
   e. Add a typed note with text relating to the content.
   f. Use the Share button to email the annotated page to yourself.
   g. Close the Markup toolbar, then close Microsoft Edge.

4. Add contacts to People.
   a. Open the People app.
   b. Create a new contact, and specify the account to which you want to save it.
   c. Type **Eric Choy** in the Name text box, type **555-555-5555** as the Mobile phone number, then type **echoy@earth.com** in the Personal email box.
   d. Save the contact, then close the People app.

5. Send messages with Mail.
   a. Open the Mail app. If you have more than one email account, select the account in the Accounts pane that you want to use for this exercise.
   b. Create a new mail message; begin typing **Eric Choy** in the To: box, then select his contact when it appears.
   c. In the Subject box, type **Tax documents.**
   d. In the Message pane, type **I received the tax documents today. Many thanks.**
   e. Apply bold formatting to the word Many.
   f. Replace Eric's email address with your own, then send the message.

6. Receive and respond to messages.
   a. After you receive the email message, reply to your own email address, adding the reply text **Great, thanks.**
   b. Use the Sync this view button if necessary to receive messages.

Skills Review (continued)

    c. After you receive the reply, forward it to a friend, your instructor, or a technical support person, with the following text at the top of the message: **Please note this for billing purposes.**

    d. Close the Mail app.

7. Use instant messaging.

    a. Open the Messaging app. Create a new instant message.

    b. Select the name of your instructor, technical support person, or someone else you know.

    c. In the message text box, type and send a message, then wait for a response. Continue to converse in this manner.

    d. If you have a Skype account, type a message to a Skype contact, send it, then close the Messaging app.

8. Manage events with Calendar.

    a. Open the Calendar app, then display the next month on your calendar.

    b. Go to today on the calendar, display the Day format, then display the Month format.

    c. Create a new event for next Monday with information of your choice then save the event.

    d. Point to the event on the calendar, and observe the pop-up window containing event information.

    e. Delete the event, then close the Calendar app.

9. Store information on OneDrive.

    a. Open a web browser such as Microsoft Edge, then go to www.onedrive.live.com

    b. Upload the pictures **Lighthouse.jpg** and **Fog.jpg** from the location where you store your Data Files to your OneDrive Files folder.

    c. Select the Lighthouse picture, then also select the Fog picture.

    d. Move the pictures to the Pictures folder on your OneDrive.

    e. Return to the main OneDrive screen, then close your browser.

Independent Challenge 1

You will soon graduate from college with a degree in business. You decide to check the web for current job possibilities.

    a. Open Microsoft Edge and search for jobs for recent college graduates. Use search text such as **jobs for college grads** or something similar.

    b. Click or tap links to explore the search results, narrow your search as necessary, and choose the three sites that you find the most interesting.

    c. For the first interesting site, click or press and hold in the address bar to select the URL, and open the pop-up menu.

    d. Copy the URL using the Copy command.

    e. Open the WordPad app, then paste the copied URL into the document. Type a short description of the site.

    f. Repeat Steps c–e to paste two more sites into the WordPad document and add brief descriptions.

    g. Add your name to the bottom of the document, save the WordPad document as **College Grad Jobs.rtf** to the location where you store your Data files, then submit the file to your instructor. Exit WordPad, then close the Microsoft Edge app.

Independent Challenge 2

As a part-time college student, you want to explore employment opportunities at your school. You search the web and send an email to ask for more information.

    a. Open Microsoft Edge, then locate the website for your school or for any school in your state.

    b. In the search box on the school's site, search using the term **student employment**.

    c. Explore the search results, narrow your search as necessary, and locate a job you'd like to apply for.

Independent Challenge 2 (continued)

    d. Open the Mail app, then address an email to your own email address.

    e. Type an email inquiring about the position. Briefly state your major and your qualifications for the job. Ask for more information on how to apply. Type your name and email address at the end of it.

    f. Send the message, then close Microsoft Edge and the Mail app.

Independent Challenge 3

You are working as an assistant manager for your city's zoo. You want to discuss a new animal care position with a colleague who is at another location.

    a. Open the People app.

    b. Select a colleague or fellow student who has access to the Messaging app in Windows 10, then add him or her as a contact.

    c. Close the People app.

    d. Choose a time for instant messaging, then open the Messaging app.

    e. Create a new instant message with your contact.

    f. Wait for a response, then continue to converse in this manner within the thread.

    g. Close the Messaging app.

    h. Open the People app, delete any contacts that you added, then close the People app.

Independent Challenge 4: Explore

You are thinking of starting your own event-planning service. You decide to do more research on the field using the web.

    a. Start Microsoft Edge, and search for event-planning websites. Use search text such as **event planning, party planning companies**, and the like.

    b. Click or tap links, and narrow your search as necessary to learn more about the business: what it involves, what skills are required, and the types of events that event planners create.

    c. When you find one page that is especially helpful, highlight any term you want to learn more about, right-click or press and hold on the selected term, then select Ask Cortana. Examine the information that Cortana finds.

    d. If the Reading view button is available, view the page in Reading view.

    e. Locate a particular paragraph that you find interesting or helpful, open the Markup toolbar, then click or tap the Clip button . Drag across the paragraph, which places the paragraph on the clipboard.

    f. Open the Mail app, address a new email to your instructor, then enter the email subject **Party Planning**, followed by your last name. In the message body, briefly summarize the results of your research, then paste in the clip that you copied in Step e. Add your name at the end of the email.

    g. Return to the page, close the Markup toolbar, copy the page's URL from the address bar, then paste that into the email as well.

    h. Send the email to your instructor.

Visual Workshop

Re-create the screens shown in **FIGURE 4-24** and **FIGURE 4-25**. If you can use your computer's PrintScreen key, take a screenshot of each screen, paste it into a WordPad document using the Paste command in the Clipboard group on the Home tab, add your name to the end of the document, then print it out and submit it to your instructor.

FIGURE 4-24

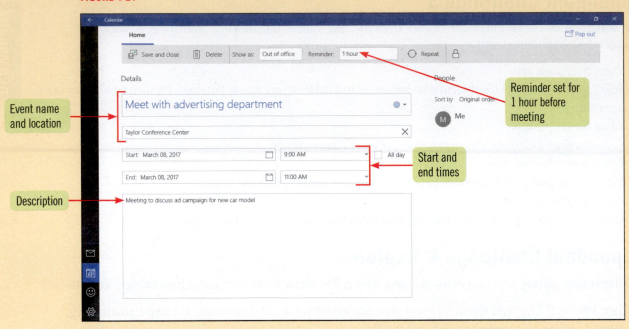

FIGURE 4-25

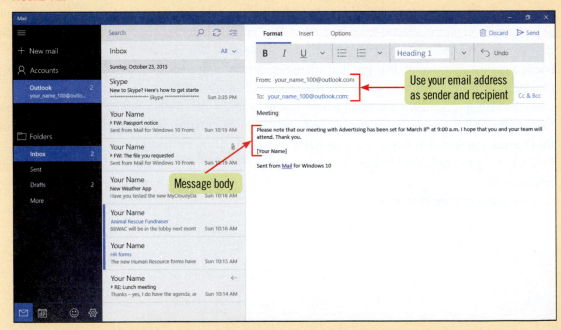

Using Apps to Manage Media

CASE ▶ Windows 10 comes with apps that help you find information and use media on the Internet. You want to learn how to use apps to get news, maps, and other information; get and play music, videos, and games; and read documents. *Note: With the release of Windows 10, Microsoft now provides ongoing updates to Windows instead of releasing new versions periodically. This means that Windows features might change over time, including how they look and how you interact with them. The information provided in this text was accurate at the time this book was published.*

Module Objectives

After completing this module, you will be able to:

- Get information with media apps
- Take photos and videos with the camera
- View and edit photos
- Get and play music or videos

- View and play games
- Use Windows Media Player
- Work with media in File Explorer
- View and read documents

In Lesson 3, you'll copy the Photos folder to the This PC > Pictures folder, and move the Media folder to the This PC > Videos folder. At the end of the module, you'll delete these folders.

Files You Will Need

5-Photos folder	Basket.jpg
	Flowers.jpg
	Melissa.jpg
	The Grad.jpg
5-Media folder	WIN 5-1.wmv
	WIN 5-2.wav
	WIN 5-3.oxps
	WIN 5-4.wmv
	WIN 5-5.mp3
	WIN 5-6.pdf

Get Information with Media Apps

Learning
Outcomes
• Identify media information apps
• Open a media information app
• Perform a calculation with a financial app

Windows 10 comes with a host of media-related apps that allow you to get specialized information, capture photos and video, watch movies and TV shows, listen to music, and play games. If you need information on a specific topic, Windows has specialized apps, such as Money, Maps, News, Sports, and Weather, that provide targeted content supplied by MSN, the Microsoft web portal. The Maps app provides maps and directions on Windows 10 PCs, tablets, and phones and, on some devices, provides voice-guided navigation. The Money app displays current financial information for worldwide financial markets. You can access the media apps from the Start menu. **CASE** ▸ *You use Maps to explore a popular New York attraction and Money to explore financial options.*

STEPS

1. **Click or tap the Start button ⊞, click or tap the Maps tile, then maximize the app window if necessary**

   The Maps app opens, displaying a map. The options bar on the right lets you change the map's orientation and tilt, show your current location, switch between aerial and road view, and zoom in and out. The menu bar on the left lets you search for and get directions to locations and explore selected world cities in 3D view. If you are starting Maps for the first time, you may be asked for permission for the app to use your current location. You can accept or decline.

2. **Click or tap the menu expand button ☰, click or tap Search, type Empire State Building NY, press [Enter] or tap 🔍, then, if you see more than one suggestion, click or tap Empire State Building in the suggestion list**

   A map showing the location of the Empire State Building appears, and the menu displays a clickable Streetside view, as well as links to nearby venues, such as restaurants and hotels. See **FIGURE 5-1**.

3. **On the menu, click or tap the 3D Cities button 🏛, then scroll down and click or tap Chicago, IL**

   An aerial 3D view of Chicago appears, as shown in **FIGURE 5-2**. You can drag to view different parts of the city.

4. **Click or tap the Map app window's Close button ✕**

   The Map app closes.

5. **Click or tap the Start button, click or tap the Money tile, then maximize the app window if necessary**

   The Money app opens, showing financial news stories and snapshots of up-to-the-minute market trends.

6. **Click or tap the menu expand button ☰, then click or tap Markets**

   You see a summary of the major U.S. stock markets and world markets. The Movers, Commodities, Bonds, and Rates tabs at the top of the window provide more information on the most active stocks and other current financial information. Depending on your screen size, your layout may differ.

7. **Click or tap ☰, then click or tap Mortgage Calculator**

   The Mortgage Calculator shows what the monthly payment would be for a loan of a given amount, at a given interest rate, for a given number of years, assuming a given amount of loan fees.

8. **Set the loan amount to $200,000, the Loan Fees to 1,000, the Annual Interest (%) to 4.5, and the number of years to 15 (or enter different amounts if you wish), then click or tap Calculate**

   The payment amount changes, as shown in **FIGURE 5-3**. A chart shows how the ending balance decreases and the cumulative payment increases over the life of the loan. The cumulative payment begins to exceed the ending balance in the seventh year of the loan.

9. **Click or tap the Money app window's Close button ✕**

FIGURE 5-1: Maps app showing New York's Empire State Building

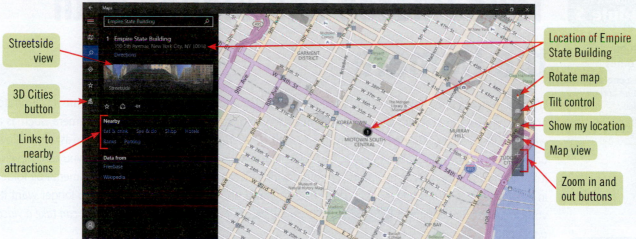

Streetside view

3D Cities button

Links to nearby attractions

Location of Empire State Building

Rotate map

Tilt control

Show my location

Map view

Zoom in and out buttons

FIGURE 5-2: 3D aerial view of Chicago

FIGURE 5-3: Money app showing mortgage payment calculation

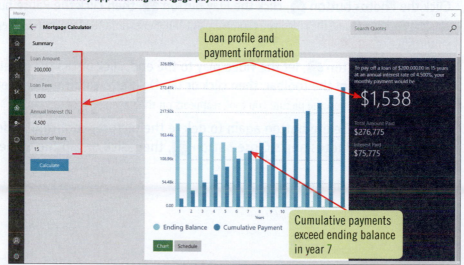

Loan profile and payment information

Cumulative payments exceed ending balance in year 7

Take Photos and Videos with the Camera

Learning Outcomes
• Take a photo
• Capture and play a video
• Delete a photo and a video

With the Camera app that comes with Windows 10, you can use a digital camera to capture a still photo or video. To use the Camera app to take photos and video, you need to have a digital camera, such as a webcam, installed on your device. When you open the Camera app for the first time, you're asked to allow or block the use of your webcam and microphone. Once you capture a photo or a video, you can preview it in the Photos app. After you capture a photo or video, it's automatically saved in the Camera Roll folder in the This PC > Pictures folder. If you don't like the way a photo or video came out or no longer want it, you can delete it at any time. **CASE** ▶ *You try out the Camera app to see how effectively it can take a video and a photo.*

STEPS

TROUBLE
If you don't have a camera on your device, the Camera app does not appear.

1. **Click or tap the Start button ⊞, type Camera, click or tap the Camera app, if you are asked to enable the use of your webcam and microphone click or tap Allow, then maximize the camera window if necessary**

   The Camera app opens, displaying the video image from the current view of your computer's digital camera. See **FIGURE 5-4**. The sides of the screen display buttons, summarized in **TABLE 5-1**, that let you take and view pictures. You may also be asked whether to let Windows Camera access your location; you can click or tap Yes to allow it or No to decline.

2. **Click or tap the Camera button ◉ to take a picture of yourself**

   The Photos button in the upper-left corner shows a reduced image of the picture you took.

QUICK TIP
Your Photos button may look different; the look of this icon changes to reflect the last photo you took.

3. **Click or tap the Photos button ▣**

   The Photos app opens, showing the picture you just took, as well as a toolbar with controls that let you work with the image. You learn more about the Photos app in the next lesson.

4. **Click or tap the Camera app button ▣ on the taskbar to return to the Camera**

5. **Click or tap the Video button ▣ to switch to Video mode, then click or tap ▣ to start recording a video of yourself**

   The timer at the bottom of the screen reflects the time elapsed in the video.

6. **After a few seconds, click or tap ▣ to stop recording**

QUICK TIP
After you have more than one photo or video in your This PC > Pictures > Camera Roll folder, the Photos window shows Back ❮ and Forward ❯ navigation arrows that you can click or tap to browse through your images.

7. **Click the Photos button ▣, click the Play button ▷, then click the Pause button ❚❚**

   The Photos app appears, the video you captured plays and pauses, and the Stop button is replaced by a Play button ▷. See **FIGURE 5-5**.

8. **Click the Play button ▷, let the video play to the end, click or tap the Delete button 🗑 on the right side of the toolbar, then click or tap Delete to confirm the deletion**

   The video is deleted, and the picture you took reappears on the screen.

9. **Click or tap the Delete button again to delete the picture, confirm the deletion, click or tap the Photos app's Close button ✕, then click or tap the Camera app's Close button ✕**

   The Camera app and the Photos app close.

FIGURE 5-4: Camera app showing live image from computer's camera

Photos app button

Options button

Change camera button

Video button

Camera button

FIGURE 5-5: Playing a video in the Photos app

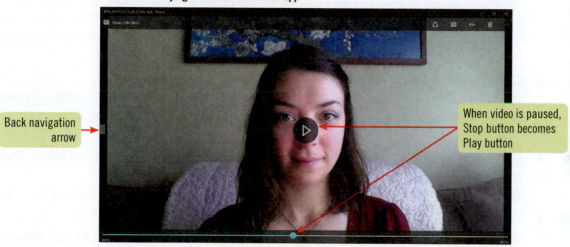

Back navigation arrow

When video is paused, Stop button becomes Play button

TABLE 5-1: Camera and image control buttons

button	image	lets you
Camera mode		Take still photos
Video mode		Take videos
Photos		View, edit, and share photos and videos you've taken with this device
Change camera		If your device has two cameras, switch between them; use to adjust lightness and darkness when shooting
Options		Access Photo timer and Settings

Setting camera options

To change the settings for the camera app, click or tap the Options button ●●● in the upper-right corner of the screen. Click or tap Photo timer to set a time delay of 2, 5, or 10 seconds or to have the camera continue taking pictures every five seconds until you click to tap the camera button again. Click or tap Settings to set other options. For example, you can have the camera shoot a "burst," or rapid succession, of photos when you press and hold the camera button. You can also reset the **aspect ratio**, the proportion of photo height to width; the default is 16:9, but you can change it to 4:3. Camera lets you turn on a framing grid to help you compose your pictures. You can use the Related settings links to change where photos and videos are saved, to choose whether the camera can use your location information, and to change privacy settings. If you are using the Camera app on a Windows tablet, Windows phone, or an external web cam, you will see additional settings appropriate to your device, such as flash settings if your device has a flash.

View and Edit Photos

Learning
Outcomes
• Navigate the
Photos app
• View photos or
videos
• Crop a photo

The Photos app that comes with Windows 10 provides a centralized place to view your photos, pictures, and videos from the Pictures folder, OneDrive, Facebook, Flickr, or any attached devices, such as a camera. Photos and videos you capture using the Camera app are automatically saved in the Pictures folder in the Camera Roll folder. Within the Photos app, you can navigate or view photos and videos with a simple click or tap of a folder or image. **CASE** *After taking some photos and storing them in the Pictures folder, you want to view them and edit one of them using the Photos app. IMPORTANT: Before starting this lesson, move a copy of the 5-Photos folder to the This PC > Pictures folder, then move a copy of the 5-Media folder to the This PC > Videos folder.*

STEPS

QUICK TIP

To display the contents of another folder in your Collection, click or tap Settings, under Sources click or tap Add a folder, then select the folder you want to add. To import pictures from a camera, connect the device, then click or tap the Import button 🖼 in the Photos app window.

1. **Click or tap the Start button ⊞, click or tap the Photos tile, then maximize the app window if necessary**

   The Photos app opens, displaying the Collection of your photos organized by date, with the most recent collection first. See **FIGURE 5-6**. The Collection consists of all the photos in your This PC > C: > Users > Your Username > Pictures folder, grouped by date. If you store your camera pictures on OneDrive, then your OneDrive photos also appear.

2. **Click or tap Albums**

   The Albums screen groups the photos in your Pictures folder based on folder names that the app creates, such as Camera roll and Saved pictures. They might also be grouped by date, location, and possibly facial recognition.

3. **Click or tap Folders, click or tap the Pictures folder, click or tap the 5-Photos folder, then click or tap the photo of the couple**

   The photo opens, and a toolbar appears above the photo. **TABLE 5-2** describes the tools available on the toolbar.

QUICK TIP

To create a new album, click or tap the New album button ➕, select pictures you want to include, click or tap the Done button ✓, select the default name (the date) if necessary, and type a new name, then click or tap the Save button 💾.

4. **Click or tap the Edit button ✏ on the toolbar**

   The photo is now in Edit mode. Buttons representing editing categories appear on the left, and buttons in the selected category appear on the right. The buttons let you change the picture's cropping, light, and color and apply effects.

5. **Click or tap the Basic fixes button on the left if it's not already selected (white), then click or tap the Crop button on the right**

   Handles appear around the photo that let you **crop**, or trim, the photo. See **FIGURE 5-7**.

6. **Drag the cropping handles and the photo itself until only the two people's faces are included, and they are centered in the cropped area**

   You can also drag the picture itself to adjust its position in the cropped area.

7. **Click or tap the Apply button ✓ on the toolbar, then click or tap the Save a copy button 💾**

   The Save a copy button saves a copy of the original with your changes, named The Grad (2), in your Pictures folder, leaving the original photo unchanged. Clicking or tapping the Save button saves changes to the original photo instead. The Cancel button cancels any changes you made.

8. **Click or tap the Back button ← to return to Folders**

   The 5-Photos folder now contains both the original, uncropped photo and the cropped version.

9. **Click or tap the Photo app's Close button ✕**

FIGURE 5-6: Photos app

Collection is selected

Your pictures will differ

FIGURE 5-7: Cropping a photo

Cancel button cancels changes

Apply button accepts changes

Cropping handles

TABLE 5-2: Photos app tools

tool	icon	lets you
Share		Share the photo via email, Facebook, Messaging, or Twitter (options vary depending on what you have installed)
Slideshow		Show an automatically running slide show of your pictures
Enhance		Apply automatic enhancements such as color, brightness, and straightening; changes are not saved to file (A checkmark on the icon indicates a photo is already enhanced)
Edit		Adjust a photo's rotation, cropping, straightness, lighting, color, or apply special effects
Rotate		Rotate a photo 90 degrees right with each click or tap
Delete		Send the photo to the Recycle Bin
See more		Copy or print a photo; or set it as your lock screen, desktop background, or photos tile

Trimming videos

You can use the Photos app to edit the length of any video you've captured using your camera. Navigate to a Photos app folder that contains a video, then click or tap a video and begin playback. During playback, or after it finishes, click or tap the Trim button in the toolbar. Drag the solid white circles on the left and right until you reach the points where you want to the video to start and end. Click or tap the Play button to show the shortened video. To save your changes, click or tap the Save a copy button.

Get and Play Music or Videos

You can get music from the Internet and play it on your Windows 10 devices. To do this, you use the **Groove Music** app, which also lets you play music stored in your Music folder. You can view your music according to album, artist, or song. The Groove Music app lets you create and edit **playlists**, which are named lists of selected recording names in a particular sequence. To download music for offline listening, or listen to unlimited music radio, you first need to go to the Store and purchase a monthly subscription to **Groove**, the Microsoft online music catalog and streaming service. **Streaming music** is music you can listen to as it is being downloaded from the web. A Groove subscription is called a **Groove Music Pass**, and you can use it to listen to music on the web, a Windows phone, the Apple iOS operating system, Android, and Xbox. But you can explore the Groove catalog and listen to samples without having to make a purchase. **CASE** ▶ *You like to play music in the background while you work, so you decide to use the Music app to find an appropriate selection.*

STEPS

1. **Click or tap the Start button ⊞, click or tap the Groove Music tile, maximize the app window if necessary, then click or tap the menu expand button ☰ to display the category names if they do not already appear**

   The Groove Music app opens, as shown in **FIGURE 5-8**. The Albums category is blue, indicating it is selected, and albums representing any recordings you currently have appear on the right. If you have no albums, you see links for getting music and/or telling Windows where on your device to look for music. Any named playlists appear in the middle section of the menu. If you have a Groove Music pass, you may have more selections on your menu than those shown in the figure, such as a Radio selection.

2. **Click or tap Artists on the menu, then click or tap Songs**

   Your musical selections appear by artist and then by song.

3. **Click or tap Get music in Store on the menu**

   The Microsoft Store opens with the Music tab in front. The Music tab shows a scrolling banner of current music, with links to top songs and genres, as well as a search box that lets you search the Groove catalog of over 38 million tracks. To stream complete selections, you need a Groove Music Pass, but anyone can preview a music selection.

4. **Click or tap any featured album, point to or tap a song, then click or tap its Preview button ▷, as shown in FIGURE 5-9**

   A preview of the selection plays. As it is playing, the Preview button becomes the Stop button.

5. **Click or tap in the search box, type movie themes, then press [Enter]**

   The search results appear, showing albums and songs featuring movie themes.

6. **Click or tap one of the album images, scroll down, point to or tap a selection, then click or tap its Preview button ▷**

   A sample of the selected song begins to play. If you have paid for a Groove Music Pass, you will see a Listen with your music pass button next to the album price so you can listen to any selection.

7. **Click or tap the Store window's Close button ✕, then click or tap the Groove Music window's Close button ✕**

   The app closes, and the desktop reappears.

FIGURE 5-8: Groove Music app

Menu expand button

Albums listing is selected

Any playlists appear here (yours will differ)

Albums appear here (yours will differ)

FIGURE 5-9: Previewing a song

Pointing to or tapping a song highlights it

Clicking the Preview button

Playing videos in the Movies & TV app

You can manage and play videos and TV shows from your own collection using the Movies & TV app. To start the app, click or tap the Movies & TV tile on the Start menu, or locate it in the All apps list. Expand the menu if necessary, then click or tap Movies, TV, or Videos to see collections that are already available on your device. These may include videos you've bought from the Movies & TV tab in the Microsoft Store; any you rented or purchased on Xbox 360 or Xbox One, Windows, Windows Phone, or the web; and any of your own videos. To locate more movies and shows, click or tap Shop for more on the menu. The Store opens, with the Movies & TV tab in front, where you can browse top movie rentals, new TV shows, and featured collections. For movies, click or tap the Watch trailer button under the movie title. For TV shows, you can buy a season pass for the entire season or select an episode. Click or tap the price button, then follow the instructions to purchase it.

View and Play Games

Learning Outcomes
- Open the Xbox app
- Install a game app
- Play then uninstall a game

Using the Xbox app that comes with Windows 10, you can play games that you download from the Windows Store. In the Xbox app, you have a **user profile** that identifies you to other game players and tracks your gaming achievements. Your user profile includes a **gamertag**, consisting of numbers and letters, and a customizable **avatar**, an electronic image or character that represents you in a game to other players. Although you can play games on your Windows computer in the Xbox app, you will have a richer experience if you use hardware such as the **Xbox One** gaming system, a console and wireless handheld controller featuring sophisticated electronics, graphics, and controls. If you have an Xbox One, Windows 10 lets you stream games from your Xbox to your Windows 10 computer using a wireless signal. You can purchase games from **Xbox Live**, the Microsoft digital gaming community and media delivery service. You log into Xbox Live using an existing Xbox account or your Microsoft account. **CASE** ▶ *In your off-hours from work you like to play games, so you decide to see what free games are available using the Xbox app.*

STEPS

1. Click or tap the Start button ⊞, then click or tap the Xbox tile

2. If the Let's get you an alter ego message box opens, click or tap Next, then follow the onscreen instructions to choose a gamertag; otherwise, skip to Step 3

3. Maximize the app window if necessary, then click or tap the menu expand button ☰ to display the category names if they do not already appear

   The Xbox app opens, as shown in **FIGURE 5-10**. You see the menu on the left, recent games, and an activity feed in the center and a Find people pane on the right. The menu lets you track games, messages, and activities, access the Store, and connect with a console, if you have one available. The recent list shows recently downloaded games and featured games, and the activity feed shows other players you might want to follow. The Find people pane lists players you might want to add as "friends" and interact with.

4. Click or tap Store on the menu

   The Xbox Store opens, displaying a list of available games for Windows 10.

5. Click or tap Show all Windows Store games, in the Store window click or tap the search box, type Wordament, press [Enter], then click or tap the Wordament game, or another free game if Wordament is unavailable

   An install button appears, as well as a notation that the app contains in-app purchases. The Store offers numerous free games you can download and play, and in those cases, the button reads "Free." Some games are free to download but offer purchases for various levels or features once you begin playing, often called **in-app purchases**.

6. Read the product description, then click or tap the Free button

   You see the progress of the download and installation, which takes a couple of minutes. When the installation is complete, the Open button appears.

7. Click or tap Open, drag across or swipe PLAY, then play the game as directed by the app, as shown in **FIGURE 5-11**

8. Click or tap the Wordament game window's Close button ⊠, then click or tap the Store window's Close button ⊠

9. Click or tap the Start button, click or tap All apps, right-click or press and hold Wordament, click or tap Uninstall, then click or tap Uninstall

   The Wordament app is removed from your system, and the desktop appears.

Using Apps to Manage Media

FIGURE 5-10: Xbox app window

Menu expand button

Menu

Store command

Recent games and activity feed

Find people pane

FIGURE 5-11: Wordament game window

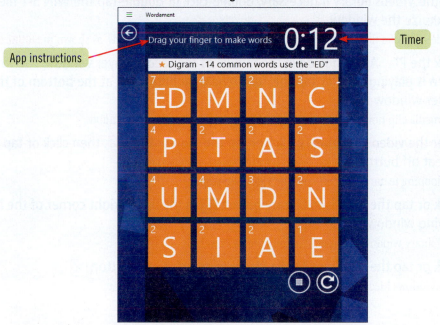

App instructions

Timer

Windows 10

Use Windows Media Player

Learning Outcomes
- View media in Windows Media Player
- Open a library
- Play a media clip in a library

Windows 10 comes with a built-in accessory called Windows Media Player, which you can use to organize and play video, audio, and mixed-media files, known as **clips**. You can play clips stored on your system, a CD, a DVD, a local network, or the Internet. Windows Media Player organizes your media in libraries. A **library** is a virtual (electronic) location that gathers filenames from different locations and shows them as a single collection. Although they appear to be in one place, the files remain in their original folders and storage locations. You can add storage locations to any library. When you play a media clip, it opens in a separate window, but you can easily return to the Library. As in Groove Music, you can organize clips into playlists. See **TABLE 5-3** for other tasks you can perform with Windows Media Player. **CASE** *You want to learn how to use Windows Media Player to play video and audio clips.*

STEPS

TROUBLE

If the menu bar does not appear at the top of the window, right-click or press and hold the toolbar, then click or tap Show menu bar.

1. **Click or tap the Start button ⊞, type Windows Media Player, click or tap Windows Media Player - Desktop app, click or tap the Recommended settings option button and then Finish if necessary to set up the app, then maximize the window if necessary**

   The Windows Media Player window opens, as shown in **FIGURE 5-12**, displaying media you currently have stored on your system. A toolbar with tabs appears at the top of the window, and player controls that look similar to those on a CD or DVD player are along the bottom. A menu bar with five menus appears below the title bar. On the system shown in the figure, the Music library is open, with its contents arranged alphabetically by artist.

2. **In the Windows Media Player navigation pane on the left side of the window, click or tap the Videos library if necessary, double-click or double-tap the WIN 5-1 file, then maximize the window**

   A video clip of a flower opening plays once in the Now Playing window, as shown in **FIGURE 5-13**.

QUICK TIP

To play an audio track from the Library, double-click or double-tap the track you want to play.

3. **Click the Play Again button in the middle of the Media Player window, then while the video is playing, click or tap the Turn repeat on button ⟳ at the bottom of the Media Player window**

   The media clip now plays repeatedly, or **loops**, in the Now Playing window.

4. **After the video clip repeats, click or tap the Stop button ☐, then click or tap the Turn repeat off button ⟳**

   The looping feature turns off, and the video clip stops.

QUICK TIP

To make sure you are using the most recent version of Windows Media Player, click or tap the Help menu, then click or tap Check for updates.

5. **Click or tap the Switch to Library button ⊞ in the upper-right corner of the Now Playing window**

   The Library window opens in Windows Media Player.

6. **Click or tap the Windows Media Player window's Close button ✕**

   The Windows Media Player app closes, and the desktop appears.

FIGURE 5-12: Library window in Windows Media Player

Menu bar

Toolbar

Music library contents displayed by artist (your content and view may differ)

Navigation pane

Player controls

FIGURE 5-13: Playing a video clip in the Now Playing window

Switch to Library button

Turn repeat on button

kovalvsmedia/shutterstock.com

TABLE 5-3: Additional Windows Media Player tasks

task	to
Rip music tracks or CDs	Copy them to your system, and create your own jukebox or playlist of media
Burn media to CDs or DVDs	Create CDs or DVDs with music or videos; copy music and videos to MP3 players, phones, or other mobile devices
Stream media from the Internet	Play videos, live broadcasts, and music tracks
Download media files to your system	Play them at any time

Using Apps to Manage Media

Work with Media in File Explorer

Learning Outcomes
• Open a media folder
• Play a media clip from a media folder

You can view and play music and video files from the Music folder or Videos folder in File Explorer. Both folders are specifically designed to play and manage music and video files. When you copy music files from a CD (using Windows Media Player) or download music or videos from the Store via the Groove Music app or Videos & TV app, the files are copied to the Music or Videos folder unless you specify a different location. The Music and Videos folders contain tabs with specialized tools that let you play the media. You can also add media files from the Music or Videos folder to a playlist in Windows Media Player. **CASE** *You decide to play some music from the File Explorer window.*

STEPS

1. **Click or tap the File Explorer button 🗔 on the taskbar**

2. **Navigate to the This PC > Videos folder, then double-click or double-tap the 5-Media folder**

   The This PC > Videos folder is where you stored your 5-Media folder earlier in this module.

3. **Click or tap WIN 5-2.wav, then click or tap the Music Tools Play tab**

   When you select a music or video file, the Music Tools Play tab or Video Tools Play tab appears on the Ribbon. Because WIN 5-2 is an audio file (WAV), the Music Tools Play tab appears, displaying buttons to play the selected file in the Groove Music app. See **FIGURE 5-14**. If you selected a video file, such as an MP4 file, the Video Tools Play tab would appear, displaying buttons to play the selected file in the Movies & TV app.

4. **Click or tap the Play button on the Play tab**

   The Groove Music app opens and starts to play the song. The playback controls appear in a blue bar at the bottom of the Groove Music screen. When the song is over, the playback controls are dimmed, and the Groove Music app remains open on the screen.

5. **Click or tap the Groove Music app window's Close button ☒**

   The Groove Music app closes and displays the File Explorer window again. The WIN 5-2 file remains selected.

6. **Click or tap the File Explorer window's Close button ☒**

   The File Explorer app closes.

Creating a sound file

Using the Voice Recorder app, you can record your own sound files. Voice Recorder creates Windows Media Audio files with the .m4a file extension. Voice Recorder both records and plays sound files. In order to use Voice Recorder, you need to have a sound card, speakers, and a microphone installed on your computer. In the Start menu, click or tap the All apps button, then navigate to and click or tap Voice Recorder. In the Voice Recorder app, click or tap the Record button, then record the sounds you want. When you're finished recording, click or tap the Stop recording button. The recording appears in the list. Right-click or press and hold it, then use the shortcut menu to share, delete, rename, or navigate to where the file is stored. When you're done, click or tap the Voice Recorder window's Close button.

FIGURE 5-14: Viewing media files in File Explorer

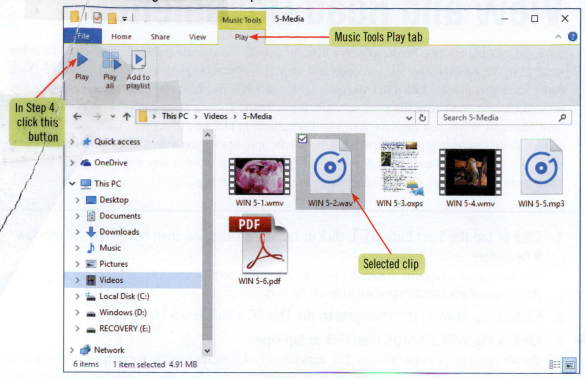

Associating a sound with an event

You can add sound effects to common Windows commands and functions, such as starting and exiting Windows or emptying the Recycle Bin. To do so, open the Sound dialog box by clicking or tapping the Start button, typing Sound, then selecting Sound Control panel. Click or tap the Sounds tab, then click or tap any Program Event in the list. The Sounds field displays the current sound associated with the event, if any. Click or tap the Sounds list arrow, select the desired sound in the list, then click or tap OK. You can also add your own .wav sound file by placing it in the This PC > Local Disk (C:) > Windows > Media folder (you need administrator permission to add files), then clicking or tapping Browse in the Sound dialog box to assign it to an event.

View and Read Documents

Have you ever used Adobe Reader to view a PDF document? You can use the Reader app to perform the same task. The **Reader app** lets you open and view PDF (Portable Document Format) and XPS (XML Paper Specification) files. **XPS** is the Microsoft version of a PDF file. With PDF or XPS, you can share files with others who don't have the same software. For example, if you are working with people who don't have Microsoft Word, you can save your Word document in PDF or XPS format. Then your coworkers without Word can open the document using the Reader app. Reader preserves the document's format, so it will look the same in Reader as it does in Word. **CASE** *You want to view a meeting report that was saved as an XPS document, so you decide to open it using the Reader app.*

STEPS

1. **Click or tap the Start button ⊞, click or tap the Reader tile, then maximize the window if necessary**

   The opening screen appears, shown in **FIGURE 5-15**. A Browse button appears at the top of the screen, with thumbnails of any recently opened documents below it.

2. **Click or tap Browse, then navigate to the This PC > Videos > 5-Media folder**

3. **Click or tap WIN 5-3.oxps, then click or tap Open**

   The file opens in the Reader window. The .oxps file extension means that this document is in **Open XPS** format, a more recent version of XPS. Open XPS documents cannot be opened in Windows versions earlier than Windows 8.0.

4. **Click or tap the Zoom in button ⊞ in the lower-right corner of the window, then click or tap the Zoom out button ⊟; with a touch screen, pinch to zoom**

   The current zoom percentage appears briefly in a red circle on the top left corner of the screen.

5. **Right-click the page, deselect the Continuous button ⬇, then select the One page button ⬆; on a touch screen, tap the menu expand button, tap App commands, deselect ⬇ then tap ⬆**

   The page controls that appear when you right-click or tap the screen let you view, search, save, and print the document.

6. **Point to the right side of the screen until the Next page button ▶ appears, then click or tap it to view the second page**

7. **Right-click the screen or open the app commands, then select the Two pages button ⬕**

   As shown in **FIGURE 5-16**, both document pages appear.

8. **Right-click or open the app commands, point to the document thumbnail in the bar at the top of the screen, then click or tap its Close button ☒**

9. **Click or tap the Reader app Close button ☒**

   The Reader app closes.

FIGURE 5-15: Reader app opening screen

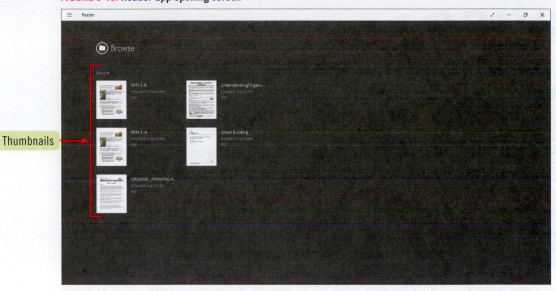

FIGURE 5-16: Viewing a document in two-page view

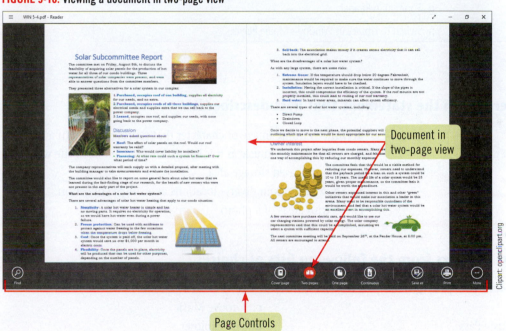

Clipart: openclipart.org

Windows 10

Practice

Concepts Review

Match each screen element on the left with the correct description on the right.

Element	App function
1. ▷	a. Accept cropping changes in Photos
2. ✚	b. Preview a music selection in Groove Music
3. ✓	c. Show two pages in Reader
4. ☰	d. Expand a menu in Maps, Money, Groove Music, or Xbox
5. 🗑	e. Take a video in Camera
6. ◖	f. Delete a video in Photos
7. ⬜	g. Zoom in in Reader
8. ⊞	h. Switch to Library in Windows Media Player

Match each term with the statement that best describes it.

9. **Library**   **a.** An electronic image or character that represents you in a game

10. **OneDrive**   **b.** A way to play music as it is being downloaded from the web

11. **Crop**   **c.** A cloud-based storage area

12. **Stream**   **d.** Shows files from diverse locations as a single collection

13. **Avatar**   **e.** To trim areas of a photo

Select the best answers from the following lists of choices.

14. **Which app lets you play games you download from the Windows Store?**
    a. Xbox
    b. Groove Music Pass
    c. Groove Music
    d. File Explorer

15. **Which folder does the Camera app use to store photos and videos?**
    a. Media
    b. Camera Roll
    c. Pictures
    d. Videos

16. **Which of the following is a named list of recordings in a particular sequence?**
    a. OneDrive
    b. Playlist
    c. Avatar
    d. Library

17. **Which term means to copy music tracks to your device?**
    a. Burn
    b. Stream
    c. Clip
    d. Rip

18. Which of the following file extensions represents a Windows Media Audio file?
 a. .xps
 b. .m4a
 c. .pdf
 d. .oxps

19. Which app allows you to calculate a mortgage payment?
 a. Maps
 b. Groove Music
 c. Reader
 d. Money

20. When you create a CD or DVD, the process is known as:
 a. ripping.
 b. burning.
 c. copying.
 d. synchronizing.

21. Which of the following apps allows you to play music and videos?
 a. Xbox
 b. Video
 c. Windows Media Player
 d. Photos

22. The term PDF stands for:
 a. Page Document Format.
 b. Portable Document File.
 c. Page Document File.
 d. Portable Document Format.

23. The term XPS stands for:
 a. XML Paper Specification.
 b. XML Page Specification.
 c. XML Paper Specialization.
 d. XML Page Specialization.

24. Which of the following apps allows you to crop a photo?
 a. Maps
 b. Groove
 c. Photos
 d. XPS Viewer

Skills Review

1. Get information with media apps.
 a. Open the News app, maximize the window, then scroll through the content.
 b. Use the tabs at the top of the app to view different types of news content, such as Top Stories and Technology.
 c. Click or tap an image or article, then scroll to view it.
 d. Use the Back button at the top of the window to return to the Home screen, then click or tap the All tab.
 e. Expand the app menu, explore another category such as Local or Videos, then close the News app.
 f. Open the Sports app, maximize the window, then expand the menu to view the categories.
 g. Select a sports category, explore a story in that category, then close the Sports app window.

2. Take photos and videos with the camera.
 a. Open the Camera app, then verify that the app is in Camera mode.
 b. Take a picture of yourself, use the Photos app button to view the photo, then delete the photo.
 c. Use the taskbar to return to the Camera app.
 d. Switch to Video mode, take a short video of yourself, then stop the recording.
 e. View the video in the Photos app, then delete the video.
 f. Close the Photos app and the Camera app.

3. View and edit photos.
 a. Open the Photos app.
 b. View your collection, scrolling if necessary.
 c. View your albums, if any, scrolling if necessary.
 d. Return to your collection, open a photo, then switch to Edit mode.
 e. In the Basic fixes category, crop the photo, save a copy of the photo, then close the Photos app.

4. **Get and play music or videos.**
   a. Open the Groove Music app, then maximize the window, and display the menu categories if necessary.
   b. Verify that you are viewing your albums, then view your music by artist and then by song. (If you do not have music on your device, skip this step.)
   c. Use a link on the menu to go to the Music tab in the Store.
   d. Select an album, scroll down, then preview a selection.
   e. Use the search box to display folk music.
   f. Select an album, then preview a selection.
   g. Close the Store and the Groove Music app.

5. **View and play games.**
   a. Open the Xbox app, then maximize its window and expand its app menu if necessary.
   b. Open the Xbox store, then show all Windows Store games.
   c. Locate the Hangman Pro game, install it, then open it.
   d. Choose a player name and level if prompted, and play the game. (Do not make any in-app purchases if asked.)
   e. After you finish one round, close the app, close the Windows store, close the Xbox app, then uninstall the game.

6. **Use Windows Media Player.**
   a. Open the Windows Media Player app, then maximize the window.
   b. Navigate to the Videos library if necessary, then play the WIN 5-4.wmv video, maximizing its window.
   c. Set the video to loop continuously, then play it again, watching it begin again automatically.
   d. Stop the video, turn off looping, then return to the Library and close the Windows Media Player app.

7. **Work with media in File Explorer.**
   a. Open File Explorer, then navigate to the This PC > Videos > 5-Media folder.
   b. Select the WIN 5-5.mp3 file, then display the Music Tools Play tab.
   c. Play the Win 5-5.mp3 file using the Play button on the Music Tools Play tab.
   d. Close the Groove Music app and File Explorer.

8. **View and read documents.**
   a. Open the Reader app and maximize its window if necessary.
   b. Browse to the This PC > Videos folder, open the 5-Media folder, select the WIN 5-6.pdf file, then open it.
   c. Zoom in and then zoom out.
   d. View it in two-page view.
   e. Close the document, then close the Reader app.
   f. Open File Explorer, then delete the 5-Photos folder from your Pictures folder and the 5-Media folder from your Videos folder.

Independent Challenge 1

You are doing research for a financial services firm. You want to monitor the latest financial news stories and locations where they occur. You decide to use the Money app to find important stories and the Maps app to find out where the stories are occurring.

a. Open the Money app, and use the News tab to locate a financial news story that mentions a location you find interesting. Open and read the story.

b. Copy the title of the story, open WordPad, and paste it. Save the document as **Financial News.rtf**.

c. Copy the first paragraph of the story, and paste that into the WordPad document.

d. Return to the article in the Money app, and find a location mentioned, such as a city, state, or country, then copy it.

e. Open the Maps app, paste the location name in the search box, add any additional description necessary to specify the location, and have the Maps app locate it.

f. Click or tap the Banks links, and note how many banks are located in the area. See **FIGURE 5-17** for examples.

g. Close the Maps app, return to the WordPad document, then type the number of banks in that location. Add your name to the document and save it, then close all apps.

FIGURE 5-17

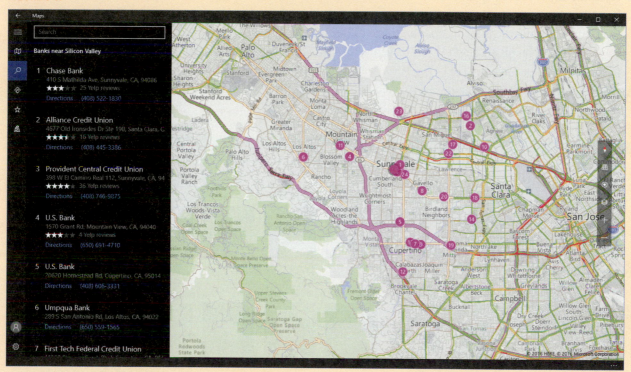

Independent Challenge 2

You are in the process of looking for a job. You want to capture a photo to insert into your written résumé as well as put together a video résumé. Before you get started on the video portion, take a moment to write out a short, three- to four-sentence script including your name and describing your qualifications and interests.

a. Open the Camera app, then switch to Video mode, if necessary.

b. Start the video, read the script (because video files are large, it should be a maximum of ten seconds long), then end the video.

Independent Challenge 2 (continued)

c. Switch to Camera mode, then take a photo of yourself.

d. Go to the Photos app, play the video, then view the photo. Close the Camera app.

e. If necessary, to show your photos, right-click the photo and click View all photos. Click or tap Folders, click or tap Pictures, then click or tap the Camera Roll folder; play the video, and view the photo.

f. If instructed to do so, share the photo and video with your instructor via email.

g. Delete the video and the photo, then close the Photos app.

Independent Challenge 3

You are a college student taking a survey course in music. As part of your studies, you need to listen to different types of music and identify examples of each one. You want to use the Groove Music app and the Store to locate sample music selections from different genres, preview the songs, then list your findings.

a. Open a blank WordPad document, then save it in the location where you store your Data Files as **Music Examples.rtf**.

b. Open the Groove Music app, then use a link there to go to the Store.

c. Preview at least one song in the following genres: Jazz or Blues; Rock; Hip Hop; Country; and Classical. (*Hint*: Use the Genres link and use the categories on the left side of the screen. If necessary, select a subgenre, as shown in **FIGURE 5-18**.) As you play each one, note its genre, the artist's or the collection name, and the names of the selection in the WordPad document.

d. Add your name to the document, save and close it, then close the Store and Groove Music apps.

FIGURE 5-18

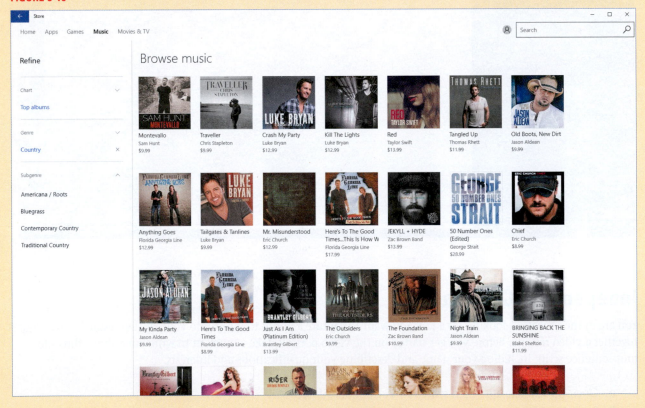

Independent Challenge 4: Explore

You are taking a business class, and have been assigned the task of selecting a technology stock and following its stock performance. You begin by searching technology financial news in the Money app, and then putting a company's stock on a watchlist, where you'll be able to see its progress.

a. Open the Money app, then open the News tab.

b. Use the Showing list arrow to show Technology news. Scroll through the articles, and skim the contents of a few that interest you.

c. In one of the articles, locate the name of a company that interests you. Open an article that mentions the company, then copy the first paragraph of it.

d. Open WordPad, paste the paragraph you copied, then save the document in the location where you store your Data Files as **Stock Performance.rtf**.

e. Use a button on the taskbar to return to the Money app, in the app menu select Watchlist, select the Add to watchlist button (the plus sign ➕), type the company name, then when the dropdown list opens click or tap the company name.

f. In the watchlist, view the stock's recent performance. Notice the general trend, whether upward, downward, or mixed, as indicated by its current price in relation to its 52-week range. See **FIGURE 5-19** for an example.

g. Switch to WordPad, add the stock name and its stock symbol above the paragraph you copied, then write two sentences about its stock performance in the last year.

h. Add your name to the document, then save and close it. Close the Money app.

FIGURE 5-19

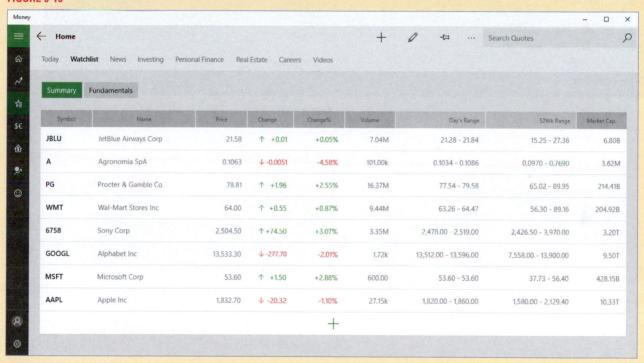

Visual Workshop

Re-create the screen shown in **FIGURE 5-20**, which shows the Maps app displaying Grand Teton National Park. Note that the view has been tilted using the tilt control, the Map view is aerial, and Traffic is on. If you can use your computer's PrintScreen key, take a screenshot of each screen, paste it into a WordPad document using the Paste command in the Clipboard group on the Home tab, add your name to the end of the document, then print it out and submit it to your instructor.

FIGURE 5-20

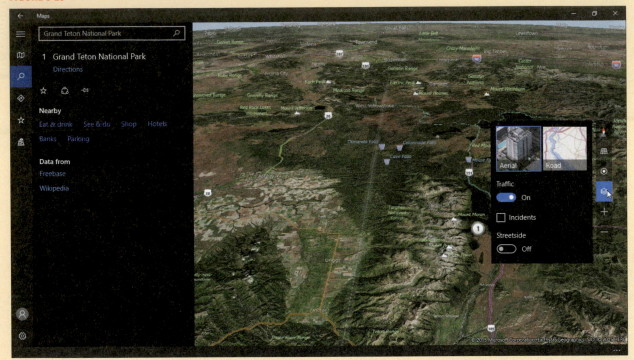

Customizing Windows

CASE ▶ Windows 10 lets you customize the way you work to suit your objectives and preferences. You want to view and customize your settings in order to personalize Windows 10. *Important*: If you are concerned about changing aspects of Windows 10 and do not want to customize, or if you are in a setting that does not allow you to change Windows 10 settings, then read through this module without completing the steps. *Note: With the release of Windows 10, Microsoft now provides ongoing updates to Windows instead of releasing new versions periodically. This means that Windows features might change over time, including how they look and how you interact with them. The information provided in this text was accurate at the time this book was published.*

Module Objectives

After completing this module, you will be able to:

- View Windows settings
- Personalize the desktop, theme, and lock screen
- Change user account settings
- Change notification settings
- Change Cortana and search settings
- Change general settings
- Change share and privacy settings
- Use the Control Panel

Files You Will Need

White Building.jpg   Beacon.jpg

View Windows Settings

Windows 10 lets you customize your work environment using the Settings app. The **Settings app**, available from the Start menu, contains nine touch-friendly categories of the most commonly used Windows options that you can set to help you work more efficiently. For example, **Personalization settings** let you change the pictures and colors that appear on the lock screen, screen background, and Start menu. **Time & language settings** let you set your computer's time zone, region, and language. Other settings are located in the **Control Panel**, a desktop app that lets you control less frequently used or more advanced Windows settings. **CASE** *You examine Windows settings.*

STEPS

1. **Click or tap the Start button ⊞, then click or tap Settings**

   The Settings app screen opens, as shown in **FIGURE 6-1**, showing the nine app categories and a search box.

2. **Click or tap the System category**

   The System subcategories appear on the left side of the Settings app windows. See **FIGURE 6-2**. **System settings** let you control your screen display, notifications, apps, power, and storage. The first subcategory, Display, is highlighted, and the Display settings appear on the right side of the window.

3. **Scroll down if necessary to view the available Display settings**

   Many settings screens contain more options than are initially visible. If you are using a pointing device and move the pointer off the Settings app window, the scroll bar may not be visible. You need to point to the window again to see it. On a touch screen, you can swipe up to view additional options.

4. **Click or tap the Power & sleep subcategory**

   The Power & sleep settings control when your screen turns off and when your PC goes to sleep.

5. **Click or tap the Back button ← at the top of the Settings app screen**

6. **At the Settings screen, click or tap the Network & Internet category**

   If you are using Wi-Fi, your Wi-Fi connection and status appear, as well as a list of available networks. Below the network list, blue links let you manage your Wi-Fi settings.

7. **Click or tap Advanced options at the bottom of the window, scroll down if necessary to view the information, click or tap the Back button ←, then under Related settings click or tap Network and Sharing Center**

   The Network and Sharing Center Control Panel opens, as shown in **FIGURE 6-3**. Sometimes, clicking a link in a Settings screen takes you to the Control Panel. The available options represent more advanced network settings, so they appear in the Control Panel, rather than in the Settings app.

8. **Click or tap the Network and Sharing Center Close button ☒, then click or tap the Settings app Close button ☒**

   The Control Panel and the Settings app close.

Choosing between the Settings app and the Control Panel

Early Windows versions contained all settings in the Control Panel. But the Settings app brings an easier-to-use, touch-friendly interface to commonly used Windows settings. Microsoft is gradually moving more Control Panel settings over to the Settings app. Many settings are available in both the Settings app and the Control Panel, while others are available only in the Control Panel. Instead of trying to remember the exact location of a particular setting, you can easily search for settings using Cortana or the Control Panel Search text box; doing so opens or displays the appropriate app and takes you directly to the setting you need.

FIGURE 6-1: Settings app categories

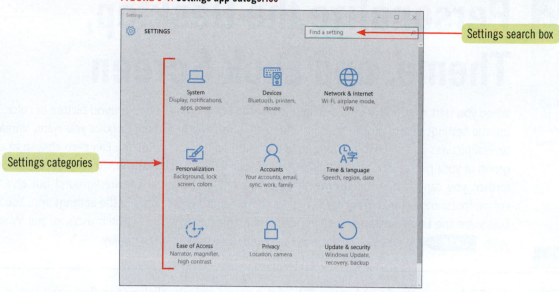

Settings search box

Settings categories

FIGURE 6-2: Display subcategory in System settings

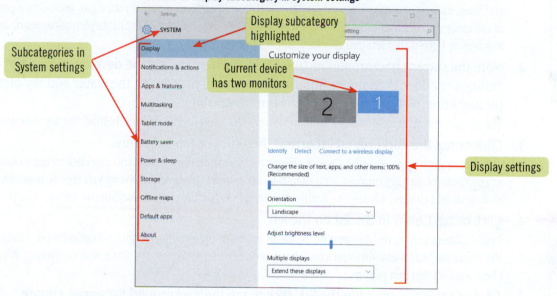

Display subcategory highlighted

Subcategories in System settings

Current device has two monitors

Display settings

FIGURE 6-3: Network and Sharing Control Panel

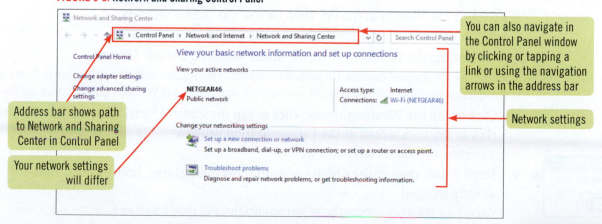

You can also navigate in the Control Panel window by clicking or tapping a link or using the navigation arrows in the address bar

Address bar shows path to Network and Sharing Center in Control Panel

Your network settings will differ

Network settings

Customizing Windows

Personalize the Desktop, Theme, and Lock Screen

Learning Outcomes
- Display Personalization settings
- Create a picture screen background
- Select a theme

When you start Windows 10 and sign in, the desktop appears with a background picture or color. You can use the Settings app to customize the desktop so it displays the picture or color you want. Windows has several pictures you can choose from, or you can use one of your own. You can even choose to display a group of your pictures in the form of a rotating display called a **slideshow**. To customize Windows even further, you can change the **theme** that governs not only the desktop background but also window colors, fonts, and sounds. You choose desktop backgrounds and themes in the Settings app. You can also customize the **Lock screen**, which appears when you start Windows, switch users, or put Windows to sleep. **CASE** ▸ *As you review Windows 10 settings, you customize your display.*

STEPS

1. **Click or tap the Start button ⊞, click or tap Settings, click or tap Personalization, then verify that your Settings window is restored down and not maximized**

   The Personalization settings appear, displaying the subcategories Background, Colors, Lock screen, Themes, and Start. Background is highlighted, and the Background options appear on the right, including a preview of the current background that fills the screen. See **FIGURE 6-4**. A group of available pictures appears, as well as a Browse button that lets you choose your own picture.

2. **Note the current background picture in the Preview and on the desktop behind the Settings window, then under Choose your picture, click or tap the water and sky picture (or any other picture if water and sky is not available)**

   The picture you selected appears in the preview window and on the desktop behind the Settings window.

3. **Click or tap the Background list arrow, then click or tap Slideshow**

   A Browse button appears under Choose albums for your slideshow, which you can click or tap to navigate to any folder of pictures on your computer. Below the Browse button, options let you specify how often the picture should change, whether to shuffle the order, how to fit the picture within the screen.

4. **Click or tap Colors in the list on the left**

   Under Choose a color, the Automatically pick an accent color from my background option is on. That is why the miniature Start menu tiles and icons changed color when you chose the water and sky picture; Windows chose a color from that picture.

5. **Click or tap Background in the list, click or tap the Background list arrow, choose Picture, then select the original picture that appeared as your desktop background (if a color appeared, go to the Colors subcategory and reselect the color)**

6. **Click or tap Themes in the list, then click or tap Theme settings**

   The Personalization Control Panel opens, showing three groups of themes.

7. **Click or tap the Windows 10 theme under Windows Default Themes**

   The screen background changes. The icons at the bottom of the window indicate that the current theme features a slideshow for the desktop background, an automatic set of colors, and Windows default sounds. See **FIGURE 6-5**.

8. **Click or tap the Windows theme, click or tap the Control Panel Close button ⊠, then click or tap Lock screen in the Personalization window**

   A preview of the current lock screen appears.

9. **Scroll down, then under Choose apps to show quick status, notice which apps are already selected**

   You can use the seven icons to choose various apps that will show information on the lock screen.

FIGURE 6-4: Personalization settings showing Background options

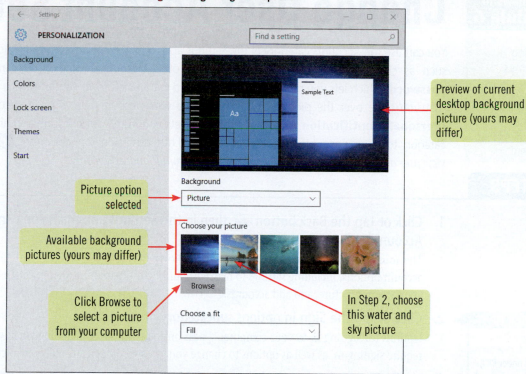

Preview of current desktop background picture (yours may differ)

Picture option selected

Available background pictures (yours may differ)

Click Browse to select a picture from your computer

In Step 2, choose this water and sky picture

FIGURE 6-5: Windows 10 Theme characteristics

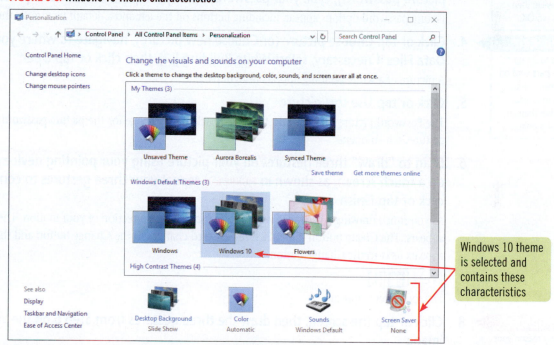

Windows 10 theme is selected and contains these characteristics

---

Adding Lock screen apps

The lock screen lets you view status information and notifications without having to unlock your system. These notifications are called **Lock screen apps**, and they can give you information such as the temperature in your area, the strength of your wireless signal, and whether or not you have new email messages. You can add information from other apps using the Personalization screen. To add Lock screen apps, click or tap the Start button, then click or tap Settings > Personalization > Lock screen. You can get detailed status for one app and quick status for up to seven apps. Click or tap an Add button (+), then select an available app from the scrollable list. To remove an app, click or tap the app icon, then click or tap another app, or click or tap None.

Change User Account Settings

You can use the Accounts category of the Settings app to manage aspects of your Microsoft user account, such as changing your sign-in procedure and other account settings. You can create a **picture password**, which lets you replace a typed password with a picture you choose and a set of three gestures that you trace over the picture to gain access to your account. Or you can specify a four-digit **PIN (Personal Identification Number) code** that lets you in to your account. You also use the Accounts category to assign accounts to family members and other users on your computer. **CASE** *You want to view user account settings and create a picture password for added security.*

STEPS

1. **Click or tap the Back button ←, then in the Settings app main app window click or tap Accounts**

   The Your email and accounts settings appear, as shown in **FIGURE 6-6**, and the right pane displays email and account options, including settings to manage your Microsoft account, sign in with a local account, change your account picture, and add accounts.

2. **Click or tap the Sign-in options subcategory on the left**

   Options for signing in to your computer appear on the right pane, including when you want Windows to require signing in, as well as options to change your password or create a PIN or a picture password.

3. **Under Picture password, click or tap Add (or Change, if your device already uses a picture password), type your password at the prompt, then click or tap OK**

   Picture password options appear, including buttons on the left and a default picture on the right.

4. **Click or tap Choose picture (or Choose new picture), navigate to where you store your Data Files if necessary, select White Building.jpg, then click or tap Open**

   A picture of a white building appears in right pane.

5. **Click or tap Use this picture**

   The Password Picture image is selected as the background image for the picture password. The Set up your gestures screen opens.

6. **Drag to "draw" three gestures on your picture using your pointing device or your finger on a touch screen, as shown in FIGURE 6-7, repeat your three gestures to confirm, then click or tap Finish**

   As you finish drawing a gesture, a white arrow confirms the direction of your motion. The Accounts screen appears. The Create button under Picture password changes to the Change button and the Remove button appears next to the Change button.

7. **Press [⊞][L]**

   The lock screen appears.

8. **Click or tap the screen, then draw the three gestures from Step 6 on the White Building image**

   The Settings screen appears, displaying the Accounts category Sign-in options.

9. **Click or tap Remove under Picture password in the right pane, then click or tap the Back button ← to return to the main Settings screen**

   The picture password is removed. The Change button under Picture password changes back to the Add button.

FIGURE 6-6: Email and accounts settings

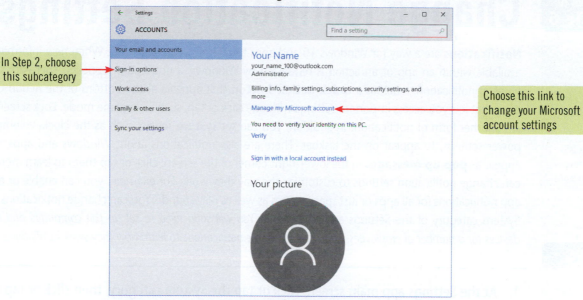

In Step 2, choose this subcategory

Choose this link to change your Microsoft account settings

FIGURE 6-7: Creating a picture password

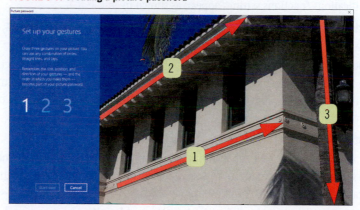

Creating a user account

When you sign in with a Microsoft account, your account settings are maintained online. You can continue to manage your account online or change it to a local one. A **local account** keeps usernames and passwords on the device as opposed to accessing the information online, and local account settings can't be synced to other devices. If you have an administrator account or belong to the current Administrators group, you can create a new user account with a separate identity. This allows the user to keep files private and customize the operating system with personal preferences. The name you assign to the user appears on the Sign-in screen and the Start menu. The steps to add user accounts differ, depending on whether your system is part of a workgroup or domain network. When you add an account, you specify a password, which you can change at any time. Good passwords are typically at least seven characters and include letters (uppercase and lowercase), numbers, and symbols. In Windows 10, you can use multiple security passwords or codes, such as text or pictures.

Deleting a user account

If you are logged in as an administrator, you can delete an existing account. To delete an account, right-click the Start button, click or tap Control Panel, then click or tap the User Accounts icon in Small icons or Large icons view. Click or tap Manage another account, select the account you want to delete, click or tap Delete the account, click or tap Delete Files to remove all account files or Keep Files to save account folders (with username) to the desktop, click or tap Delete Account, then click or tap the Close button. If you choose to Keep Files, Windows automatically saves the content of the user's desktop and Documents, Favorites, Music, Pictures, and Video folders to a new folder (named the same as the user) on your desktop.

Customizing Windows

Windows 10

Windows 125

Change Notification Settings

Learning Outcomes
- Display system notifications and actions settings
- Hide and redisplay a taskbar notification icon
- Display lock screen notification icons

Notifications are a way for Windows 10 and apps to communicate with you. When new information is available within an app or an action is requested by Windows, a notification appears. There are several types of notifications, such as a **quick action button** that appears at the bottom of the Action Center pane that lets you access important settings with one click or tap, such as Airplane mode. Lock screen apps are another form of notification. In addition, you can set **system icons**, such as the clock, volume, and power settings, to appear on the taskbar. There are also notifications about Windows and apps, which appear as **pop-up messages** in the lower-right corner of the screen; click or tap them to learn more. You can change notification settings to customize the way they work. For example, you can enable or disable app notifications for all apps or just specific ones as well as play sounds. You can change notifications in the System category of the Settings app. **CASE** ▶ *You will soon need to set up the computers and mobile devices for a number of employees. You want to enable notifications to learn how they work in Windows 10.*

STEPS

1. **At the Settings app main screen, click or tap the** System **category, then click or tap the** Notifications & actions **subcategory**

   The Notifications & actions settings appear, as shown in **FIGURE 6-8**.

2. **Scroll down to view the three sections** Quick actions, Notifications, **and** Show notifications from these apps, **then scroll back up**

   The Quick actions section lets you customize up to four tiles in the Windows Action Center, so that actions you use frequently, such as writing a note or switching to tablet mode, are immediately available, even when the Action Center is collapsed. Clicking or tapping one of these icons opens a menu of available actions you can assign to that tile.

3. **Click or tap** Select which icons appear on the taskbar

   Some icons are currently set to appear on the taskbar, as shown in **FIGURE 6-9** (Your settings will differ based on your system and configuration). You can drag any of the sliders to the on (right) position to display them on the taskbar or the off (left) position to hide them.

4. **Drag any** On slider **to the left, display the taskbar if necessary and observe that the icon no longer appears, drag the same** slider **to the right to turn it on again, click or tap the** Back button ⬅, **then view the taskbar again**

   Your selected icon again appears in the taskbar.

5. **Scroll down to view the Notifications section and the Show notifications from these apps sections**

   The apps that will show notifications are those switched On in the lower section. You can click or tap any app name to see sliders for specific notification actions, such as whether banners appear or sounds play.

6. **Drag the** Show notifications on the lock screen **slider in the Notifications section to** On, **if necessary**

   This option displays notifications on the lock screen.

7. **Press [⊞][L]**

   The lock screen appears, where you can view notification icons. The icons that appear are the ones specified on the lock screen settings screen under Personalization > Lock screen.

8. **Click or tap the** lock screen, **enter your password, then click or tap the** Submit button

   The PC settings screen appears with the Notifications category selected.

9. **Click or tap the** Back button ⬅ **to return to the Settings screen, then click or tap the Settings window** Close button ☒

FIGURE 6-8: Notifications & actions settings

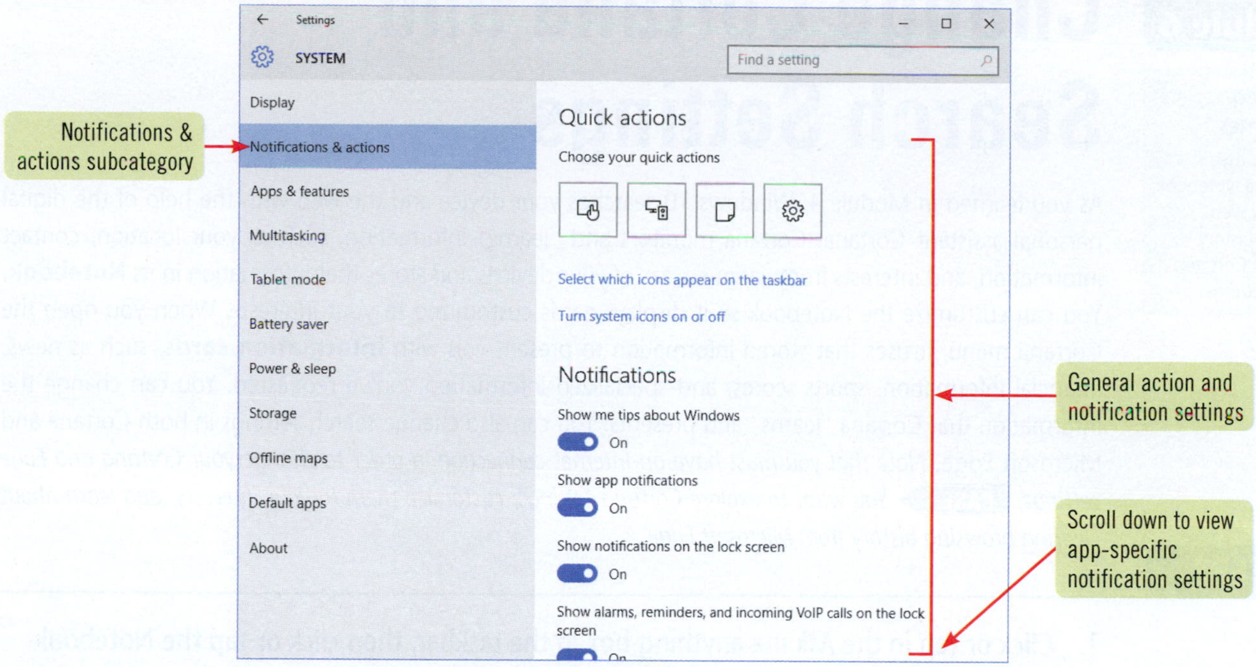

Notifications & actions subcategory

General action and notification settings

Scroll down to view app-specific notification settings

FIGURE 6-9: Selecting taskbar icons

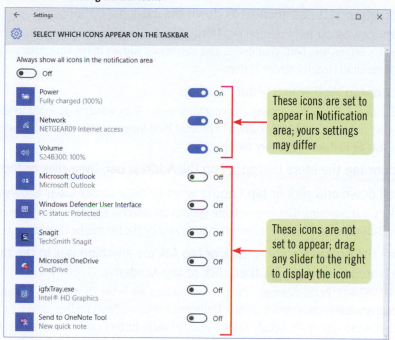

These icons are set to appear in Notification area; yours settings may differ

These icons are not set to appear; drag any slider to the right to display the icon

Syncing Windows settings on other devices

When you sign in to Windows 10 with a Microsoft account, you can enable the system to automatically synchronize your system and some app settings with other devices that use the same Microsoft account. In the Settings app, click or tap the Accounts category, then click or tap Sync your settings. Your account email address appears at the top of the screen. You can drag the Sync settings slider to the On position. Then you can enable or disable individual sync settings, such as theme, browser settings, and Language preferences. If you enable Other Windows settings, Windows syncs selected device settings, such as printer settings, File Explorer settings, and your notification preferences. To sync devices you must sign into the same Microsoft account or link your Microsoft account to your school or work account. If you can't select Sync settings, your organization may have disabled this feature.

Windows 10

Change Cortana and Search Settings

As you learned in Module 4, Windows 10 searches your device and the web with the help of the digital personal assistant Cortana. Cortana monitors and "learns" information, such as your location, contact information, and interests from various areas of your devices and stores that information in its **Notebook**. You can customize the Notebook so it displays cards customized to your interests. When you open the Cortana menu, it uses that stored information to present you with **information cards**, such as news, financial information, sports scores, and specialized information you've requested. You can change the information that Cortana "learns" and presents. You can also change search settings in both Cortana and Microsoft Edge. *Note that you must have an Internet connection in order to change your Cortana and Edge settings.* **CASE** *You want to explore Cortana settings, customize them to your interests, and learn about clearing browsing history from Microsoft Edge.*

STEPS

1. **Click or tap in the Ask me anything box in the taskbar, then click or tap the Notebook button ▣ on the Cortana menu**

   The Cortana Notebook appears, showing categories of information that Cortana maintains. See **FIGURE 6-10**.

2. **Click or tap Settings, then scroll down the available options**

   Below the Cortana response options, Device search history and Web search history options are On by default. Cortana uses both your device and web search history to improve future searches. You can click or tap Clear all to clear the device history.

3. **Click or tap Web search history settings**

   A Microsoft Edge window opens, showing your recent Bing searches, grouped by day. See **FIGURE 6-11**. You can click the slider to the Off position to prevent Bing from maintaining your search history, and/or click or tap Clear all to delete all history listings.

4. **Click or tap the More button ⋯ on the Address bar, then click or tap Settings**

5. **Scroll down and click or tap Choose what to clear under Clear Browsing data**

   Under Clear browsing data, one or more options are selected (display a checkmark). If you click or tap the Clear button, all the selected information indicated by the list will be cleared.

6. **Close the browser window, click or tap Ask me anything box in the taskbar, click or tap the Notebook button ▣, then click or tap Academic**

   See **FIGURE 6-12**. In the Academic category, all options are in the On position by default, so Cortana is set to display Academic cards, which include Conference updates, News updates, and New papers on any scholarly field. You can specify a scholarly field of study to make history card contents relevant to your interests.

7. **Click or tap Add scholar field of study, type History (or a field that interests you), click or tap a field in the list of suggestions, turn on or off the conference, news, and new papers options for that field of study, then click or tap Add**

   The field of study is added to the bottom of the Notebook.

8. **Click or tap the Cortana Home button ⌂, scroll down, then verify that a History section showing History cards (or cards for the field you selected) now appears**

9. **Click or tap anywhere outside the Cortana menu to close it**

FIGURE 6-10: Cortana Notebook

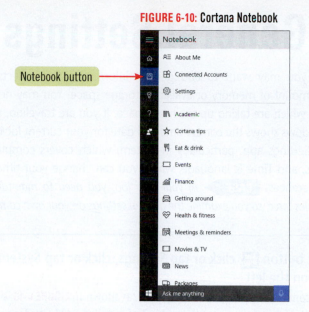

Notebook button

FIGURE 6-11: Bing search history in Edge

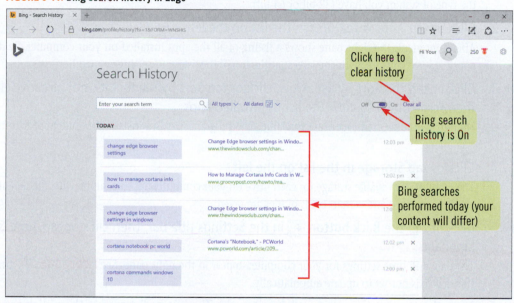

Click here to clear history

Bing search history is On

Bing searches performed today (your content will differ)

FIGURE 6-12: Academic area of the Cortana Notebook

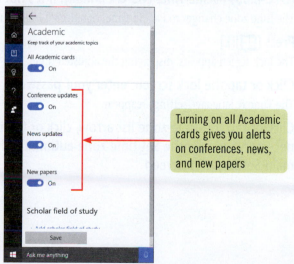

Turning on all Academic cards gives you alerts on conferences, news, and new papers

Customizing Windows

Windows 129

Windows 10

Change General Settings

Learning Outcomes
• Display system characteristics
• Display installed applications by size
• Change a device's time zone settings

As you use Windows 10, you may want to find general information that affects your computer's performance, such as the amount of memory or available storage space. You may need to know which apps are installed and learn which are taking up the most space. If you are traveling, you might want to adjust the time zone so Windows shows the correct time and date for your current location. You can learn all this information in the Settings app, particularly in System, which covers computer characteristics, performance, and programs, and Time & language, where you can change your time zone, date, time, language, and speech preferences. **CASE** *In your new job, you need to maintain the Windows 10 computers for the traveling sales force, so you examine the general settings on your own computer to get started.*

STEPS

1. **Click or tap the Start button ⊞, click or tap Settings, click or tap System, then click or tap About in the list on the left**

   Information about your computer appears in the right pane, as shown in **FIGURE 6-13**, such as the edition of Windows you are using, the type of processor, the amount of installed RAM (random access memory), and the type of system you have (32-bit or 64-bit).

2. **Click or tap Apps & features in the list on the left**

   After a moment, the right pane shows a listing of all the apps installed on your computer. By default, the apps are sorted by size, with the largest at the top of the list; your settings may differ.

3. **Click or tap the Sort by list arrow, click or tap Sort by name if it's not already selected, then scroll down to view the list of installed apps**

   Your apps are re-sorted according to Name. The program size and installation date appear to the right of each name.

4. **Click or tap Storage in the list on the left**

   The amount of available storage for each drive on your computer appears, along with the default locations about where apps and certain types of files are saved.

5. **Click or tap the Back button ← in the Settings title bar, then click or tap Time & language**

   The date and time settings for your computer appear in the right pane. See **FIGURE 6-14**. The time zone on this device is not set to update automatically.

6. **Note the current time zone, click or tap the Time zone list arrow, then click or tap (UTC-8:00) Pacific Time (US & Canada), if it's not already selected**

   The time zone changes to Pacific Time, as reflected in the time displayed near the top of the pane.

7. **Press [⊞][L]**

   The lock screen appears, displaying the adjusted time.

8. **Click or tap the lock screen, enter your password, then click or tap the Submit button →**

   The Time & language settings reappear.

9. **Click or tap the Time zone list arrow, click or tap the original time zone setting if necessary, or drag the Set time zone automatically setting to On, then return to the main Settings app screen**

FIGURE 6-13: Computer system information

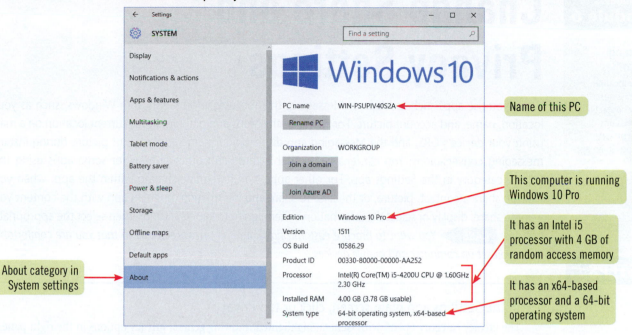

Name of this PC

This computer is running Windows 10 Pro

It has an Intel i5 processor with 4 GB of random access memory

It has an x64-based processor and a 64-bit operating system

About category in System settings

FIGURE 6-14: Date and time settings

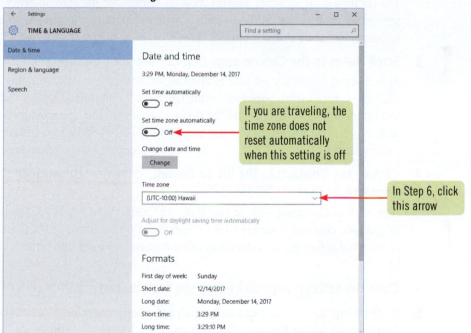

If you are traveling, the time zone does not reset automatically when this setting is off

In Step 6, click this arrow

Reinstalling Windows 10

If your system is not running well, you can refresh the Windows software without affecting your personal files. Or, if you want to start over from scratch with a new Windows installation, you can reset your system to the factory settings, but your files will not be preserved. *Use care before selecting any Windows reinstall option, and make sure that you are choosing the options you want to avoid inadvertent loss of your important files.* To refresh, open the Settings app, open the Update & security category, then click or tap Recovery in the list. Under Reset this PC, click or tap Get started. Follow the onscreen instructions to keep your files or remove them and then reinstall Windows. To do a complete reinstall using installation files on a USB or DVD drive, click or tap Restart now under Advanced startup. *Be aware that a full reinstall will delete all your files, apps, and customizations.*

Change Share and Privacy Settings

Learning Outcomes
- View location permissions
- View contacts permissions
- View privacy settings in an app

When you use apps such as Maps or Messaging, the app uses information from Windows, such as your location, name, and account picture. For example, the Maps app pinpoints your current location on a map using your device's GPS, and the Messaging app displays your name and account picture during instant messaging conversations. You can enable or disable these and other options for some apps using the Privacy category in the Settings app. For other apps, you determine sharing within the app, when you want to share a contact, picture, or the like. To share app information, open an app with the content you want to share, display or select the information or item, go to the app's settings, then select the appropriate options. **CASE** *You want to practice customizing share and privacy settings so that you are comfortable when you set up computer and mobile devices.*

STEPS

1. **In the Settings app main screen, click or tap Privacy**

   The Privacy category opens, with General highlighted, showing general privacy options in the right pane.

2. **Click or tap Location in the list on the left**

   The Location pane indicates whether location services for the current device are on or off. If location services are on for your account, Cortana and any apps accessing this setting can, for example, make recommendations of available businesses nearby.

3. **Scroll down to the Choose apps that can use your location section**

   Apps that can potentially use your location are listed; those currently permitted to do so are switched on, while those not currently permitted are off. On the device shown in **FIGURE 6-15**, for example, Camera, Mail and Calendar, and Maps can all use the device's location, so they can provide location-specific information such as indicating where a picture was taken. You can drag a slider to the left or right to allow or disallow location access.

4. **Click or tap Contacts in the list on the left, then view the apps that can access your Contacts**

   Apps such as Messaging + Skype and Mail and Calendar can access your contacts, unless you turn the settings off. This way, you only have to enter your Contacts once, in the Contacts app, and they appear in the other apps whenever you want. Other Privacy categories with settings you can control are shown in **TABLE 6-1**.

5. **Close the Settings app, click or tap the Start button ⊞, then click or tap the Maps app tile**

6. **Click or tap the Menu expand button ☰, click or tap Settings at the bottom of the menu, then under Privacy, click or tap Open location settings**

   The Privacy category of the Settings app opens from inside the Maps app, with the Location subcategory active.

7. **Close the Settings app, then in the Maps app click or tap the Use location data to improve maps list arrow**

   This menu lets you choose whether maps can use your location data at any time or only when you're using the Maps, to improve the app. If you choose Always, the Maps app will share your location data with Microsoft, even when you're not using the Maps app. See **FIGURE 6-16**.

8. **Click or tap the Map app Close button ✕**

   The app closes.

FIGURE 6-15: Apps that can use your Location settings

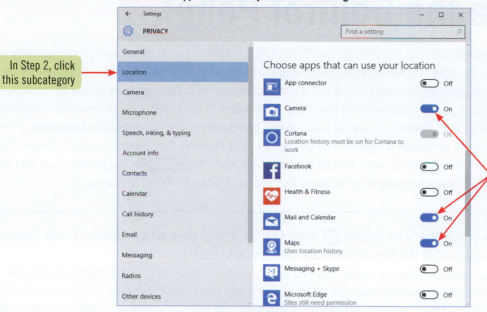

In Step 2, click this subcategory

These apps have permission to use your location (your app list and permissions may differ)

FIGURE 6-16: Specifying when to use location data in Maps app

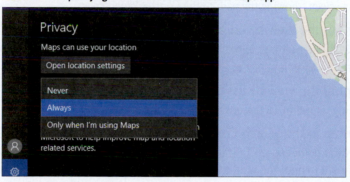

TABLE 6-1: Selected settings in the Privacy category of the Settings app

subcategory	what it does	used by
General	Shares info like the advertising ID number associated with your device or account (not your name), so apps can display advertising content tailored to your interests	Websites, ads within apps
Camera	Determine which apps can use your camera	Messaging + Skype, Facebook, OneNote
Speech, inking, & typing	Collects information about your voice and writing to make better suggestions for you	Cortana
Calendar	Gives apps access to your Calendar	Mail and Calendar apps and the App connector, which gives third-party programs access to your contacts, location, camera, and so forth

More Microsoft privacy controls

To learn more about personalized ads that may appear in Edge as you browse the web, open the Privacy category of the Settings app. In the General subcategory, click or tap Manage my Microsoft advertising and other personalization info. Edge opens, displaying a Microsoft webpage that describes its use of "interest-based advertising." The page also contains a switch that lets you turn off personalized ads in the current browser. You can also use the Privacy Statement link in the Settings app Privacy > General screen to read the Microsoft Privacy Statement, describing the data they collect and how they use it. Links to Frequently Asked Questions and the Microsoft Services Agreement provide more details.

Windows 10

Use the Control Panel

As you learned earlier in this module, the Control Panel contains more advanced or less frequently used settings in Windows 10. Although Microsoft is gradually moving more features from the Control Panel to the Settings app, the Control Panel is still a useful collection of utilities you can access to manage how Windows both appears and works on your PC or mobile device. Control Panel windows may contain small applications called **applets**, as well as icons, dialog boxes, and questions series called **wizards**. If you're not sure where an option is located, you can search for it by using the search box in the Control Panel. See **TABLE 6-2** for a variety of ways you can open the Control Panel. **CASE** ▸ *You want to open the Control Panel and search for the background setting so that you know where to make the change.*

STEPS

1. **Click or tap the Start button ⊞, type Control Panel, then when Control Panel, Desktop app appears at the top of the Start menu, press [Enter]**

    The Control Panel window opens, as shown in **FIGURE 6-17**, showing links to Control Panel categories. The View by list indicates the currently selected view: Large icons, Small icons, or, as shown in the figure, Category. Category view displays utilities in functional categories based on tasks, with some direct links, while Small or Large icons view displays an icon for each utility program. A navigation bar appears at the top of the screen, showing the path to the Control Panel screen.

2. **Click or tap the View by list arrow, then click or tap Small icons**

    A list of computer settings appears by small icons and type, in alphabetical order. This view can make it easier to find a specific applet or setting.

3. **Click or tap the View by list arrow, then click or tap Large icons**

    The settings appear by large icons and type, again in alphabetical order.

4. **Click or tap in the Search Control Panel text box**

    The insertion point appears in the search box, where you can enter text related to a Control Panel option that you want to find. You want to learn more about ease of access in Windows 10.

5. **Type access**

    Control Panel settings that relate to ease of computer access appear in the Control Panel window, as shown in **FIGURE 6-18**.

6. **Click or tap Ease of Access Center, then scroll down to observe the available settings**

    The Ease of Access Center includes links to start assistive tools such as Magnifier, On-Screen Keyboard, Narrator, and High Contrast. Links in the lower part of the screen cover alternative topics.

7. **Click or tap Control Panel Home at the top of the left pane**

    You return to the main window of the Control Panel, in Large icons view.

8. **Click or tap the Control Panel window Close button ⊠**

TROUBLE
If you hear a narrator announcing selected options, deselect the Always read this section aloud check box.

Customizing desktop icons

Icons on the desktop provide easy access to programs, folders, and system-related shortcuts. But if your desktop is getting cluttered, you can quickly show or hide these icons. In addition, you can customize the desktop to show or hide the familiar icons: Computer, User's Files, Network, Recycle Bin, or Control Panel. You can also quickly sort, resize, and rearrange desktop icons by right-clicking or tap-holding the desktop and then using commands on the View and Sort by submenus. To show

or hide desktop icons, right-click or tap-hold a blank area on the desktop, then click or tap Personalize. In the Personalization Settings screen, click or tap Themes in the list, then click or tap Desktop icon settings. Select or clear the check boxes in the Desktop Icon Settings dialog box to show or hide icons. To change the appearance of an icon, select the icon in the dialog box, click or tap Change Icon, select an icon, then click or tap OK. Click or tap OK, then close the Settings window.

FIGURE 6-17: Control Panel

- Navigation bar
- Control Panel categories
- Search Control Panel text box
- View is currently set to Category

FIGURE 6-18: Ease of Access settings

- Ease of Access Center
- Search text

TABLE 6-2: Ways to access Control Panel options

method	steps to access
Start menu	All Apps list > Windows System folder
Utility menu	Right-click or press and hold the Start button to display utility menu, then click or tap Control Panel
Settings windows	Links to specific Control Panel screens
Typing in Cortana Ask me anything box	May display a Control Panel option
Add a shortcut to the desktop	Right-click or press and hold a Control Panel applet, then click or tap Create Shortcut
Pin a shortcut to Quick Access in File Explorer	Right-click or press and hold a Control Panel applet, then click or tap Pin to Quick access
Pin to Start menu	Right-click or press and hold a Control Panel applet, then click or tap Pin to Start

Practice

Concepts Review

FIGURE 6-19

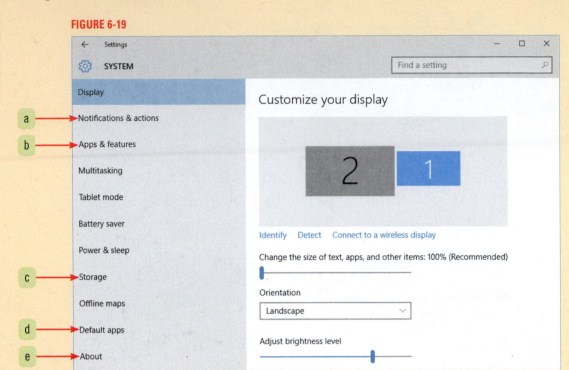

Match the statements below with the elements labeled in the screen shown in FIGURE 6-19.

1. Which element lets you see how much space is available on your hard drive?
2. Which element lets you see all the apps installed on your computer?
3. Which element lets you control which app opens when you double-click or double-tap a file?
4. Which element lets you see the amount of memory your computer has?
5. Which element lets you customize the icons that appear in the top row of the Action Center?

Match each term with the statement that best describes it.

6. Control Panel   a. News presented by Cortana
7. Lock screen app   b. A series of photographs displayed in succession
8. System icons   c. A desktop app to control higher-level or less frequently used Windows settings
9. Theme   d. A type of notification you can receive without having to unlock your system
10. Information card   e. Determines colors, fonts, and sounds
11. Slideshow   f. Images on the taskbar representing a clock, power, and volume

Select the best answers from the following lists of choices.

12. In which of the following location paths can you change the lock screen?
    a. Control Panel > Ease of Access   c. Settings > System
    b. Settings > Personalization   d. Settings > Lock Screen

13. Which of the following lets you create a picture password?

a. Personalization

b. Update & security

c. Time & Language

d. Accounts

14. Which of the following allows you to choose a theme?

a. Personalization

b. Devices

c. Privacy

d. System

15. Which of the following is *not* a method of transmitting notifications?

a. Pop-up message

b. Lock Screen app

c. Quick Action button

d. PIN Code

Skills Review

1. View Windows settings.

a. Open the Settings app, then open the System category.

b. Select the Multitasking subcategory, and read the available options, noting which ones are on.

c. If you are using a laptop or tablet device, go to Battery saver and read its options, then use the Back button to return to the Settings app category screen. If not, proceed to step d.

d. Return to Settings if necessary, open the Ease of Access category, display the High contrast options, and observe the choices available when you select the Choose a theme list arrow.

e. Return to Settings, go to the Devices category, display options for connected devices, then select Devices and printers in the right pane to display the Devices and Printers Control Panel.

f. View the contents of the window, close the Control Panel, then return to the main Settings screen.

2. Personalize the desktop, theme, and lock screen.

a. In the Settings app, display the Personalization category.

b. Note the current background picture, then choose another available picture.

c. Display the Colors subcategory, then specify that Windows should choose an accent color from your background.

d. Return to the Background settings, then return to the original background picture.

e. Go to the Colors category, and if necessary, specify that Windows should not pick an accent color from your background.

f. Go to the Themes subcategory, display the theme settings, then choose a different theme.

g. Observe the effects of your chosen theme, then return to the Windows theme.

h. Close the Control Panel, then in the Settings app return to the main app screen.

3. Change user account settings.

a. In the Settings app, go to the Accounts category, then scroll down the Your email and accounts options.

b. Display the Sign-in options subcategory, then go to the Picture password settings, entering your account password.

c. Add a picture password, using the file **Beacon.jpg**, located where you store your Data Files. Use gestures that follow the lines around the green area surrounding the lighthouse image, as shown in **FIGURE 6-20**.

d. Display the lock screen by pressing [⊞][L], press [Spacebar], then enter your picture password.

e. Return to the Sign-in options subcategory, then remove the picture password.

4. Change notification settings.

a. Go to the Settings main app window, go to the System settings, then display the Notifications & actions subcategory.

b. Scroll to the Show notifications from these apps section, then hide or display notifications from any app. If no apps have provided notifications yet, hide or display an option under Notifications instead. Reverse the change.

c. Display one of the Quick actions icon menus, then close it without changing the selection.

d. Display the screen that determines which icons appear on the taskbar, then display an icon that was previously hidden.

e. On the taskbar, verify that the icon appears.

f. Turn off the display for the icon, then verify that it no longer appears on the taskbar. Close the Settings app.

FIGURE 6-20

5. Change Cortana and search settings.

   a. Open the Cortana Notebook, then scroll to view the available options.

   b. Under Settings in the Notebook menu, locate the control to clear the device search history, then clear it.

   c. Return to the Notebook menu, add a Scholar field of study, then verify that it appears on the menu.

   d. Return to the Notebook menu, open the Notebook settings for Movies & TV, then close the Cortana Notebook.

6. Change general settings.

   a. Open the Settings apps, and use a subcategory in the System category to display your system's characteristics.

   b. Display a listing of the applications installed on your device, then sort them by size.

   c. Display the storage characteristics of your device.

   d. Return to the Settings main screen, then display the Time and language settings.

   e. Change the time zone to the Hawaii time zone (UTC-10:00) (turn off the Set time zone automatically setting if necessary), then observe the time displayed on the taskbar.

   f. Reset your device's time to the correct zone or, if desired, have it set your time zone automatically.

7. Change share and privacy settings.

   a. Go to the Privacy Settings, then open the Location subcategory.

   b. Turn the Location option off, observe that no apps can use your location, then turn the option on again.

   c. In the list of apps that can use your location, turn off two, then turn them on again.

   d. View the Email subcategory, then view the app(s) that can access your email.

   e. Open the Weather app, view its Settings, then click or tap the link to view its Privacy statement.

   f. Scroll through the statement, close the Weather app, then close the Settings app.

8. Use the Control Panel.

   a. Open the Control Panel, view the contents by large icons, then by small icons.

   b. Use the Control Panel search box to locate information on fonts. In the search results, go to the link that lets you make text and other items larger and smaller.

   c. Use the Control Panel address bar to return to the Control Panel main window in large or small icon view.

   d. Go to the Control Panel's Programs and Features area, then scroll the list of installed programs on your device.

   e. Use the Control Panel options to locate Personalization settings, then close the Control Panel.

Independent Challenge 1

You have taken a job at a startup company that specializes in teaching technology to people who want to improve their job skills. You want to personalize your taskbar and have Cortana help you stay up to date on technology news.

a. Open the Settings app, go to the System category, and then to the Notifications & actions subcategory.

b. Locate the "Select which icons appear on the taskbar" link, then add three additional icons that you would like to appear on the taskbar.

c. Display the taskbar if necessary, and verify that the three newly selected icons appear.

d. Return to the Settings app, turn off the display of the three icons you just selected, then close the Settings app.

e. Open the Cortana Notebook, and display the News category. Scroll down to display the "News categories you're tracking" section, select Add a category, then select Technology headlines and select Add.

f. Scroll down the News category, and verify that Technology headlines has been added, then save your changes.

g. Go to Cortana Home, scroll down, and verify that Science Technology News appears, then close the menu.

Independent Challenge 2

You work as a consultant for Emerson Enterprises, which provides business consulting services for small businesses. The company has assigned you a laptop and has asked you to document the machine for insurance purposes.

a. Open the Settings app, then display the System category.

b. Display the Storage subcategory, then if possible use the [PrintScreen] key to take a screenshot of your Settings window. (If you cannot use the [PrintScreen] key, write down the information.)

c. If you took a screenshot in Step b, open WordPad and paste the copied screen. Save the document in the location where you store your Data Files as **6-My Computer.rtf**.

d. Use Settings to determine how much RAM your device has.

e. Display your apps and sort them by size. Write the name and size of the four largest apps.

f. Using the Location Privacy settings, determine then list apps that have access to your location.

g. Add your name to the document, then submit it to your instructor. Close the document and the Settings app.

Independent Challenge 3

You work at Elfy Software, a developer of software that teaches American sign language. You are preparing for a demonstration of the company's software to a group of teachers from a local community college, and you want to make sure that your computer settings are appropriate for the demonstration.

a. Open the Control Panel, then view the options by category.

b. In the Search Control Panel text box, enter **File Explorer**, then select File Explorer Options.

c. Select the View tab, then in the Advanced settings list, under Files and Folders, verify that the "Hide extensions for known file types" check box is not checked (remove the checkmark if necessary), so file extensions appear in the title bar and in dialog boxes.

d. On the General tab, in the Privacy category, verify that "Show recently used files in Quick access" and "Show frequently used folders in Quick access" are selected, then click OK and close the Control Panel.

e. Open Cortana, go to the Notebook > Settings category, then click or tap the Web search history settings link.

f. In Microsoft Edge, use the More button on the Edge address bar to locate Edge settings.

g. Clear whatever browser data you wish, then close Edge.

h. Create a picture password, using a picture that would be appropriate to the topic and audience. If you can use the [PrintScreen] key, open the picture you are using, take a screenshot of it, paste it into a Word document, add your name in the line below the screenshot, save the document as **6-Elfy Sign-in.rtf** where you store your Data Files, close the document, then submit it to your instructor. Delete the picture password.

Independent Challenge 4: Explore

You are a freelance photographer. You want to create a slideshow background for your desktop that displays your best work. *Note:* To complete this independent challenge, you'll need to locate a group of pictures and place them in a new folder within the Pictures folder.

a. Open File Explorer, then navigate to the This PC > Pictures folder.

b. Create a new folder in the Pictures folder called **Best Work**. Copy at least five of your best photos into it.

c. In Personalization settings, display the Background subcategory, then create a slideshow background.

d. Browse to and select the Best Work folder you created in Step b, then choose the folder.

e. Specify that the picture should change every minute, whether you want to shuffle the photos, how to fit the pictures to the screen, and whether or not to allow the slideshow while your device is on battery power.

f. In the Themes area in the Control Panel, save the unsaved theme as **Picture Theme**.

g. Minimize all windows, and observe your desktop for a few minutes, noting the pictures as they change.

h. Experiment with different Fit options, and observe the effect of each choice.

i. In the Control Panel, return to the Windows theme, delete your Picture Theme by right-clicking or pressing and holding it and selecting Delete theme, then close the Control Panel and the Settings app.

Visual Workshop

Re-create the screen shown in **FIGURE 6-21**. Notice that the Your Name icon has been customized. If you can use the [PrintScreen] key, capture an image of your desktop, paste it into a WordPad document, add your name, save the document in the location where you store your Data Files as **My Desktop.rtf**, then submit it to your instructor.

FIGURE 6-21

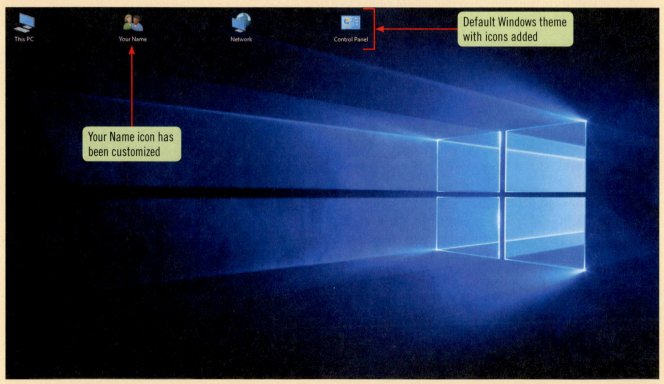

Managing Windows Security

CASE ▶ Windows 10 makes communicating with other devices over the Internet more secure and easier than ever. You want to view and customize your settings to make Windows 10 secure from online hackers or malicious software. **Important: To perform some of the lessons in this module, you need to use the administrator password or use an administrator account. See your instructor or technical support person for more information.** *Note: With the release of Windows 10, Microsoft now provides ongoing updates to Windows instead of releasing new versions periodically. This means that Windows features might change over time, including how they look and how you interact with them. The information provided in this text was accurate at the time this book was published.*

Module Objectives

After completing this module, you will be able to

- Use Security and Maintenance
- Manage Windows Firewall
- Manage automatic updates
- Defend against malicious software

- Protect your Internet privacy
- Delete Internet information
- Set Family Safety controls

Files You Will Need

No files needed.

Use Security and Maintenance

Learning
Outcomes
• Access Security
  and Maintenance
• View Security and
  Maintenance
  settings
• View User Account
  Control settings

Security and Maintenance lets you manage system security by providing a single place to view alerts and take action on security and maintenance issues with your system. Security and Maintenance makes it easy to find information about the latest virus or security threat, check the status of essential security settings, quickly get support from Microsoft for a security-related issue, and access the Control Panel utilities that allow you to set additional security and privacy settings. Security and Maintenance displays important and recommended alerts to help protect your system and keep Windows running smoothly. As you work, Windows 10 displays security alerts and icons in the Action Center and in the notification area on the taskbar to make you aware of potential security risks, such as a new virus, out-of-date antivirus software, if an important security option is turned off, or other security-related issues from Microsoft. To open Security and Maintenance, you can click or tap on an alert, access it from the Control Panel, or click or tap a notification icon in the Action Center. In Security and Maintenance, you can also find links to troubleshooters and system restore tools. **CASE** *You want to make sure company computers are properly protected from outside threats, so you examine the current security settings on your computer.*

STEPS

1. **Click or tap the Start button ⊞, type Control Panel, click or tap Control Panel - Desktop app, then click or tap the View by list arrow and verify that the Control Panel items are shown as Small icons**

   The Control Panel opens and shows items listed in alphabetical order by small icons.

2. **Click or tap Security and Maintenance**

   The Security and Maintenace window opens, displaying current security and maintenance information, as shown in **FIGURE 7-1**. The window has sections for Security and for Maintenance, each with its own Expand button that lets you show more detail. If there are no security or maintenance issues, both the Security and Maintenance sections are closed. In this case, there is only one recommended issue, flagged with a yellow bar: a request to verify the user's saved identity credentials on the current PC.

3. **Click or tap the Expand button ⊙ for the Security area, then scroll down to view all the available settings**

   The Security area shows any pending notifications, as well as the notification status of important areas, including your network firewall, Windows Defender virus and spyware protection, and your Microsoft Account. To change these notification settings, you need to open a related window.

4. **In the list on the left, click or tap Change Security and Maintenance settings**

   The Change Security and Maintenance settings dialog box opens, where you can turn security and maintenance message options on or off.

5. **Click or tap Cancel to close the dialog box without making changes**

6. **In the list on the left, click or tap Change User Account Control settings**

   The User Account Control Settings dialog box opens, displaying a notification slider you can drag to help prevent potentially harmful programs from making changes to your system. See **FIGURE 7-2**.

7. **Click or tap Cancel to close the dialog box without making changes**

8. **Click or tap All Control Panel Items in the Address bar**

   The Control Panel items reappear.

Using Security and Maintenance with third-party protection programs

Although Windows protects your device with Windows Firewall and Windows Defender, it can work with third-party protection programs as well, such as Norton Security. If your system has more than one firewall, antivirus, or antispyware program, you will see a link in Security and Maintenance that you can click or tap to show a list of those programs and turn any of them on or off.

FIGURE 7-1: Security and Maintenance categories

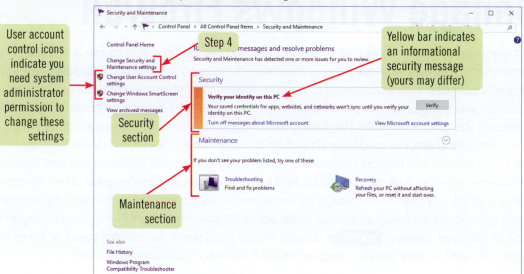

User account control icons indicate you need system administrator permission to change these settings

Step 4

Yellow bar indicates an informational security message (yours may differ)

Security section

Maintenance section

FIGURE 7-2: Changing notification frequency with User Account Control

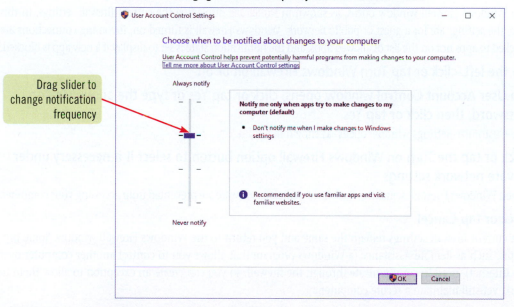

Drag slider to change notification frequency

Protecting against malware

A **computer virus** is a program that attaches itself to a file, reproduces itself, and then spreads to other files. A virus is typically "caught" from programs and files downloaded from the Internet, electronic mail attachments, or shareware disks containing free or inexpensive software or illegally obtained pirated software. When you open an app or file with the computer virus, the computer becomes infected with the virus and can corrupt or destroy data or disrupt program or Windows functionality. A **worm** is like a virus, but it can spread without human action across networks. For example, a worm might send email copies of itself to everyone in your email address book. A worm can consume memory, causing your computer to stop responding or even take it over. A **Trojan** horse, like its mythological counterpart, is an app that appears to be useful and comes from a legitimate source but actually causes problems, such as gathering personal information or deleting files. **Antivirus software**, or virus detection software, examines the files stored on a disk to determine whether they are infected with a virus, then destroys or disinfects them. Antivirus software provides protection when you start Windows and checks for viruses whenever your computer is on. Windows 10 includes **Windows Defender**, free software that protects your computer against viruses and spyware. You can also purchase commercial antivirus software, such as Norton Security and McAfee AntiVirus Plus. New viruses appear all the time, so it is important to keep your antivirus software up to date.

Manage Windows Firewall

Learning Outcomes
• View firewall status
• View firewall settings

If your computer is directly connected to the Internet, you need a firewall program. A **firewall** is a protective barrier between your computer or network and others on the Internet. **Windows Firewall** protects your computer from unauthorized access from others on the Internet by monitoring communication between your computer and the Internet and preventing unsolicited inbound traffic from the Internet from entering your private computer. Windows Firewall blocks all unsolicited communications from reaching your computer unless you specifically allow them to come through. Windows Firewall is enabled by default for all Internet and network connections. However, some computer manufacturers and network administrators might turn it off, so you need to check before you start using the computer. When Windows Firewall is enabled, you might not be able to use some communication features, such as sending files with a messaging program or playing an Internet game, unless the program is listed in the Allowed Programs window in Windows Firewall. **CASE** ▶ *Because firewall protection is an essential aspect of computer protection, you want to make sure your Windows Firewall is running so your information is safe.*

STEPS

▶ 1. **In the All Control Panel Items window, click or tap Windows Firewall**

The Windows Firewall window opens, as shown in **FIGURE 7-3**, displaying the current firewall settings. In this case, the settings are for a guest or public network: Windows Firewall is turned on, incoming connections are blocked to apps not on the list of allowed apps, and the notification state is set to display if a new app is blocked.

2. **On the left, click or tap Turn Windows Firewall on or off**

3. **If a User Account Control window opens, click or tap Yes or type the administrator password, then click or tap Yes**

The Customize Settings window opens, as shown in **FIGURE 7-4**.

▶ 4. **Click or tap the Turn on Windows Firewall option button to select it if necessary under Private network settings**

When Windows Firewall is enabled, hackers or malicious software are prevented from accessing your computer.

5. **Click or tap Cancel**

The current firewall settings remain the same and you return to the Windows Firewall window. Some programs, such as Remote Assistance (a Windows program that allows you to control another computer over the Internet), need to communicate through the firewall, so you can create an exception to allow them to work, yet still maintain a secure computer.

▶ 6. **On the left, click or tap Allow an app or feature through Windows Firewall**

The Allowed apps window opens, displaying the current programs or connection ports allowed to communicate through the firewall. Connection ports link devices such as printers to your computer so you can use them.

7. **Scroll down the list, then click or tap the Windows Media Player Network Sharing Service (Internet) check box in the Private column to select it**

Selecting this option enables the Windows Media Player program to freely communicate over the Internet for network-sharing purposes through the firewall.

▶ 8. **Click or tap to deselect the Windows Media Player Network Sharing Service (Internet), then click or tap OK**

The Windows Firewall window reopens.

9. **Click or tap the Control Panel window Close button ☒**

Managing Windows Security

FIGURE 7-3: Windows Firewall window

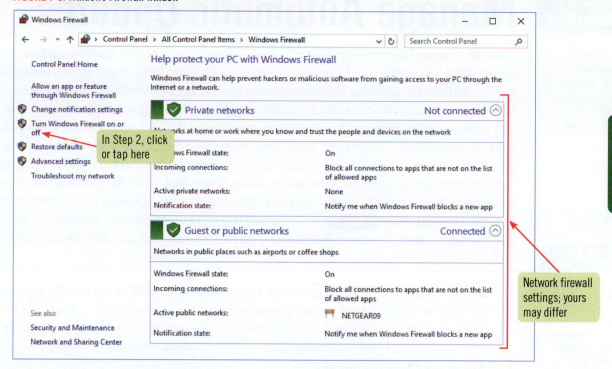

FIGURE 7-4: Customize Settings window

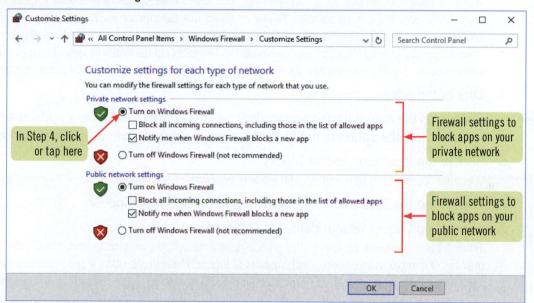

Blocking unsafe websites and programs with Windows SmartScreen

Windows 10 blocks malicious websites and downloads with **Windows SmartScreen Filter**. Windows SmartScreen is especially useful against **phishing**, when a realistic-looking but fake email, pop-up, or website asks you to confirm your password or other personal information and then uses that information to defraud you. When SmartScreen is enabled, visiting an unsafe website displays a message that lets you close the tab or display more information. To turn on the SmartScreen Filter in Microsoft Edge, click or tap the More button on the toolbar, click or tap Settings, then click or tap View advanced settings. Scroll down, then turn on the Help protect me from malicious sites and downloads with SmartScreen Filter option. To protect against unsafe apps and file downloads, open the Control Panel Security and Maintenance window, then click or tap Change Windows SmartScreen settings on the left side of the screen. Here you can choose whether to require system administrator approval before running an unrecognized app from the Internet, to simply present a warning, or to turn off SmartScreen; when you're finished, click or tap OK.

Managing Windows Security

Manage Automatic Updates

Microsoft continues to improve Windows 10 with new features or security fixes, known as **updates**. Windows Update allows you to keep your PC up to date with the latest system software and security updates over the Internet. **Automatic updating** provides protection to make sure your Windows software is up to date and safe. Windows Update provides a central location where you can view currently installed updates, and install new updates and device drivers. **Device drivers** are programs that control devices attached to your computer, such as printers, monitors, and video cards. Windows Update confidentially and continuously scans your PC for updates that need to be installed. Windows Update can review device drivers and system software on your computer, compare those findings with a master database on the web, and then recommend and install updates specifically for your computer. You can also restore a previous device driver or system file using the uninstall option. **CASE** *You're not sure how long it's been since your computer has been updated with the latest Windows 10 software. You want to check your computer for updates and current settings.*

STEPS

1. **Click or tap the Start button ⊞, click or tap Settings, then click or tap Update & security**

   The Update & Security category of the Settings app opens, as shown in **FIGURE 7-5**, displaying the current status for Windows Update. The dialog box shows that for the current device, Windows is up to date and the date and time it was last checked. Updates are set to download and install automatically.

2. **Click or tap Check for updates**

   Windows displays a Checking for updates message, then, after a moment, lists any necessary updates that have been downloaded but not yet installed. **FIGURE 7-6** shows that the current machine needs a virus definition update. Your results will differ. The virus definition update is automatically installed, and the Check for updates screen reappears. Although updates are downloaded and installed automatically by default, you can reschedule when Windows restarts your machine for major updates, which take longer and usually require a system restart.

3. **Click or tap Advanced options**

4. **Click or tap the Automatic (recommended) list arrow under Choose how updates are installed, note the option to notify you to schedule a restart, then press [Esc] to close the list**

5. **Click or tap View your update history**

   Windows displays a list of recent updates made to your system. See **FIGURE 7-7**.

6. **Click or tap the Back button ← at the top of the Settings window**

7. **Click or tap Choose how updates are delivered**

   When Microsoft releases updates to the general public, the updates are sent to, and downloaded by, many millions of computers worldwide. Such updates of identical information take a great deal of time and can slow transmission rates. To speed the update process, Microsoft lets your computer send updates to other computers, either on your local network or to other PCs on the Internet. If you change this setting to On, you can then select whether to use only PCs on your local network or your own network plus PCs on the Internet.

8. **Click or tap the Back button ← three times to return to the Settings window**

Updating device drivers

Although Windows Update automatically checks for updates to both Windows and device drivers, it may not detect some drivers, so you may need to install them separately. To do so, open the Control Panel in Small icons or Large icons view, then click or tap Device Manager. Click or tap the Expand arrow ▸ next to the device you want to update, right-click or press and hold the driver or device name, then click or tap Update Driver Software. Specify whether you want to search automatically for updated driver software or browse your computer for previously downloaded drivers to have Windows install them. Windows will locate and install the updated driver or inform you if the most up-to-date driver is already installed.

FIGURE 7-5: Windows Update window

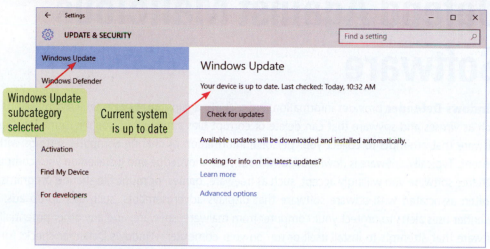

Windows Update subcategory selected

Current system is up to date

FIGURE 7-6: Checking for available updates

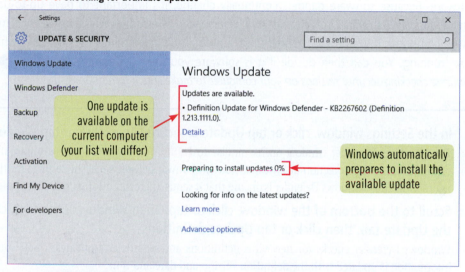

One update is available on the current computer (your list will differ)

Windows automatically prepares to install the available update

FIGURE 7-7: Viewing Update history

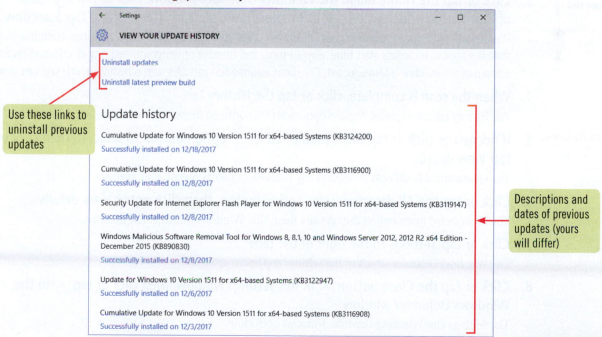

Use these links to uninstall previous updates

Descriptions and dates of previous updates (yours will differ)

Defend Against Malicious Software

Learning Outcomes
• Obtain definition updates
• Scan for system problems
• View Windows Defender settings

Windows Defender provides information and security against **malware**, which is malicious software, such as viruses and spyware that can delete or corrupt files and steal personal information. **Spyware** is software that attempts to collect your personal information or change computer settings without your consent. Typically, spyware is downloaded without your knowledge and installed on your computer along with free software you willingly accept, such as freeware, games, or music file-sharing programs. Spyware is often associated with adware software that displays advertisements, such as pop-up ads. Windows Defender uses alerts to protect your computer from malware, spyware, and any other potentially harmful software that attempts to install itself or run on your computer. Windows Defender checks for potential problems by using definitions. A **definition** provides instructions on how to defend against malware software. Because software dangers continually change, it's important to have up-to-date definitions, which you can get online. You can perform a quick scan of essential Windows files or a full scan of your entire computer. If Windows Defender finds a problem, it quarantines the software, which prevents it from running. You can then decide if it is software you indeed want to run. **CASE** *You want to continue checking security settings on your computer to make sure information is safe.*

STEPS

1. **In the Settings window, click or tap Update & security, then click or tap Windows Defender**

   The Windows Defender window opens, similar to **FIGURE 7-8**, displaying status information about your computer's current protection against malicious and unwanted software. The settings for the device in the figure show that Windows Defender is on and that it sends Microsoft information about potential problems.

2. **Scroll to the bottom of the window, click or tap Open Windows Defender, click or tap the Update tab, then click or tap Update definitions**

   Windows Defender checks for new virus definitions and installs any updates. Upon completion, status information is updated with the definition version and date and time.

3. **Click or tap the Home tab in the Windows Defender window, click or tap the Quick option button under Scan options to select it if necessary, then click or tap Scan now**

   Windows Defender scans the essential files on your computer, as shown in **FIGURE 7-9**. Upon completion, scan statistics appear, including start time, elapsed time, and number of items scanned. Status information at the bottom of the window is also updated. The status information includes scan schedule, which you can modify.

4. **When the scan is complete, click or tap the History tab**

   The History tab information displays options for Quarantined items, Allowed items, and All detected items.

5. **If necessary, click or tap the Quarantined items option button to select it, then click or tap View details**

   The Quarantined items option displays any items identified as potential problems.

6. **Click or tap the All detected items option button, then click or tap View details**

   The All detected items option displays any items that Windows Defender has detected.

7. **Click or tap Settings to the right of the tabs**

   The Windows Defender screen in the Settings app opens again.

8. **Click or tap the Close button ☒ in the Settings window, then click or tap ☒ in the Windows Defender window**

   The Settings and Windows Defender windows both close.

FIGURE 7-8: Windows Defender in the Settings app

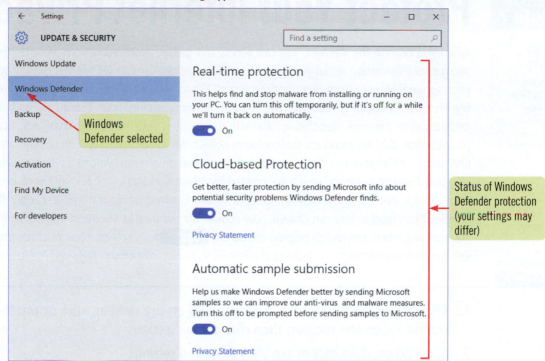

FIGURE 7-9: Scanning for malware using Windows Defender

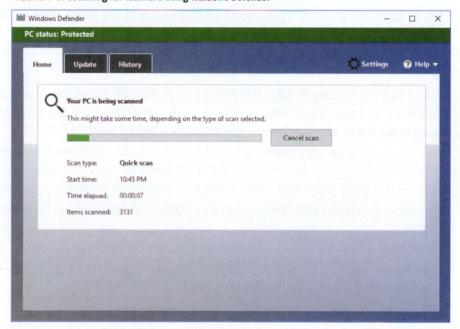

Monitoring and managing programs using Windows Defender

You can use Windows Defender to monitor all the programs on your system or just specific ones. To set monitoring options in the Windows Defender window, click or tap the History tab. To remove or restore quarantined programs, click or tap the Quarantined items option, click or tap View details, select an app, then click or tap Remove or Restore. To remove an app from the allowed (not monitored) list, click or tap the Allowed items option button, click or tap View details, select a program, then click or tap Remove.

Windows 10

Protect Your Internet Privacy

**Learning
Outcomes**
• View privacy
settings in Edge
• View privacy
settings in Internet
Explorer

When you browse the Internet, you can access and gather information from websites, but websites can also gather information about you without your knowledge. You can set Internet privacy options to protect your personal identity from unauthorized access. When you visit a website, the site creates a **cookie** file, known as a **first-party cookie**, which stores information on your computer, such as your website preferences or personal identifiable information, including your name and email address. The next time you visit that site, it can access the cookie to collect this information. Not all cookies are harmful; many first-party cookies save you time reentering information on a return visit to a website. However, there are also **third-party cookies**, which are created by advertisers and can track your web browsing, even for sites you are not currently viewing. Once a cookie is saved on your computer, only the website that created it can read it. You can change how cookies are handled in Microsoft Edge or in Internet Explorer. You can also block unwanted pop-up messages. **CASE** ▶ *As you continue to check the current security settings on your computer, you want to check privacy settings in Microsoft Edge and in Internet Explorer.*

STEPS

1. **Click or tap the Microsoft Edge button 🅴 on the taskbar, click or tap the More button ⋯ on the toolbar, then click or tap Settings**

2. **Scroll down, then click or tap View advanced settings**

3. **Scroll down to the Cookies section, then click or tap the Cookies list arrow**

   Options for handling cookies are listed, as shown in **FIGURE 7-10**. You can choose to block all cookies, only third-party cookies, or no cookies. You can also block unwanted pop-up ads that may place spyware on your device.

QUICK TIP
If you have a
third-party pop-up
blocker, you can turn
off the Block
pop-ups option in
the Advanced
settings pane.

4. **Click or tap the list arrow again, scroll up to the top of the pane, then verify that Block pop-ups is set to On**

   When pop-up blocking is on, Edge will display a message whenever it blocks a pop-up window. In the message you can choose to allow the pop-up once or always.

5. **Click or tap the Microsoft Edge window Close button ✕, open the Control Panel in Small icons or Large icons view, click or tap Internet Options, in the Internet Properties dialog box click or tap the Privacy tab, then click or tap Sites**

   In case you decide to use the Internet Explorer 11 browser, you can change how cookies are handled in the Control Panel. The Per Site Privacy Actions dialog box shown in **FIGURE 7-11** opens. These Control Panel options let you specify any website whose cookies you want to allow or block.

6. **Type www.questspecialtytravel.com in the Address of website text box, then click or tap Allow**

   The website address moves to the Managed websites list, with the current setting, Always Allow.

7. **Click or tap questspecialtytravel.com in the Managed websites list, click or tap Remove, then click or tap OK**

8. **Click or tap Advanced**

   The Advanced Privacy Settings dialog box opens, where you can accept or block first-party or third-party cookies. See **FIGURE 7-12**. You can also choose Prompt, which will show an onscreen prompt asking whether to accept or block cookies of each type. You can also allow **session cookies**, which are temporary cookies that let websites "remember" your choices from one page of a website to another. Session cookies are erased when you leave a website.

9. **Click or tap OK to maintain the current settings, click or tap Cancel, then close the Control Panel window**

FIGURE 7-10: Cookies options in Microsoft Edge

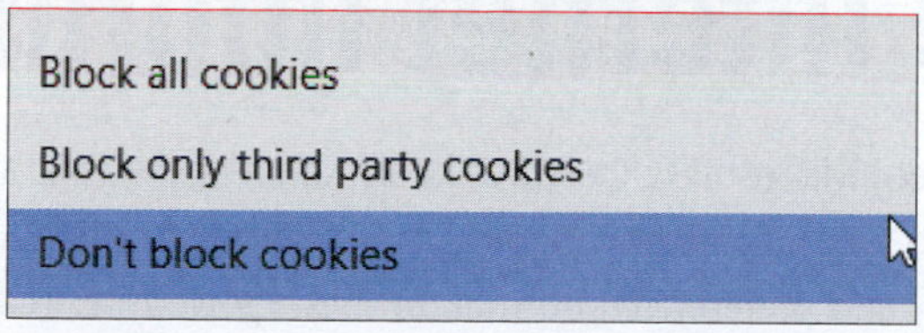

Block all cookies
Block only third party cookies
Don't block cookies

FIGURE 7-11: Managing cookies in Internet Explorer

Per Site Privacy Actions
Manage Sites
You can specify which websites are always or never allowed to use cookies, regardless of their privacy policy.
Type the exact address of the website you want to manage, and then click Allow or Block.
To remove a site from the list of managed sites, select the name of the website and click the Remove button.
Address of website:
Block
Allow
Managed websites:
Domain
Setting
Remove
Remove all
Type address of website here
Managed websites list
Buttons become active after a website is added to the Managed websites list

FIGURE 7-12: Specifying cookie types in Internet Explorer

Advanced Privacy Settings
You can choose how cookies are handled.
Cookies
First-party Cookies
Accept
Block
Prompt
Third-party Cookies
Accept
Block
Prompt
Always allow session cookies
OK
Cancel
First-party Cookies settings
Third-party Cookies settings
Select to allow session cookies

Using InPrivate browsing

If you're using a computer at a friend's house, another office, a hotel, or an Internet café and you don't want to leave any trace or evidence of your web activity, you can use InPrivate browsing. **InPrivate browsing** doesn't retain or keep track of browsing history, searches, temporary Internet files, autofill entries, form data, cookies, or usernames and passwords. You can start an InPrivate browsing session using Microsoft Edge. Click or tap the More button on the toolbar, then click or tap New InPrivate window. A Browsing InPrivate window opens. An InPrivate indicator appears on the leftmost tab when the feature is turned on. To stop InPrivate browsing, close the browser window to end the InPrivate browsing session.

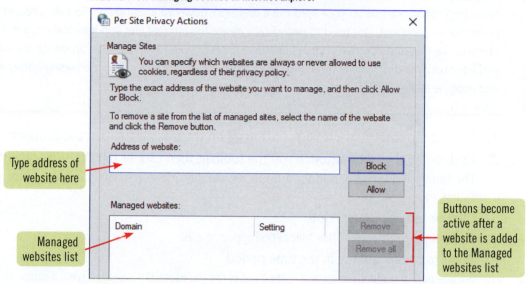

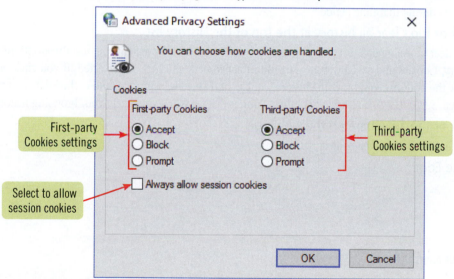

Delete Internet Information

Learning Outcomes
• Delete unwanted Internet files
• Set browsing history settings

As you browse the web, Microsoft Edge stores information about your activities, including the information you have provided to websites when you log on (passwords) or fill out a form, the location of sites you have visited (history), and preference information used by websites (cookies). Edge also saves webpages, images, and media (temporary Internet files) for faster viewing in the future. If you frequently browse the web, Edge can gather and store a large amount of Internet-related data (including normal and InPrivate browsing), which can fill up your hard drive and slow down your computer. To help prevent computer performance problems, you need to periodically delete the Internet files and information; yet you can still preserve the files and information for your trusted sites in your Favorites. You can delete the Internet files and information individually or all at once. **CASE** *You decide to delete your browsing history information and examine related settings.*

STEPS

1. **Click or tap the Microsoft Edge button** 🅔 **on the taskbar to open the browser**

2. **Click or tap the Hub button** ☰ **on the toolbar, then click or tap the History button** 🕘
   The History listing opens, showing a list of the websites you've browsed, grouped by time period. See **FIGURE 7-13**.

3. **Click or tap any time period**
   The sites you visited during that time period appear in a list.

4. **Point to or tap any site in the time period**
   A Close button for that site appears to the right of the site name. On a touch screen, a submenu opens. You can click or tap a Close button for an individual site to erase the history of that site visit or, on a touch screen, tap Delete. You can also click or tap the Close button next to any time period to erase the history of all visits during that time period.

5. **Click or tap Clear all history at the top of the History list**
   The Clear browsing data list appears, as shown in **FIGURE 7-14**. By default, the top three options (Browsing history, Cookies and saved website data, and Cached data and files) are selected. If you click or tap Clear below the options, your browsing history, cookies and saved website data, and cached data and files will be deleted. See **TABLE 7-1** to learn what information is deleted when you delete your browsing history.

6. **Click or tap anywhere on the webpage**
   The Clear browsing data pane closes.

7. **Close Edge**

TABLE 7-1: Effects of clearing browsing history

category	what it deletes
Browsing history	List of visited sites
Cookies and saved website data	Information that websites store on your device to remember your preferences (e.g. usernames and location)
Cached data and files	Copies of webpages stored on your device for faster loading in the future
Download history	The list of files (not the files themselves) you've downloaded from the web
Form data	Personal information you've entered into forms, such as your billing address
Passwords	Site passwords you have saved

FIGURE 7-13: History list in Microsoft Edge

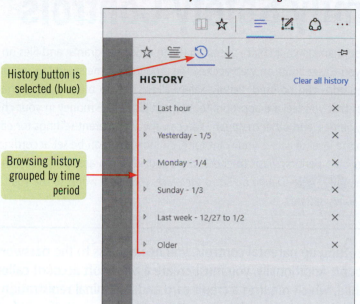

History button is selected (blue)

Browsing history grouped by time period

FIGURE 7-14: Clearing Browsing data

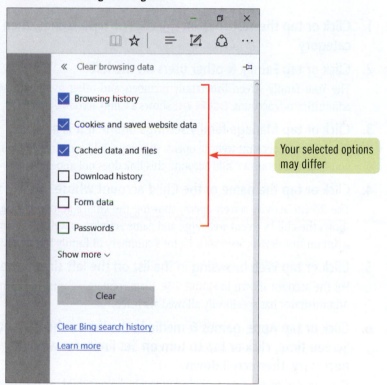

Your selected options may differ

Clearing browsing history in Internet Explorer

Internet Explorer is the browser that preceded Microsoft Edge and was included in earlier versions of Windows. It is still included with Windows 10. If you choose to use Internet Explorer, you can clear your browsing history by opening the Internet Options windows in the Control Panel. The Internet Properties dialog box opens, with the General tab in front. The Browsing history section lets you choose what to delete. Under

Browsing History, click or tap Delete, specify which elements of your browsing history you want to delete, such as temporary files, cookies, history, saved passwords, and web form information, then click or tap Delete. A progress box appears as the files are being deleted, then the Delete Browsing history dialog box closes and the Internet Properties dialog box reopens with the General tab displayed.

Set Family Safety Controls

Family Safety helps you manage your child's access to the Internet, programs, and files on your computer. Family Safety allows you to set limits on web access, the amount of time spent logged on the computer, and which games and apps can be used. Family Safety allows you to block inappropriate websites and allow specific websites that you feel are appropriate. You can also place money in your child's account for the purchase of apps, games, and other materials. You can specify different settings for each user account on your computer, so the level of access you want for each individual can be set accordingly. You can also review activity reports on a periodic basis to check what your children are specifically doing during their time on the computer. **CASE** ▶ *During a visit to the office, your child wants to use your computer, so you want to set up Family Safety settings.*

STEPS

Important: Before setting up parental controls, you need access to the password-protected Administrator account. Additionally, you must create a Microsoft account called a Child account for each child, which requires a credit card and a nominal registration fee. See the yellow box on the next page to learn how to set up a Child account. If you do not have a Child account set up, you can simply read the steps after Step 3 in this lesson.

1. **Click or tap the Start button ⊞, click or tap Settings, then click or tap the Accounts category**

2. **Click or tap Family & other users on the left**

   The Your family screen lists family members and other users with Microsoft accounts connected to the administrator's account. **FIGURE 7-15** shows a Child account.

3. **Click or tap Manage family settings online if it is available**

   The Microsoft account website opens, showing Child accounts and adult accounts that you have set up. (If you have not set up a Child account, this link does not appear.)

4. **Click or tap the name of the Child account whose settings you want to change**

   The Recent activity screen opens, showing the child's account name, picture, and email address. It also shows the child's recent web, app, and game activity, as well as the amount of time the child has recently spent on this device. See **TABLE 7-2** for a summary of Family Safety settings categories.

5. **Click or tap Web browsing in the list on the left side of the screen, then scroll down**

   For the account shown in **FIGURE 7-16**, inappropriate websites are currently blocked, and websites that the Administrator has specifically allowed are listed.

6. **Click or tap Apps, games & media in the list on the left, review the settings; click or tap Screen time, click or tap to turn on Set limits for when my child can use devices if necessary, then scroll down**

   Here you can set the time periods during which your child can use the device. On the right, you can also set the total time your child can use the device each day. Toward the end of the child's allowable time, he or she receives a warning of time remaining. After he or she reaches the limit, their files and programs stay open, and he or she can continue using them during a later permitted time slot.

7. **Click or tap Purchase & spending in the list on the left**

   Here you can add money to an account that the child can use to purchase apps and games.

8. **Click or tap Find your child in the list on the left**

   On this screen, you can track the location of your child's Windows 10 mobile device.

9. **Close the webpage and the Settings app**

FIGURE 7-15: Family and other user accounts

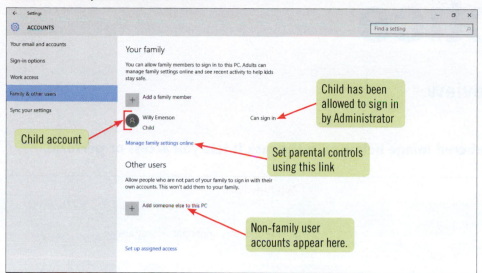

FIGURE 7-16: Web browsing settings with permitted sites

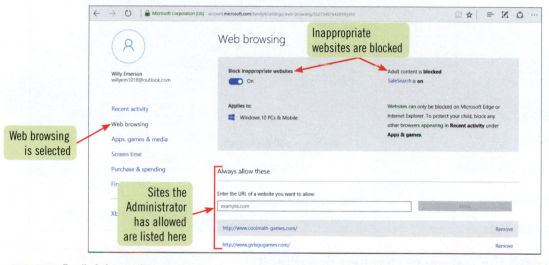

TABLE 7-2: Family Safety settings

settings	what it does
Recent activity	Summarizes web searches, completed and blocked site visits, apps used, and screen time
Web browsing	Shows website-blocking settings and lists sites you have blocked or allowed
Apps, games & media	Shows app and game-blocking settings, selected age limit, and specific apps and games you have blocked
Screen time	Shows hours during which child can use the selected device and time limit per day
Purchase and spending	Shows dollar amount remaining in child's account and their purchase history
Find your child	Shows the location of your child's Windows 10 mobile device (required to use this feature)

Creating a Child account

Like all Microsoft accounts, a Child account is stored online so that your child can log in to any Windows 10 computer and so that you can change account settings from any location. To set up a Child account, go to Settings > Accounts > Family & other users, and click or tap Add a family member. Select Add a child, then enter his or her email address or create one. Then select communications preferences. Enter contact information, your child's age, as well as a credit card number, which covers a one-time nominal charge. After you create the account, your child's account name will appear on the computer's login screen. To use the computer, your child selects the account and enters a password. For young children, a picture password (see Module 6) might make it easier for them to access the account.

Practice

Concepts Review

Match each numbered image below with the task it lets you access or perform.

Element	App function
1.	a. Hide or display important security alerts
2. Update & security	b. Prevent unsolicited inbound Internet traffic from reaching your device
3. Accounts	c. Clear Internet history from Edge
4. Windows Firewall	d. Change Family Safety Controls
5. Security and Maintenance	e. View items Windows Defender has quarantined

Match each term with the statement that best describes it.

6. Spyware	**a.** A program that tries to collect information about you
7. Virus	**b.** A security system that creates a protective barrier between your computer and others on the Internet
8. Worm	**c.** A program you open that infects your computer
9. Cookie	**d.** A program you don't need to open for it to infect your computer
10. Firewall	**e.** A file that a website stores on your computer, containing your information and preferences

Select the best answer from the list of choices.

11. Which of the following is *not* considered malware?
   a. Virus   **c.** Worm
   b. Cookie   **d.** Trojan horse

12. Which of the following programs protects you from viruses?
   a. Microsoft Edge   **c.** Windows Defender
   b. Cortana   **d.** Windows Update

13. Where would you go to view the notification status of your network firewall, Windows Defender virus and spyware protection, and your Microsoft Account?

    a. History list

    b. Family settings

    c. Security & Maintenance

    d. Microsoft Edge

14. Which Settings category would you use to verify that you have the latest version of Windows?

    a. Devices

    b. Ease of Access

    c. System

    d. Update & security

15. Which of the following is a file that stores your personal information so that websites know your information for future visits?

    a. Notification

    b. Update

    c. Cookie

    d. Firewall

16. To ensure that future users of a borrowed computer won't see the sites you've visited, you can clear your:

    a. History.

    b. Firewall.

    c. Safety controls.

    d. Cookies.

17. Which of the following does Family Safety *not* let you do for a Child account?

    a. Limit screen time.

    b. Block selected games and apps.

    c. Track browsed websites.

    d. Install Windows updates.

Skills Review

1. **Use Security and Maintenance.**

    a. Open the Control Panel, view it by small icons, then open Security & Maintenance.

    b. Expand the Security and Maintenance sections if necessary, and view their settings

    c. Go to the Change Security and Maintenance settings, then return to the Security and Maintenance settings.

    d. Go to the Change User Account Control settings, close the window, then close the Security and Maintenance window.

2. **Manage Windows Firewall.**

    a. Open the Windows Firewall window in the Control Panel.

    b. Open the Allowed apps area.

    c. Change the program exceptions to deselect Windows Media Player Network Sharing Service (Internet), if it is not already deselected.

    d. Go back to the Windows Firewall window, then close the Control Panel.

3. **Manage automatic updates.**

    a. Open the Settings app, then open the Update & security window.

    b. Go to Advanced Windows Update options and observe how updates are installed.

    c. View your update history.

    d. View how your updates are delivered, then return to the Settings app window.

4. **Defend against malicious software.**

    a. From the Settings app, click or tap Update & security, then open the Windows Defender window.

    b. Use a link at the bottom of the Windows Defender window to go to open the Windows Defender dialog box.

    c. Check to verify that your virus and spyware definitions are up to date.

    d. On the History tab, view the details of any quarantined items and any detected items.

    e. Close the Windows Defender window.

Skills Review (continued)

5. Protect your Internet privacy.

   a. Open Microsoft Edge Settings, open the Settings pane, then view Advanced settings.

   b. In the Advanced settings pane, see how cookies are handled, then verify that pop-up blocking is on. Close the Settings pane and Microsoft Edge.

   c. Open the Internet Options Control Panel, then open the Per Site Privacy Actions dialog box.

   d. Specify that the website https://www.microsoft.com/en-us is allowed, then remove it from the list of allowed sites.

   e. Open Advanced Privacy settings, view how first-party and third-party cookies are handled in Internet Explorer, then close all dialog boxes and the Control Panel.

6. Delete Internet information.

   a. In Microsoft Edge, go to the Hub to view your web history, grouped by time periods.

   b. Open a time period in the list, then delete one item.

   c. Use the Clear all history button to view which categories are selected.

   d. Return to the Edge window.

7. Set Family Safety controls.

   a. Open the Settings app and go to the Accounts category.

   b. View the Family & other users screen, and observe the current users of your device.

   c. If you have set up a Child account, view the settings for that account online.

   d. View the settings for Web browsing and Screen time, then close the webpage and the Settings app.

Independent Challenge 1

Your work at a small gourmet restaurant called Dandelions. Because you have experience with computers and the Internet, your manager asks you to document that their computer is protected against advertisers leaving unwanted commercial content and tracking users' browsing behavior. She also wants you to check the computer's security status to see if there are any security or maintenance issues that need to be addressed.

   a. Open a blank document in WordPad, then save it where you store your Data Files as **Dandelions Security.rtf**.

   b. Open Microsoft Edge, navigate to the Advanced Settings pane, then see how cookies are handled.

   c. In the WordPad document, write how cookies are handled on the current device. Explain to your manager, in your own words, what the setting means, making any necessary recommendation to accomplish the goal of protecting against browsing data being tracked.

   d. Go to the Security and Maintenance area of the Control Panel, and note any issues that need attention.

   e. In the WordPad document, list any security and maintenance issues you found.

   f. Create a list of steps that explain where your manager can find the cookies settings and the Security and maintenance settings in the future. Use formatting that will help make the information easy to understand.

   g. Add your name to the document, save it, then close all windows.

Independent Challenge 2

You are the network administrator at Dronz, Inc., a company that specializes in the production and distribution of toy drones. You want employees to update their computer systems with the latest Windows 10 system updates. You also want them to know how to clear browsing history to maintain company confidentiality. You decide to practice demonstrating the processes to them in a meeting where they can see your projected computer screen and also prepare instructions on a handout they can take with them.

   a. Open the Update & security category in the Settings app, and check Advanced options to see how updates are installed.

   b. See if any updates are available. If updates are available, install them if permitted on your system; if necessary, restart your system.

Independent Challenge 2 (continued)

c. View your update history.

d. Open Microsoft Edge, and view your browsing history for any time period, then clear it if you wish.

e. Start WordPad, then save the new document where you store your Data Files as **How to Check for Updates and Clear History.rtf**.

f. Describe the steps you performed to see how updates are installed, check for updates, and check update history. Then explain how to view your web browsing history. Use formatting and concise steps so the information can be understood by people who do not have very much experience with Windows 10.

g. Add your name to the document, save changes to it, then close all windows.

Independent Challenge 3

You and a friend are starting an ice cream manufacturing company called Cold Comfort. You have a new computer for your office and want to make sure it is protected from unsolicited Internet traffic and is also protected from malware, spyware, and viruses. You want to document your current Windows settings so that future employees can set their devices the same way.

a. Start WordPad, then save the new document where you store your Data Files as **Protecting Your Machine.rtf**.

b. Open the Control Panel, then use the search box to locate Windows Firewall settings.

c. Verify that Windows Firewall is turned on.

d. View the status of Windows Firewall on Private networks and on Guest or public networks.

e. View the list of apps that are allowed through the Windows Firewall.

f. Close the Control Panel, then open the Settings app and locate Windows Defender settings.

g. Open Windows Defender, go to the Update tab, and update your definitions if available.

h. On the Home tab, verify that Real-time protection is turned on.

i. Switch to your WordPad document, and, in your own words, summarize how to find the Firewall and Defender settings, then briefly summarize your current Windows Firewall and Windows Defender settings. Add your name to the end of the document, then save and close it.

j. Close all open windows.

Independent Challenge 4: Explore

You recently received an urgent pop-up message on your computer, saying that your computer was infected and offering to repair it for you. You discover that the sender wants a fee to repair it. You ignore the offer and decide to double-check your Windows SmartScreen Filter settings to make sure you're protected. You also want to better understand phishing scams so you can be more prepared to recognize them.

a. Open Microsoft Edge, open Settings, then display advanced settings.

b. Locate the setting for Windows SmartScreen Filter, and verify that it is set to On.

c. Close the Settings pane, then search the web on the text "how to recognize phishing."

d. Look at a minimum of three sites on the subject, and determine the top three clues that should alert you to a phishing scam.

e. Start WordPad, then save the new document where you store your Data Files as **Detecting Phishing Scams.rtf**.

f. In the document, summarize at least four clues that you learned that will help to detect phishing scams.

g. Add your name to the document, save it, then close all open windows.

Visual Workshop

Re-create the screens shown in **FIGURE 7-17** and **FIGURE 7-18**, which show Family settings. Your settings will differ, and you may not have a child account set up.

FIGURE 7-17

FIGURE 7-18

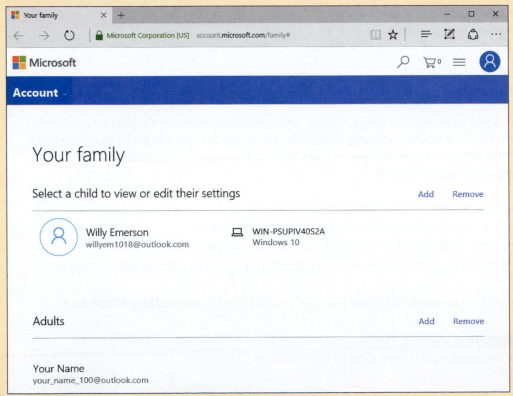

Managing Windows Devices

CASE ▶ Windows 10 allows you to install, remove, and work with devices attached to your system. As a computer specialist, you often need to install, manage, and remove various hardware devices, such as printers, to keep company computers up to date. *Note: With the release of Windows 10, Microsoft now provides ongoing updates to Windows instead of releasing new versions periodically. This means that Windows features might change over time, including how they look and how you interact with them. The information provided in this text was accurate at the time this book was published.*

Important: If you are in a computer lab or other situation where you may not have permission to alter device settings, simply read through this module without completing the steps.

Module Objectives

After completing this module, you will be able to:

- View Windows devices
- Install a printer
- View printer properties
- Share a printer
- Manage printers and print jobs
- Install hardware devices
- Remove hardware devices
- Sync your Windows 10 devices

Files You Will Need

List of Artworks.rtf

Marketing Outlook.rtf

Press Release.rtf

Sales Region Managers.rtf

Sales Report.rtf

Sales Strategies Seminar.rtf

View Windows Devices

Learning Outcomes
• View devices in the Settings app
• View devices in the Control Panel

A **hardware device**, also called simply a **device**, is any physical hardware that connects to and is controlled by your system. An example of a device is a printer, monitor, mouse, or digital camera that you connect to your computer externally or a sound card that you install internally. A device may connect to your computer with a cable that plugs into a port on your computer or via a wireless connection. **CASE** ▶ *The marketing department just purchased a printer. Before you install it, you want to see what devices are currently installed.*

STEPS

1. **Click or tap the Start button ⊞, then click or tap Settings**

2. **Click or tap the Devices category**

   The Devices window opens, letting you view the devices that are connected to your computer. See **FIGURE 8-1**. Printers & Scanners is selected, showing a list of the printers and scanners for which Windows has drivers installed. This computer has drivers installed for a Canon printer, which is currently **offline**, meaning that it's either not connected or is turned off, and a Dell printer, which was the last printer used.

   > **QUICK TIP**
   > The computer in the figure also has drivers that let the user "print" to (create) an Adobe PDF file; to Microsoft OneNote, an electronic note-taking program; and to Snagit, a screen capture program.

3. ▶ **Click or tap Connected devices on the left side**

   This screen lists other connected devices such as monitors or devices connected to a USB port. A **port** is the physical location on your computer where you connect the device cable. See **TABLE 8-1** for computer ports commonly found on newer computers. Windows uses technology called **Plug and Play** that makes it easy to install and uninstall devices quickly. In most cases, you simply connect the device to your computer, and Windows recognizes it and automatically installs related software, known as a **driver**, which allows the hardware to communicate with Windows and other software applications. Windows 10 comes with a library of thousands of built-in drivers for common devices, and Windows Update installs updated drivers when necessary. This computer has a USB receiver that communicates with a wireless mouse. **USB** refers to an external hardware interface that can connect up to 127 peripheral devices and transfer data at high speeds.

   > **QUICK TIP**
   > You may also see a Bluetooth category, which lets you connect to Bluetooth devices. You learn more about Bluetooth in the next lesson.

4. ▶ **Click or tap Mouse & touchpad on the left side**

   These settings let you adjust your mouse and touchpad responses. Additional subcategories let you specify how your device responds to other events: Typing lets you adjust spelling, typing, and keyboard responses, AutoPlay lets you specify what happens when you plug in a removable drive or memory card, and USB lets you receive notifications about issues with USB devices.

5. **Click or tap Printers & scanners again, then scroll down to the bottom of the window**

   > **QUICK TIP**
   > The window may take a minute to list all devices.

6. **Click or tap the Devices and printers link**

   The Devices and Printers window in the Control Panel opens, showing all devices at once.

7. **Right-click or press and hold any icon**

   A shortcut menu appears with commands relating to that device. See **FIGURE 8-2**.

8. **Click the Close button ☒ in the Devices and Printers window**

TABLE 8-1: Common computer ports

port	stands for	connects
USB	Universal Serial Bus	Printers, scanners, hard drives, keyboards, USB (thumb) drives, phones
DVI	Digital Visual Interface	Monitors, other video displays
DisplayPort, Mini DisplayPort		Monitors
HDMI	High-Definition Multimedia Interface	Camcorders, cameras, high-definition TVs and monitors

FIGURE 8-1: Viewing devices in the Settings app

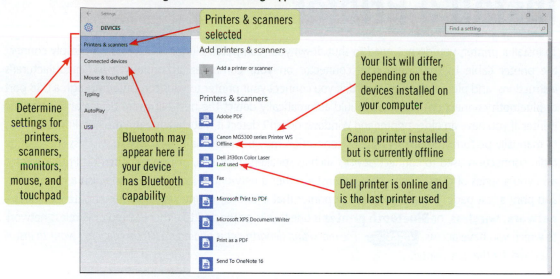

Printers & scanners selected

Determine settings for printers, scanners, monitors, mouse, and touchpad

Bluetooth may appear here if your device has Bluetooth capability

Your list will differ, depending on the devices installed on your computer

Canon printer installed but is currently offline

Dell printer is online and is the last printer used

FIGURE 8-2: Viewing devices in the Control Panel

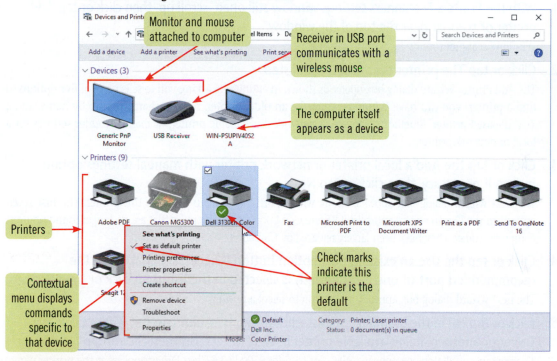

Monitor and mouse attached to computer

Receiver in USB port communicates with a wireless mouse

The computer itself appears as a device

Printers

Contextual menu displays commands specific to that device

Check marks indicate this printer is the default

Installing devices

In most cases, Windows installs your device as soon as you connect it. But occasionally, Windows won't recognize a device and you'll need to do one of the following: (1) Gather your Windows 10 installation discs or bootable thumb drive you may have created, if any, and the hardware device you want to install and the program download or discs that came with the device, if available. (2) For an internal device such as a network card or a sound card, turn off your computer before installing it. For external devices such as a USB flash drive or a camera, you don't need to turn off your computer first—these are called **hot-pluggable** or **hot-swappable** devices. But check the device's documentation because it may require you to install software before connecting it. (3) Follow the manufacturer's instructions to connect the new device to your computer. (4) Turn on your computer if necessary. Windows tries to detect the new device and install the device drivers. If it can't find the drivers, it asks you to insert the disc(s) that came with the device. If Windows still doesn't recognize the new hardware device, it might be an older device, known as a **legacy device**, which is no longer compatible. Or, the device might not have installed correctly. To manually install the device, you can use the Add a device wizard in the Devices and Printers window, then follow the instructions.

Install a Printer

Learning Outcomes
• Install a printer manually
• View printers in the Control Panel

To install a printer, you do not need to shut down your computer. Plug and Play lets you simply connect the printer cable to the appropriate connector on your computer, according to the manufacturer's instructions, and plug in the power cord. If you connect your printer to your computer through a USB port or Bluetooth connection, Windows should automatically detect the new hardware device and install the printer. If you have an older printer and Windows doesn't detect it, you can also use the Add Printer Wizard to manually perform the task. A wireless connection may be made via **Bluetooth**, a wireless short-range radio connection used to connect devices such as speakers, headsets, or printers. The Add Printer Wizard asks you a series of questions to help you install either a network or local printer, establish a connection, and print a test page. A **local printer** is a printer that is directly connected to your computer, whereas a **network, wireless**, or **Bluetooth printer** is one that is connected to either a wired or wireless network to which you have access. **CASE** ▶ *The marketing department is adding an HP LaserJet. You want to install the driver for the new printer.*

STEPS

1. **With the Printers & scanners settings window still open, scroll up, then click or tap Add a printer or scanner near the top of the window**

   Windows searches for any local or network printers.

2. **Click or tap The printer that I want isn't listed**

   The Add Printer Wizard dialog box opens, as shown in **FIGURE 8-3**, asking you to select one of five options to find a printer: you can have Windows search for an older printer, select a shared printer by name, add a TCP/IP-based printer, Bluetooth, wireless or network discoverable printer, or manually enter settings for a local or network printer.

3. **Click or tap the Add a local printer or network printer with manual settings option button if necessary, then click or tap Next**

   The next wizard dialog box appears, asking which port you want to use with this printer. The first seven options in the Use an existing port list, LPT and COM ports, are older ports that are no longer found on most computers today. They have been largely replaced by USB ports.

4. **Click or tap the Use an existing port option button if necessary, make sure the recommended port (if one is suggested) is selected in the list, then click or tap Next**

   The next wizard dialog box appears, asking you to select a printer.

5. **Click or tap HP in the Manufacturer list, click or tap HP Color LaserJet 9500 PCL6 Class Driver or another similar available printer in the Printers list, then click or tap Next**

   The next wizard dialog box appears; HP Color LaserJet 9500 PCL6 Class Driver appears as the printer name.

6. **Click or tap Next to accept the name, if the Printer Sharing window opens and you want to share the printer, click the Share this printer so that others on your network can find and use it option button, then click Next to accept the defaults**

   The next wizard dialog box appears, asking whether you want to print a test page. When you start a print job without specifying a particular printer, the job is sent to the **default printer**. The default printer is indicated in the Printers folder with a green circle containing a check mark. Printing a test page is an important final step to make sure the printer is working properly. However, in this example, the printer is not connected, so you do not print a test page.

7. **If the Set as the default printer check box appears and contains a checkmark, click to deselect it, then click or tap Finish**

   The Printers & scanners window reopens with the new printer, as shown in **FIGURE 8-4**.

FIGURE 8-3: Add Printer Wizard dialog box

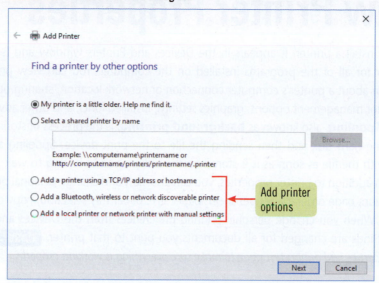

FIGURE 8-4: Printers & scanners settings showing the new printer

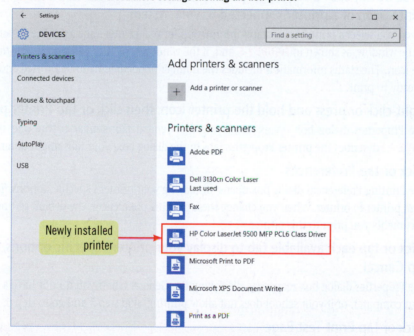

Understanding printers

Although there are many different kinds of printers, there are two main categories: inkjet and laser. An **inkjet printer** works by spraying ionized ink at a sheet of paper. Inkjet printers are less expensive and considerably slower than laser printers but still produce a good-quality output. A **laser printer** utilizes a laser beam to produce an image on a drum, which is rolled through a reservoir of toner and transferred to the paper through a combination of heat and pressure. Laser printers are faster and produce a higher-quality output than inkjets but are also more expensive. Printers are classified by two main characteristics: resolution and speed. **Printer resolution** refers to the sharpness and clarity of a printed page and is measured by the number of dots per inch (dpi). For example, a 300-dpi printer is one that is capable of printing 300 distinct dots in a line one-inch long, or 90,000 dots per square inch. The higher the dpi, the sharper the print quality. Printer speed is measured in pages per minute (ppm); the higher the ppm, the faster the print speed. In general terms, inkjet printers range from about 4 to 10 ppm, while laser printers range from about 10 to 30 ppm. The speed depends on the page's contents; text and/or one-color pages will print faster than those containing graphics and/or using multiple colors.

View Printer Properties

Once you install a printer, it appears in the Devices and Printers window and is accessible in the Print dialog box for all of the programs installed on the computer. You can view printer properties to get information about a printer's computer connection or network location, sharing options, related software drivers, color management options, graphics settings, installed fonts, and other advanced settings, such as spooling. **Spooling**, also known as **background printing**, is the process of storing a temporary copy of a file on the hard disk and then sending the file to the print device. Spooling allows you to continue working with the file as soon as it is stored on the disk instead of having to wait until the file is finished printing. In addition to printer properties, you can also view and change personal printer preferences, such as orientation, page order, pages per sheet, paper size, paper tray selection, copy count, and print quality and color. When you change personal printing preferences from the Devices and Printers window, the default settings are changed for all documents you print to that printer. **CASE** *You decide to check printer properties and print a test page to make sure everything is working properly.*

STEPS

1. **Scroll down, click Devices and printers to open the Control Panel, then, click or tap the printer icon of a printer connected to your system**

   When you select a printer icon, status information for that printer appears in the Details pane at the bottom of the window, as shown in **FIGURE 8-5**, and, if the window is in Tiles view, status information appears under the icon. The status information includes the number of documents to be printed and whether the printer is ready to print.

2. **Right-click or press and hold the printer icon, then click or tap Printer properties**

   The Properties dialog box opens, displaying the General tab, similar to the one shown in **FIGURE 8-6**. **TABLE 8-2** describes the printer Properties tabs in the dialog box; your tabs might differ.

3. **Click or tap Preferences**

   The Printing Preferences dialog box opens, displaying your printer's specific options. Tabs and options vary from printer to printer. When you change these printing preferences, the default settings are changed for all documents you print to this printer.

4. **Click or tap each available tab to display your printer's specific options, then click or tap Cancel**

   The Properties dialog box reappears, displaying the General tab. If you do not have a printer connected to your computer, or if your school does not allow printing, skip step 5 and go to step 6.

5. **Click or tap Print Test Page**

   The page prints, and then a dialog box opens, saying that the test page has been sent.

6. **Click or tap Close in the dialog box, then click or tap the Ports tab in the Properties dialog box**

   The Ports tab displays a list of ports that may be available on the computer. A check mark appears in the check box next to the port to which the printer is connected.

7. **Click or tap the Advanced tab**

   The Advanced tab displays the current printer's driver and indicates your specific printing choices, including print spooling options.

8. **Click or tap Cancel**

   The printer Properties dialog box closes and the Devices and Printers window reappears.

Managing Windows Devices

FIGURE 8-5: Devices and Printers window with a selected printer

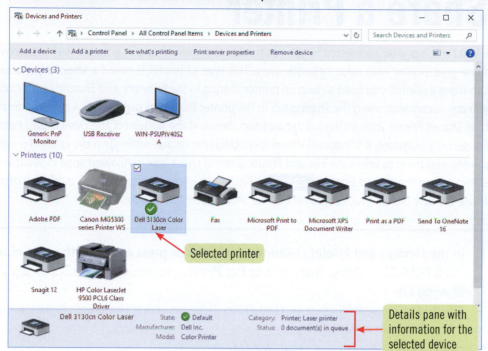

Selected printer

Details pane with information for the selected device

FIGURE 8-6: Properties dialog box with the General tab displayed

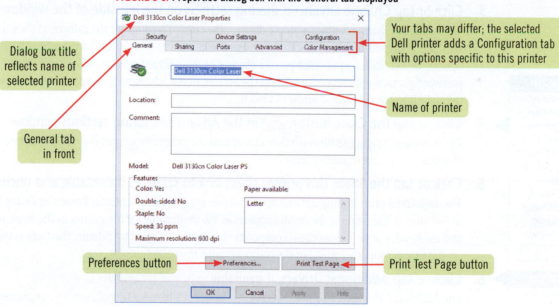

Dialog box title reflects name of selected printer

General tab in front

Your tabs may differ; the selected Dell printer adds a Configuration tab with options specific to this printer

Name of printer

Preferences button

Print Test Page button

TABLE 8-2: Printer options tabs in the printer Properties dialog box

tab	description
General	Lists general information about the printer, and allows you to print a test page
Sharing	Allows you to share the printer over a network
Ports	Lists the printer's connection port and software drivers
Advanced	Lists software drivers, and allows you to change printer options
Color Management	Allows you to adjust color settings and select color profiles to correctly print colors for a specific printer
Security	Allows you to set permissions to print and manage printers and documents
Device Settings	Allows you to change printer device and related settings

Share a Printer

If you have a printer connected to your computer and your computer is connected to a network, you can share your printer with other network users. This type of printer is called a **shared printer**. Before you can share a printer, you need to turn on printer sharing in the Network and Sharing Center window, which you can accomplish using the Sharing tab in the printer Properties dialog box. A shared printer is indicated by a Shared Printer icon on the printer and also shown at the bottom of the Devices and Printers window. For security purposes, if Windows Firewall is enabled (the default setting) on the computer with the shared printer, you need to select the File and Printer Sharing check box in Allowed apps in Windows Firewall for others to use the shared printer. **CASE** ▶ *Because all of the employees in the marketing department need to use the new printer, you want to set it up for sharing over the network.*

STEPS

QUICK TIP
To rename a printer, select the printer, right-click or press and hold the printer icon, click or tap Printer properties, type a new name on the General tab, then click or tap OK.

1. **In the Devices and Printers window, right-click or press and hold the HP Color LaserJet 9500 PCL6 Class Driver icon, click or tap Printer properties, then click or tap the Sharing tab**

   The HP Color LaserJet 9500 PCL6 Class Driver Properties dialog box opens displaying the Sharing tab options, as shown in **FIGURE 8-7**.

2. **Click or tap Network and Sharing Center**

   The Network and Sharing Center window opens, displaying network and sharing options.

3. **Click or tap Change advanced sharing settings on the left side of the window**

   The Advanced sharing settings window displays the current settings for the printer, as shown in **FIGURE 8-8**. To share your printer with other network users, you need to enable the Turn on file and printer sharing option. If you want to password-protect the use of your shared printer, you need to enable the Turn on password protected sharing option (go to the bottom of the Advanced sharing settings window then click or tap the All Networks expand arrow to view it).

QUICK TIP
To enable sharing through Windows Firewall, open the Control Panel, click System and Security, click or tap Allow an app through Windows Firewall, click or tap Change settings, change setting as desired, then click or tap OK.

4. ▶ **Click or tap the Close button** ☒ **in the Advanced sharing settings window**

   The Advanced sharing settings window closes, and the printer Properties dialog box reappears without any changes to the current printer settings.

5. **Click or tap the Share this printer check box to select it, if available and unchecked**

   The additional print sharing options now available are listed in the printer Properties dialog box, as shown in **FIGURE 8-9**. The name of the printer appears as the share name for the printer in the Share name text box, and the Render print jobs on client computers check box is selected by default. This option spools print jobs on the user's computer instead of the computer with the shared printer.

QUICK TIP
If this command is grayed out, additional drivers are not available.

6. ▶ **Click or tap Additional Drivers, if available**

   The Additional Drivers dialog box displays the drivers available for installation if your printer is going to be used by other users running different versions of Windows.

7. **Click or tap Cancel in the Additional Drivers dialog box if it is open, or skip to Step 8**

   The printer Properties dialog box reopens.

8. **Click or tap OK to close the HP Color LaserJet 9500 PCL6 Class Driver Properties dialog box**

   The dialog box closes, and a Shared Printer icon 👥 appears next to the HP Color LaserJet 9500 PCL6 Class Driver printer icon in the Devices and Printers window, indicating that this is a shared printer. If the printer is the default printer, then the Shared Printer icon will be replaced by a green check mark.

FIGURE 8-7: Properties dialog box with the Sharing tab displayed

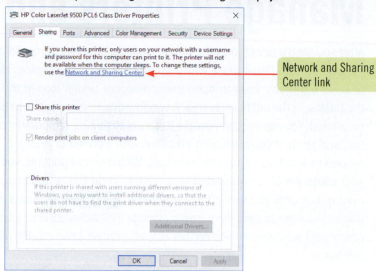

Network and Sharing Center link

FIGURE 8-8: Advanced sharing settings window

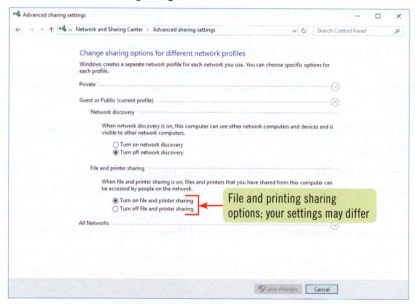

File and printing sharing options; your settings may differ

FIGURE 8-9: Printer sharing options

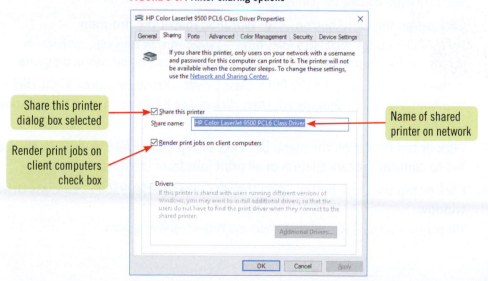

Share this printer dialog box selected

Render print jobs on client computers check box

Name of shared printer on network

Manage Printers and Print Jobs

Learning
Outcomes
• Pause a printer
• Pause and cancel a
  print job

After you send a print job to the printer, you can check its status. To quickly check status, you can display Tiles view or the Details pane with a selected device in the Devices and Printers window. To manage one or more print jobs, you can open the appropriate printer icon in the Devices and Printers window or on the taskbar in the notification area. A window opens showing the **print queue**, which is the list of files to be printed. You can use this window to cancel print jobs, temporarily pause print jobs, view printer properties, and so on. If you are having problems with a printer or print job, you can **defer**, or halt, the printing process to avoid receiving error messages. With deferred printing, you can send a job to be printed even if your computer is not connected to a printer. To do this, you pause printing, and the file remains in the print queue until you turn off pause printing. **CASE** ▷ *Because multiple employees are using the shared printer, you want to show them how to manage their individual print jobs, including how to pause a printer and cancel print jobs. Because you are not actually printing to an existing printer, you will use deferred printing in this lesson.*

STEPS

QUICK TIP

To print a document in a File Explorer window, right-click or press and hold the document icon, then click or tap Print.

1. **In the Devices and Printers window, click or tap the HP Color LaserJet 9500 PCL6 Class Driver icon if necessary, click or tap See what's printing on the toolbar, click or tap Printer on the menu bar, then click or tap Pause Printing**

   The HP Color LaserJet 9500 PCL6 Class Driver window opens, and "Paused" appears after the printer name in the title bar. The Pause Printing command prevents the computer from attempting to send a print job to the printer.

2. **Click or tap the Start button ⊞, type WordPad, then click or tap WordPad**

   WordPad opens.

3. **Click or tap the File tab, click or tap Open, navigate to where you store your Data Files, then double-click or double-tap Marketing Outlook.rtf to open the file**

QUICK TIP

To get printer status, point to the printer icon 🖨 in the notification area of the taskbar.

4. **Click or tap the File tab, click or tap Print, click or tap the HP Color LaserJet 9500 PCL6 Class Driver icon in the Print dialog box if necessary, as shown in FIGURE 8-10, then click or tap Print**

   A pop-up notification briefly appears on the screen telling you that the file was sent to the paused printer, and a printer icon appears in the notification area on the taskbar, indicating that print jobs are pending. Because you paused the printer, nothing prints; the job simply remains in the print queue until you either delete the job or unpause the printer.

QUICK TIP

To print the paused file, right-click or press and hold the file, then click or tap Resume.

5. **Click or tap the Close button ✕ in WordPad to exit the program**

   The HP Color LaserJet 9500 PCL6 Class Driver – Paused window reappears, as shown in FIGURE 8-11. The window displays the printer status in the title bar and the print job currently in the queue.

6. **In the HP Color LaserJet 9500 PCL6 Class Driver – Paused window, right-click or press and hold Marketing Outlook.rtf, then click or tap Pause to change the printing status for the file**

QUICK TIP

To delete a single job in the print queue, select the file, click or tap Document on the menu bar, click or tap Cancel, then click or tap Yes to confirm.

7. **Click or tap Printer on the menu bar, click or tap Cancel All Documents, then click or tap Yes to confirm the cancellation of all print jobs from the queue**

8. **Click or tap the Close button ✕ in the HP Color LaserJet 9500 PCL6 Class Driver - Paused window**

   The printer window closes, and the Devices and Printers window appears.

FIGURE 8-10: Printing a file to a paused printer

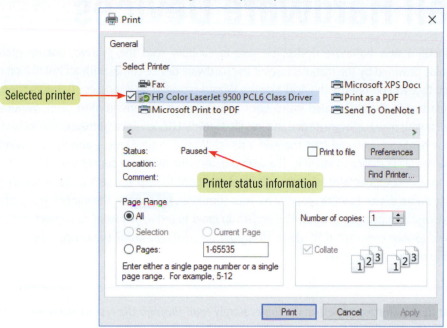

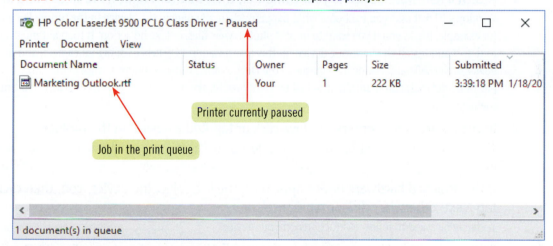

Managing devices

When you install a new operating system, such as Windows 10, it is important to make sure that you are using the latest software drivers with your system hardware. If not, your hardware devices might not work properly. You can view your system hardware using a Windows utility called Device Manager. **Device Manager** organizes all the hardware devices attached to your computer by hardware types, also known as **hardware classes**. If an exclamation point within a yellow triangle icon appears next to a specific device, it indicates a conflict with some other device. To fix it, you can try to uninstall and reinstall the device or seek technical support from the device manufacturer. With Device Manager, you can determine the software driver versions being used with your system hardware, update the software driver with a newer version, roll back to a previous

driver version if the device fails with the new one, or uninstall a driver. After viewing your software driver version numbers, you can contact the manufacturer or visit their website to determine the latest versions. Most manufacturers allow you to download drivers from their websites for free. To do so, open the Control Panel, open the Hardware and Sound category, click or tap Device Manager under Devices and Printers, then click or tap Yes to grant permission to make changes, if necessary. Select the device that you want to view; click or tap the Expand indicator, if necessary, to display the device. To view device properties, click or tap the Properties button on the toolbar. To update software drivers, click or tap the Update Driver Software button on the toolbar. To remove a device, click or tap the Uninstall button on the toolbar.

Install Hardware Devices

Before you install a new hardware device, be sure to carefully read the product documentation and installation guide provided by the manufacturer. If the hardware device comes with an installation disc, it is recommended that you do not use the Add a device Wizard provided by Windows 10. Instead, you should use the manufacturer's disc and related instructions to install the hardware. In most cases, Windows automatically detects your new hardware device and installs its related device driver software. If Windows doesn't detect the new hardware, you can start the Add a device Wizard in the Devices and Printers window and select the new hardware device to install it. The wizard detects the hardware connected (either with a cable or wirelessly) to your computer and asks you a series of questions to help you set up the necessary software for the new hardware device to work properly on your computer. **CASE** *The marketing department just received a new digital camera for an upcoming project. In order to test it, you want to connect and install the hardware device to your computer. If Windows 10 doesn't automatically install the device, you use the Add a device Wizard to search for and install it.*

STEPS

 If you do not have a hardware device available, simply read through the rest of the lessons without completing the steps.

1. **Attach a hardware device to your computer, then wait for Windows to detect and install it**

   Windows 10 first asks you to choose what happens when you plug in this device in the future. For a camera, for example, it asks you if you want to import photos, view files, or take no action. It then automatically tries to detect and install the hardware device, in this case a Canon EOS Rebel T3i digital camera, and its related device driver software. The device appears in the Devices and Printers window, as shown in **FIGURE 8-12**. If the hardware device is automatically installed by Windows 10, skip to the next lesson; otherwise, continue with the next step.

2. **In the Devices and Printers window, click or tap Add a device on the toolbar**

   The Add a device Wizard opens and starts to search for any attached hardware devices, as shown in **FIGURE 8-13**.

3. **If the attached hardware device appears in the list, select the device icon, then click or tap Next; otherwise, click or tap Cancel**

   You may be asked to follow instructions on your device.

4. **Follow the instructions to complete the installation; steps vary depending on the hardware device**

TROUBLE
If the Windows 10 installation media is not available, skip Step 5, click or tap OK, then click or tap Cancel.

5. **If necessary, insert the Windows 10 installation DVD or thumb drive in the appropriate drive, click or tap OK, then click or tap the Close button ☒ in the window**

   Windows installs the appropriate driver to complete the installation. The newly installed hardware device appears in the Devices and Printers window.

FIGURE 8-12: Windows 10 detects and installs a hardware device

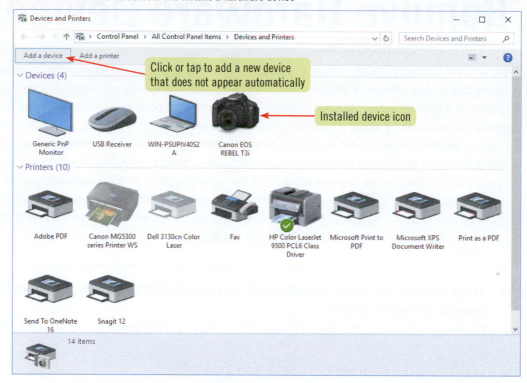

FIGURE 8-13: Add a device Wizard

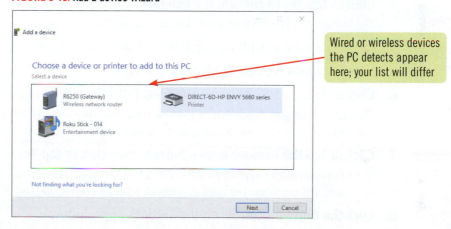

Connecting to the Internet

Microsoft Windows lets you connect your computer to the Internet and use the many services available on the World Wide Web. First, you need to select an ISP (Internet service provider), a company that provides Internet access through servers connected directly to the Internet. Your ISP gives you an Internet account and connection information that provide Internet access for a monthly rate. You can connect your computer to your ISP in one of several ways. **DSL (digital subscriber line)** provides a completely digital connection using telephone lines, whereas cable modems use cable television lines. DSL and cable are types of **broadband connections**, high-speed connections are continually connected to the Internet.

You connect to broadband Internet using DSL and cable modems. A **modem**, short for **Mo**dulate/**Dem**odulate) converts your computer's digital data to a format that can be transmitted over a cable or telephone line, and interprets that cable or telephone line data for your computer. Most newer computers let you use a wireless connection, which uses radio waves or microwaves to communicate. **FIGURE 8-13** shows a wireless network router which, when connected to a cable or DSL modem, lets you connect to the Internet wirelessly. In remote areas, you can connect with a slower dial-up modem and telephone line, which needs to be established each time you connect to the Internet.

Remove Hardware Devices

If you no longer use a hardware device, you can easily remove it from your computer. Before you remove the physical hardware device from your computer, however, you need to remove the hardware device drivers and related software. If the documentation for the hardware device recommends a specific method to remove a device, then use the manufacturer's instructions to remove it. For example, if you have a USB device, in many cases, you can remove it by simply unplugging it when the device is not actively in use. To ensure a hardware device is not in use and properly removed, Windows recommends using the Remove device button in the Devices category in the Settings app or Devices and Printers window in the Control Panel. You can also use the Devices category of the Settings app to remove hardware devices and any related device drivers. **CASE** *The marketing manager decides that the new printer and digital camera would be best suited to the needs of the advertising department. You want to delete the printer and digital camera and the related hardware device drivers that you installed.*

STEPS

1. **In the Devices and Printers window, click or tap your installed hardware device from the previous lesson to select it**
   The hardware device, in this case the Canon EOS REBEL T3i digital camera, is selected in the Devices and Printers window, as shown in **FIGURE 8-14**.

2. **Click or tap the Remove device button on the toolbar**
   The Remove Device dialog box opens, asking if you want to delete the hardware device.

3. **Click or tap Yes to confirm the deletion**
   The Devices and Printers window no longer lists your hardware device.

4. **Click or tap the Start button ⊞, then click or tap Settings**

5. **In the Settings window, click or tap Devices**

6. **Click or tap the HP Color LaserJet 9500 PCL6 Class Driver icon**
   The Devices category is selected in the task pane, and the currently installed devices appear in the right pane, as shown in **FIGURE 8-15**, along with the Add a printer or scanner button at the top.

7. **Click or tap the Remove device button, then click or tap Yes to confirm**
   The printer no longer appears in the Printers & scanners list. If a printer contains a print job, the Delete command will not work. You need to purge all print jobs before you can delete a printer.

8. **Click the Close button ☒ on the Settings app window**

FIGURE 8-14: Deleting a device in the Devices and Printers window

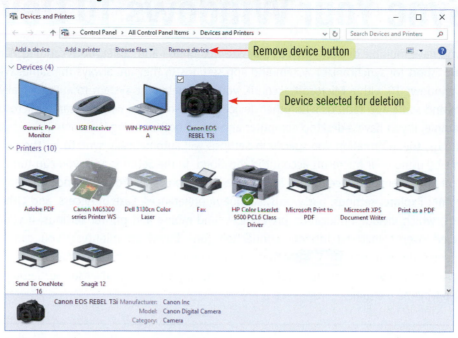

FIGURE 8-15: Deleting a device in the Settings app

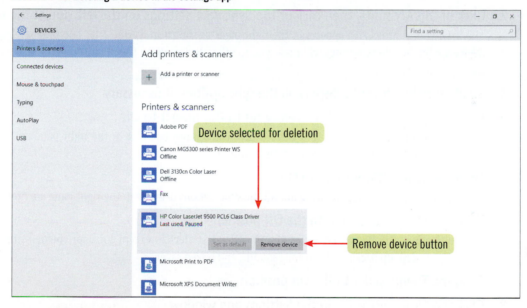

Using a second screen

If you need more screen space when working in Windows, you can add a second monitor to your system. This allows you to view and work with more than one full-size window on the screen at the same time. For example, you can work on a document in WordPad on one monitor and search for web content in Edge on the other monitor. One monitor serves as the primary display while the other serves as the secondary display. You can set the multiple displays to duplicate the displays on both monitors, extend the displays over two monitors, and show the desktop on only one or the other. In addition, you can set different screen resolutions and different orientation settings for each monitor. After you connect the secondary monitor, Windows automatically detects the new device and applies the video settings best suited to the display. To change the settings for multiple monitors, open the System category of the Settings app, then select the Display subcategory. Thumbnails representing each monitor appear; click Identify to see which monitor is which. Click the Multiple displays list arrow, and choose to duplicate or extend the displays. If you extend the displays, you can move windows across either screen; monitor 1 is the main display and shows your desktop and full taskbar. Click Advanced display settings to set more specific options for each monitor. When your settings are complete, click Apply.

Sync Your Windows 10 Devices

Learning Outcomes
• View Windows 10 sync settings
• Change sync settings

If you have multiple devices, such as a desktop computer and tablet, both running Windows, you can **sync** (short for synchronize) system and app settings so they are always the same. When you sign in to Windows 10 with a Microsoft account, you can enable the system to automatically sync your system and some app settings with other devices that also sign in with the same Microsoft account. For example, if you have a desktop computer and tablet both running Windows 10 and you turn on sync settings, the information you specify in Settings will automatically sync to be the same on both systems by using your Microsoft account in the cloud. In the Settings app, you can turn sync settings on or off for the entire device or turn individual settings on or off. You can sync your settings for themes, Internet Explorer settings, passwords, Language preferences, Ease of Access, and Other Windows settings, which include notification preferences, and mouse and printer settings. If your device is connected over a metered Internet connection (one based on minutes), you can specify whether to sync settings or not. **CASE** *Your company recently purchased a Windows 10 tablet for you to take to client locations. You want to enable sync settings on your PC and tablet so your settings on both devices will always be the same.*

STEPS

1. Click or tap the **Start button** , then click or tap **Settings**

QUICK TIP
If your sync settings are not available, your school or organization might not allow this feature.

2. Click or tap **Accounts**, then click or tap **Sync your settings** on the left side of the screen

   The Sync your settings area appears in the right pane, as shown in **FIGURE 8-16**. The sync settings for this device are on. Windows settings will now sync to other devices using the Microsoft account mentioned at the top of the window.

3. Scroll or swipe down to display all the sync options, if necessary

4. If the **Sync settings slider** is currently set to **On**, drag it to **Off**

   Sync settings for this device are now off. All the sync options below it in the right pane are grayed out, indicating that they are now unavailable, See **FIGURE 8-17**.

5. Drag the **Sync settings slider** to **On**

   Sync settings for this device are on again. All the sync options below it in the right pane are now available.

6. Drag the **Theme slider** left, to the **Off** position

   Now all features will be synced across your Windows 10 devices except for your theme settings, which include your desktop background, colors, sounds, and screen saver.

7. Drag the **Theme slider** to the **On** position

8. Click the **Close button** ☒ in the Settings app window

FIGURE 8-16: Enabled sync settings

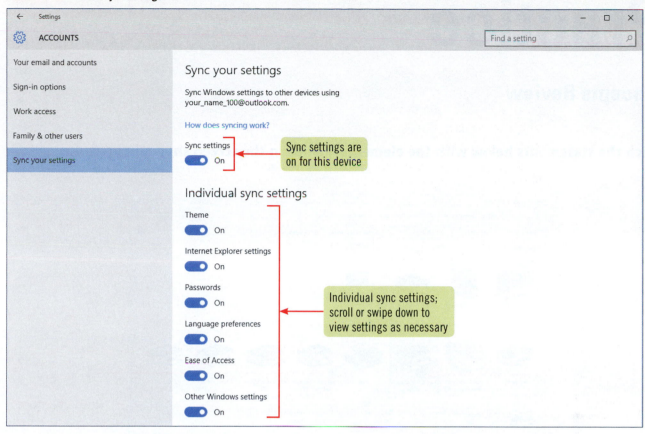

FIGURE 8-17: Disabled sync settings

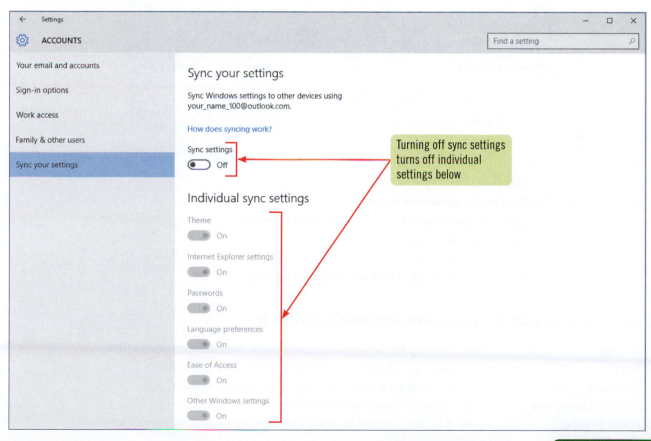

Practice

Concepts Review

Match the statements below with the elements labeled in the screen shown in FIGURE 8-18.

FIGURE 8-18

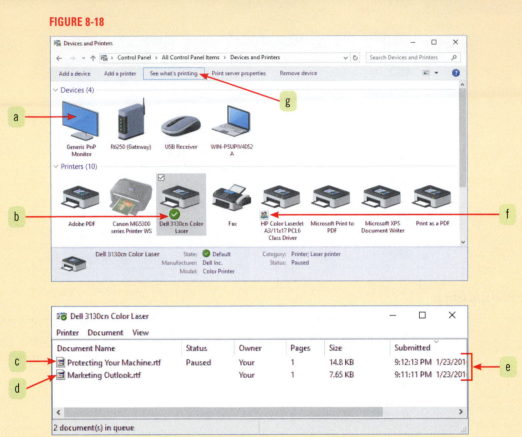

1. Which element points to a paused print job?
2. Which element points to a shared printer?
3. Which element indicates the default printer?
4. Which element points to a hardware device that is not a printer?
5. Which element points to the print queue?
6. Which element points to an unpaused file?
7. Which element would you click or tap to show the print queue?

Match each term with the statement that best describes it.

8. Driver
9. Port
10. Spooling
11. Bluetooth printer
12. Local printer

a. The way hardware communicates with Windows and other software
b. Storing a temporary copy of a file to the hard disk before printing
c. Location on a computer where you connect a cable
d. A printer connected to your computer
e. A printer attached to your computer via a short-range wireless connection

Select the best answer from the list of choices.

13. **When you install a hardware device, what is the related software that Windows installs called?**
    - **a.** Wizard.
    - **b.** Driver.
    - **c.** Port.
    - **d.** None of the above

14. **What kind of printer is indicated by an icon containing a green circle with a check mark?**
    - **a.** Shared.
    - **b.** Default.
    - **c.** Local.
    - **d.** Networked.

15. **Which of the following is a port name?**
    - **a.** DVI
    - **b.** HDMI
    - **c.** USB
    - **d.** All of the above

16. **Which of the following describes a device you can plug in while your computer is on?**
    - **a.** Inkjet
    - **b.** Background
    - **c.** Hot-pluggable
    - **d.** Synced

17. **What is the name for a collection of files to be printed?**
    - **a.** Print queue.
    - **b.** Print window.
    - **c.** Print spool.
    - **d.** Print list.

18. **Another name for spooling is:**
    - **a.** hot plugging
    - **b.** syncing
    - **c.** sharing
    - **d.** background printing

Skills Review

1. **View Windows devices.**
   - **a.** Open the Settings app, then open the Devices category.
   - **b.** View the printers and scanners attached to this device.
   - **c.** View the other devices connected to this computer.
   - **d.** Use a link in this window to view all devices in the Control Panel.

2. **Install a printer.**
   - **a.** In the Devices and Printers window, use the Add Printer wizard to add a local printer.
   - **b.** Specify an existing port of your choosing.
   - **c.** Choose EPSON as the manufacturer, then Epson ESC/P Standard 1 V4 Class Driver as the model. (If that model is already installed on your computer, select another printer or keep the existing driver.)
   - **d.** Use the default printer name (do not set the printer as the default, however), then click Finish.

3. **View printer properties.**
   - **a.** In the Devices and Printers window, open the Printer properties for a printer connected to your computer.
   - **b.** View the various printer properties, then view the printer preferences.
   - **c.** Close the Preferences dialog box without making changes, print a test page, then close the printer Properties dialog box.

4. **Share a printer.**
   - **a.** Open the printer Properties dialog box for the Epson ESC/P Standard 1 V4 Class Driver printer.
   - **b.** Open the Network and Sharing Center.
   - **c.** Make sure file and printer sharing is turned on, then close the dialog box.
   - **d.** Share the printer.
   - **e.** View the additional drivers, if available, then cancel the dialog box.
   - **f.** Close the Epson ESC/P Standard 1 V4 Class Driver Properties dialog box.

Skills Review (continued)

5. Manage printers and print jobs.

    a. In the Devices and Printers window, open the Epson ESC/P Standard 1 V4 Class Driver printer.

    b. Pause the printing for the Epson ESC/P Standard 1 V4 Class Driver printer.

    c. Open WordPad, navigate to the location where you store your Data Files, then open the **Sales Strategies Seminar.rtf** file.

    d. Print to the Epson ESC/P Standard 1 V4 Class Driver printer, then exit WordPad.

    e. Pause the printing for the Sales Strategies Seminar file.

    f. Cancel all documents, then confirm the cancellation.

    g. Close the Epson ESC/P Standard 1 V4 Class Driver printer window.

6. Install hardware devices.

    a. Attach a hardware device to your computer if you have one available, then wait for Windows to detect and install it.

    b. In the Devices and Printers window, click or tap Add a device.

    c. Choose to install hardware from a list. If no choices are available, click or tap Cancel.

7. Remove hardware devices.

    a. In the Devices and Printers window, select the device installed in Step 6a.

    b. Remove the device.

    c. Open the Settings app, then open the Devices category.

    d. Select the Epson ESC/P Standard 1 V4 Class Driver printer, then remove the device.

    e. Return to the main Settings app window.

8. Sync your Windows 10 devices.

    a. Open the Accounts category in the Settings app, then select Sync your settings.

    b. Turn off Sync settings, if necessary.

    c. Turn on Sync settings, if the option was already enabled in Step 8b.

    d. Close the Settings app.

Independent Challenge 1

You are an administrator at the U.S. Geological Survey. Your manager recently approved the purchase of a new color laser printer to help you create better reports. You want to install this printer on your computer.

a. Starting in either the Settings app or the Control Panel, start adding a printer to your computer.

b. Assume the following about the installation: The printer is local, use an open port (LPT or COM), the manufacturer is TOSHIBA, and the printer model is TOSHIBA e-STUDIO Color PCL6 V4.

c. Share the printer; do not set the printer as default and do not print a test page.

d. Open the TOSHIBA e-STUDIO Color PCL6 V4 Properties dialog box, then verify that the port and printer assignments are correct.

e. Delete the printer you just added.

f. Check the properties for an existing printer connected to your computer, then print a test page.

g. Close all open windows.

Independent Challenge 2

You are organizing an art show that will benefit ocean cleanup efforts in your coastal community. You need to mail out a press release about the show, as well as a listing of the art pieces that will be on display, to media outlets. You want to print the documents from WordPad to a printer attached to your computer.

a. Pause printing on an existing local printer connected to your computer.

b. Using WordPad, open the file named **Press Release.rtf** in the location where you store your Data Files.

c. Print the document.

d. Open the file named **List of Artworks.rtf** in the location where you store your Data Files.

e. Print the document.

f. In the printer window, cancel the print job **Press Release**.

g. Turn off Pause Printing, then print the job List of Artworks.

h. Check the status of the printer in the Control Panel, then close all open windows.

Independent Challenge 3

You are the owner of Natura, a photography studio that specializes in nature photography. You sell your photographs to magazines and online stock image companies. As a photographer and businessperson, you want to provide the best products for your clients in the most efficient and effective way. As such, you are constantly on the lookout for new cameras and other technologies. You recently bought a new digital camera, and you need to install it.

a. Attach the hardware device to your computer.

b. If the device isn't added automatically, click or tap Add a device in the appropriate window of the Control Panel.

c. Follow the steps to install the device.

d. Display the properties for this device.

e. Remove the installed device, then close all open windows.

Independent Challenge 4: Explore

Many people have more than one computer or tablet in their homes. It is helpful to set up networks so that users can share information as well as devices such as printers. You just purchased a new photo printer and you want to share it with the other users on your network.

a. Open the Settings app and view the Windows devices on your computer.

b. Click or tap the Add a printer or scanner command in the Printers & scanners screen, then install a photo printer using the Add Printer Wizard. Assume the following about the installation: The printer is local, use an open port, the manufacturer is Dell, and the printer model is Dell 1135n Laser MFP.

c. Do not set the printer as default and do not print a test page.

d. Share the printer, pause the printer, then send two print jobs of your own to the printer.

e. Delete the print jobs, delete the printer you added, then close all open windows.

Visual Workshop

Display the Devices and Printers window with the Samsung B/W Laser PS Class Driver and NEC Color MultiWriter Class Driver selected, as shown in **FIGURE 8-19**. Your other devices and printers will vary.

FIGURE 8-19

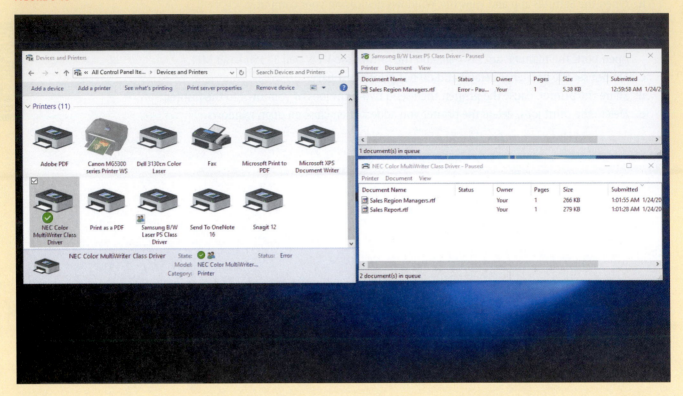

Glossary

Accessories Simple Windows application programs (apps) that perform specific tasks, such as the Calculator accessory for performing calculations. Also called Windows accessories.

Action Center Opened by clicking or tapping the Notifications button on the right side of the taskbar; shows notifications, tips, and reminders. Contains Quick Actions buttons for commonly-used Windows settings.

Active window The window you are currently using; if multiple windows are open, the window in front of other open windows.

Address A sequence of drive and folder names that describes a folder's or file's location in the file hierarchy; the highest hierarchy level is on the left, with lower hierarchy levels separated by the ▶ symbol to its right.

Address bar In a window, the area just below the Ribbon that shows the file hierarchy, or address of the files that appear in the file list below it; the address appears as a series of links you can click or tap to navigate to other locations on your computer.

Antivirus software A program that examines the files stored on a disk to determine whether they are infected with a virus, then destroys or disinfects them.

App An application program. Windows 10 apps are smaller apps available at the Windows store. Desktop apps, such as Microsoft Office, are more full-featured programs and are available from many software companies.

App window The window that opens after you start an app, showing you the tools you need to use the program and any open program documents.

Applet Small applications accessible from selected areas of the Control Panel.

Application program Any program that lets you work with files or create and edit files such as graphics, letters, financial summaries, and other useful documents, as well as view webpages on the Internet and send and receive e-mail. Also called an app.

Aspect ratio The proportion of photo height to photo width; in the Camera app, the default aspect ratio is 16:9, but you can change it to 4:3.

AutoComplete A feature that suggests possible matches with previous filename entries or Web addresses.

Automatic Updating A feature that provides the latest system software and security updates automatically to keep your PC up to date and secure.

Avatar In electronic games, an image or character that represents you to other players.

Background A picture that serves as your desktop's backdrop, the surface on which icons and windows appear; you can customize its appearance using Settings > Personalization > Background.

Background printing The process of storing a temporary copy of a file on the hard disk and then sending the file to a print device; also called spooling.

Backup A duplicate copy of a file that is stored in another location.

Blind carbon copy (Bcc) An option to send a copy of your email message to another person whose name will not appear in the email message.

Bluetooth A wireless short-range radio connection aimed at simplifying communications among Internet devices and between devices and the Internet.

Bluetooth printer A type of printer that is connected via a short-range radio connection to either a wired or wireless network to which you have access.

Bookmark To save a link to a website you visit frequently and add it to your Favorites list.

Border A window's edge; you can drag to resize the window.

Broadband High speed connections to the Internet that are continually connected and use a network setup.

Burn The process of copying files and folders to a compact disc or DVD.

Button A small rectangle you can click or tap in order to issue a command to an application program.

Calendar An app that allows you to update the appearance and organization of events and to schedule time for completing specific tasks, meetings, vacations, holidays, or for any other activity.

Canvas In the Paint accessory, the area in the center of the app window that you use to create drawings.

Carbon copy (Cc) An email option to send a copy of your email message.

Case sensitive An application program's (app's) ability to differentiate between uppercase and lowercase letters; usually used to describe how an operating system evaluates passwords that users type to gain entry to user accounts.

Character Map A Windows accessory that lets you locate and copy special characters such as symbols and small images in different fonts.

Check box A box that turns an option on when checked or off when unchecked.

Click To quickly press and release the left button on the pointing device; also called single-click. The touch-screen equivalent is a tap on the screen.

Clip A video, audio, or mixed media segment.

Clipboard A location in a computer's random access memory that stores information you copy or cut.

Close button In a Windows title bar, the rightmost button; closes the open window, app, and/or document.

Cloud storage location File storage locations on the World Wide Web, such as Microsoft OneDrive or Dropbox.

Command An instruction to perform a task, such as opening a file or emptying the Recycle Bin.

Computer virus A program that attaches itself to a file, reproduces itself, and spreads to other files, usually meant to cause harm to the infected computers.

Contact A person or company with whom you communicate.

Control Panel A collection of utility programs that determine how Windows both appears and performs on your computer or device.

Conversation thread Consists of the original message on a particular topic along with any responses that include the original message.

Cookie A file created by a website that stores information on your computer, such as your website preferences or personal identifiable information, including your name and email address, when visiting that site. Also known as a first-party cookie.

Copy To make a duplicate of a file, folder, or other object that you want to store in another location.

Cortana The digital personal assistant that comes with Windows 10 and Windows phones; can search, give you reminders, alarms, directions, news, weather, and more.

Crop To trim unwanted information from the top, bottom, or sides of a photograph; the Photos app lets you crop photographs.

Default In an app window or dialog box, a value that is automatically set; you can change the default to any valid value.

Default printer The printer that a print job is automatically sent to if a particular printer is not specified.

Defer To halt the printing process to avoid receiving error messages.

Definition Set of instructions determining how to defend against malicious software.

Desktop apps Application programs (apps), such as Microsoft Word, that are full-featured and that are often purchased, either from the Windows Store or from a software developer; also called traditional apps.

Device Any physical hardware that you plug in to and that is controlled by your system, such as a disk drive, a pointing device, or a touch screen device. Also called a hardware device.

Device driver A program that controls devices attached to your computer, such as printers, monitors, and video cards.

Device Manager A Windows utility that organizes all the hardware devices attached to your computer by hardware types.

Dialog box A window with controls that lets you tell Windows how you want to complete an application program's (app's) command.

Digital signature An electronic stamp like a written signature.

Digital Subscriber Lines (DSL) Wires that provide a completely digital path from one computer to another using telephone lines.

Digital Video Disc (DVD) A type of read-only optical disc that holds a minimum of 4.7 GB (gigabytes), enough for a full-length movie.

Display port A computer port used to connect monitors.

Document window The portion of a application program's (app's) window in which you create the document; displays all or part of an open document.

Documents folder The folder on your hard drive used to store most of the files you create or receive from others; might contain subfolders to organize the files into smaller groups.

Double-click To quickly press and release or click the left button on the pointing device twice. The touch-screen equivalent is a double-tap on the screen.

Downloads list In Microsoft Edge, a list of all the files you have downloaded.

Drag To point to an object, press and hold the left button on the pointing device, move the object to a new location, and then release the left button. Touch-screen users can press and hold a location, then move along the screen with a finger or stylus.

Drag and drop To use a pointing device (or for touchscreen users, a finger or stylus) to move or copy a file or folder directly to a new location instead of using the Clipboard.

Drive A physical location on your computer where you can store files.

Drive name A name for a drive that consists of a letter followed by a colon, such as C: for a hard disk drive.

Driver Related software that Windows installs when you install a hardware device in order for the hardware to communicate with Windows and other software applications.

Dropbox A free online storage site that lets you transfer files that can be retrieved by other people you invite. *See also* Cloud storage location.

DVI (Digital Visual Interface) port A computer port used to connect monitors and other video displays.

E-mail *See* Electronic mail.

Edit To make changes to a file.

Electronic mail A system used to send and receive messages electronically. Also known as email.

Emoji Small graphics used in electronic communication, that express a feeling. Also called emoticons.

Emoticon *See* Emoji.

Event Activity that you schedule using the Calendar app for organizational purposes.

Favorites list Located in the Navigation pane, it provides links to commonly used folders and saved searches to reduce the number of clicks or taps it takes to locate a file or folder. Also called a bookmarks list.

File A collection of information stored on your computer, such as a letter, video, or app.

File Explorer A Windows app that allows you to navigate your computer's file hierarchy and manage your files and folders.

File extension A three- or four-letter sequence, preceded by a period, at the end of a filename that identifies the file as a particular type of document; for example, documents in the Rich Text Format have the file extension .rtf.

File hierarchy The tree-like structure of folders and files on your computer.

File list A section of a window that shows the contents of the folder or drive currently selected in the Navigation pane.

File management The ability to organize folders and files on your computer.

File syncing Changes to files stored in the Cloud are automatically synced to all devices.

Filename A unique, descriptive name for a file that identifies the file's content.

Filter To show only a selected group of files; click or tap the arrow icon to the right of a field name in a File Explorer window.

Firewall A protective barrier between a computer or network and others on the Internet.

First-party cookie *See* Cookie.

Folder An electronic container that helps you organize your computer files, like a cardboard folder on your desk; it can contain subfolders for organizing files into smaller groups.

Folder name A unique, descriptive name for a folder that helps identify the folder's contents.

Gamertag In playing Windows Store games, a series of numbers and letters that identifies each player.

Gesture An action you take with your fingertip directly on a touch screen, such as tapping or swiping, to make a selection or perform a task.

Groove The Microsoft online music catalog and streaming service.

Groove Music A Windows 10 app that lets you download music from the Internet and play music stored in your Music folder.

Groove Music Pass A subscription to Groove, the Microsoft online music catalog and streaming service; used to listen to music on the web, a Windows phone, the Apple iOS operating system, Android, and Xbox.

Group In a Microsoft app window's Ribbon, a section containing related command buttons.

Grouping A way of viewing apps on the Start menu, grouped by letter of the alphabet.

Hard disk A built-in, high-capacity, high-speed storage medium for all the software, folders, and files on a computer. Also called a hard drive.

Hardware classes Hardware types that Device Manager utilizes when organizing all the hardware devices attached to your computer.

HDMI (High-Definition Multimedia Interface) port A computer port used to connect camcorders, cameras, high-definition TVs and monitors.

Highlighted Describes the changed appearance of an item or other object, usually a change in its color, background color, and/or border; often used for an object on which you will perform an action, such as a desktop icon.

History list In Microsoft Edge, a list of the webpages you have previously viewed.

Hits A list of matched results from an Internet search.

Home page The main webpage around which a website is built that opens every time you start a browser.

Hot pluggable Devices such as many USB drives and printers that you can connect or disconnect to your device while the device is on. Also called hot swappable.

Hub In Microsoft Edge, a button on the address bar that lets you view your Favorites or Reading list.

Hyperlink (link) Highlighted text or graphic in a webpage that opens another webpage or location when you click or tap it.

Icon A small image that represents an item, such as the Recycle Bin on your Windows desktop; you can rearrange, add, and delete desktop icons.

In-app purchase In electronic gaming and other apps, purchases that can be made to upgrade the user experience after you begin using the app; may include new levels, content, or features.

Inactive window An open window you are not currently using; if multiple windows are open, the window(s) behind the active window.

Information card An area on the Cortana Home menu containing information, such as news, financial information, or academic information in fields you choose.

Inkjet printer A less expensive, slower but good quality device which utilizes sprayed ionized ink.

InPrivate browsing A way to browse the Web without keeping track of browsing history, searches, temporary Internet files, form data, cookies, and user names and passwords.

Insertion point In a document or filename, a blinking, vertical bar that indicates where the next character you type will appear.

Instant message(IM) An online typewritten conversation in real time between two or more contacts.

Internet A global collection of millions of computers linked together to share information.

Keyword A descriptive word or phrase you enter to obtain a list of results that include that word or phrase. *See also* Search engine.

Laser printer A print device that utilizes a laser beam in combination with heat and pressure to produce a fast, high-quality, but expensive printout.

Layout In File Explorer, an arrangement of files or folders in a window, such as Large icons or Details. There are eight layouts available.

Legacy devices Older hardware devices which Windows may not recognize due to lack of compatibility.

Library A special folder that catalogs specific files and folders in a central location, regardless of where the items are actually stored on your device.

Link Text or an image that you click or tap to display another location, such as a Help topic, a website, or a device. *See also* Hyperlink.

List box A box that displays a list of options from which you can choose (you may need to scroll and adjust your view to see additional options in the list).

Live tile Updated, "live" content that appears on some apps' tiles on the Windows Start menu, including the Weather app and the News app.

Load The process of displaying a webpage in a browser from a server.

Local account A Microsoft account that keeps usernames and passwords on the device instead of online; local accounts cannot be synced to other devices.

Local printer A printer that is directly connected to your computer.

Lock screen A full screen image that appears when you first start Windows, consisting of time, date, and notification icons (with app status).

Log in To select a user account name and enter a password when a computer starts up, giving access to that user's files. Also called sign in.

Loop An option that repeatedly plays a media clip until you stop it.

Malware Malicious software, such as viruses and spyware, that can delete or corrupt files and gather personal information.

Maximize button On the right side of a window's title bar, the center button of three buttons; used to expand a window so that it fills the entire screen. In a maximized window, this button changes to a Restore button.

Maximized window A window that fills the desktop.

Menu A list of related commands.

Messaging A Windows 10 app that lets you send and receive instant messages, online text-based conversations in real time between two or more contacts.

Microsoft account A web service that lets users sign on to one web address so they can use Windows 10 computers and Outlook.com.

Microsoft Edge New in Windows 10, the Microsoft Web browser that is intended to replace Internet Explorer.

Microsoft Internet Explorer In Windows versions through 8.1, a browser program that helps you access the World Wide Web; in Windows 10, replaced by Microsoft Edge (although Internet Explorer is included in Windows 10 for legacy users.)

Microsoft OneDrive A Microsoft website where you can obtain free file storage space, using your own account, that you can share with others; you can access OneDrive from a laptop, tablet computer, or smartphone.

Microsoft Store A website, accessible from the Store icon in the Windows 10 taskbar, where you can purchase and download apps, including games, productivity tools, and media software.

Microsoft Windows 10 An operating system.

Minimize button On the right side of a window's title bar, the leftmost button of three buttons; use to reduce a window so that it only appears as an icon on the taskbar.

Minimized window A window that is visible only as an icon on the taskbar.

Mouse pointer A small arrow or other symbol on the screen that you move by manipulating the pointing device; also called a pointer.

Move To change the location of a file, folder, or other object by physically placing it in another location.

Multitasking Working with more than one Windows program at the same time.

Navigate down To move to a lower level in your computer's file hierarchy.

Navigate up To move to a higher level in your computer's file hierarchy.

Navigation pane The left pane in a window that contains links to folders and device locations; click or tap an item in the Navigation pane to display its contents in the file list, or click or tap the ⌄ or ⟩ symbols to display or hide subfolders in the Navigation pane.

Network printer A type of printer that is connected to either a wired or wireless network to which you have access.

Notebook The area where Cortana monitors, learns, and stores information about you, such as your location, contact information, and interests; you can customize it to display information cards containing news, financial information, sports score, or specialized information. *See also* Information card.

Notification A message from Windows 10 informing you of new information within an app or when action is requested; *see also* Quick action buttons, System icons, pop-up message.

Notification area An area on the right side of the Windows 10 taskbar that displays the current time as well as icons representing selected information; the Notifications button displays pop-up messages when a program on your computer needs your attention. Click or tap the Notifications button to display the Action Center. *See also* Action Center.

Offline The condition of a device that is not usable because it is not connected to a computer or is turned off.

Operating system A program that manages the complete operation of your computer and lets you interact with it.

Option button A small circle in a dialog box that you click or tap to select only one of two or more related options.

Outbox An email storage folder where an outgoing email message is placed temporarily before it is sent automatically to the recipient.

Pane A section of a window, such as the Navigation pane in the File Explorer window.

Password A special sequence of numbers and letters that users can employ to control who can access the files in their user account area; keeping the password private helps keep users' computer information secure.

Paste To place a copied item from the Clipboard to a location in a document.

Path An address that describes the exact location of a file in a file hierarchy; shows the folder with the highest hierarchy level on the left and steps through each hierarchy level toward the right. Locations are separated by small triangles or by backslashes.

PDF Stands for Portable Document Format, a document format created by Adobe System, Inc., that can be opened and read by a freely available reading program such as Reader.

Personal Identification Number (PIN) code In Windows 10, a four-digit number you select to allow access to your computer account.

Personalization settings A Settings app category that lets you change the pictures and colors that appear on the lock screen, screen background, and Start menu.

Phishing Sending a realistic-looking, but false, email, pop-up or website that asks for the recipient's personal information and then uses that information to defraud the recipient.

Photos app A Windows 10 app that lets you view and organize your pictures.

Picture password A replacement for a text password that gives you access to your device; instead of typing characters, you swipe across a picture using gestures you previously set for that image.

PIN code *See* Personal Identification Number.

Pinch On touch screens, moving your thumb and finger close together or spaced apart to correspondingly make a screen element appear smaller or larger.

Pinned Item Shortcuts that let you open an app or accessory using one click or tap; can be located on the Start menu or the taskbar; create by right-clicking or pressing an item, then selecting Pin to taskbar or Pin to Start.

Playlist In a music application such as Groove Music, a named list of selected recording names in a particular sequence.

Plug and play Technology that Windows uses for hardware that makes it easy to install and uninstall devices quickly.

Point To position the tip of the mouse pointer over an object, option, or item.

Pointer *See* Mouse pointer.

Pointing device A device that lets you interact with your computer by controlling the movement of the mouse pointer on your computer screen; examples include a mouse, trackball, touchpad, pointing stick, on-screen touch pointer, or a tablet.

Pointing device action A movement you execute with your computer's pointing device to communicate with the computer; the five basic pointing device actions are point, click, double-click, drag, and right-click.

Pop-up ad An advertisement that appears on your screen that, if you click or tap it, may place spyware on your computer.

Pop-up message A Windows notification that appears as a message in the lower-right corner of the screen.

Port The physical location on your computer where you connect the printer cable.

Power button The physical button on your computer that turns your computer on.

Preview pane A pane on the right side of a File Explorer window that shows the actual contents of a selected file without opening an app; might not work for some types of files, such as databases.

Print queue The list of files to be printed in a print job

Program A set of instructions written for a computer, such as an operating system program or an application program; also called an application or an app.

Properties Information that Windows automatically adds to a file when it is created, such as the filename, creation date, modified date, and size.

Quick Access buttons Buttons that appear at the bottom of the Windows Action Center; click or tap to perform common actions such as turning WiFi on or off.

Quick Access toolbar A small toolbar on the left side of a Microsoft application program window's title bar, containing icons that you click or tap to quickly perform common actions, such as saving a file.

Quick Access view A list of frequently-used folders and recently used files that appears when you first open File Explorer.

Quick action button A type of notification that appears at the bottom of the Action Center pane that lets you access important settings with one click or tap, such as Airplane mode.

RAM (Random Access Memory) The storage location that is part of every computer, that temporarily stores open apps and document data while a computer is on.

Reader A Microsoft app that lets you open and view PDF (Portable Document Format) and XPS (XML Paper Specification) files.

Reading list A list of websites you save for future reference; available through the Hub button in Microsoft Edge.

Reading View In the Microsoft Edge web browser, a view that lets you view webpages without advertisements or unnecessary content in an easy-to-read format.

Recycle Bin A desktop object that stores folders and files you delete from your hard drive(s) and enables you to restore them.

Remote Desktop Connection A Windows accessory that lets you connect to another Windows computer on the same network or on the Internet.

Removable storage Storage media that you can easily transfer from one computer to another, such as DVDs, CDs, or USB flash drives.

Restore Down button On the right side of a maximized window's title bar, the center of three buttons; use to reduce a window to its last non-maximized size. In a restored window, this button changes to a Maximize button.

Ribbon In many Microsoft app windows, a horizontal strip near the top of the window that contains tabs (pages) of grouped command buttons that you click or tap to interact with the app.

Rich Text Format (RTF) The file format that the WordPad app uses to save files.

Right-click To press and release the right button on the pointing device; use to display a shortcut menu with commands you issue by left-clicking.

Rip To copy individual music tracks or entire CDs to your computer and create your own jukebox or playlist of media.

RTF *See* Rich Text Format.

ScreenTip A small box containing informative text that appears when you position the mouse over an object; identifies the object when you point to it.

Scroll To adjust your view to see portions of the app window that are not currently in a window.

Scroll arrow A button at each end of a scroll bar for adjusting your view in a window in small increments in that direction.

Scroll bar A vertical or horizontal bar that appears along the right or bottom side of a window when there is more content than can be displayed within the window, so that you can adjust your view.

Scroll box A box in a scroll bar that you can drag to display a different part of a window.

Search box A text box that searches to find installed programs and other Windows items.

Search critera The words or phrases you type to describe what you want to find in a web search; also called keywords.

Search engine A program provided by a search provider's website that lets you search through a collection of information found on the Internet.

Search provider A company that provides a search engine directly from Edge or Internet Explorer to look for information found on the Internet.

Search Tools tab A tab that appears in the File Explorer window after you click or tap the Search text box; lets you specify a specific search location, limit your search, repeat previous searches, save searches, and open a folder containing a found file.

Select To change the appearance of an item by clicking, double-clicking, or dragging across it, to indicate that you want to perform an action on it.

Select pointer The mouse pointer shape that looks like a white arrow pointing toward the upper-left corner of the screen.

Settings app A Windows 10 app containing nine touch-friendly categories of the most commonly used Windows settings; more advanced settings are found in the Control Panel desktop app.

Shared printer A type of print device that can be used with other network computers.

Shortcut An icon that acts as a link to an app, file, folder, or device that you use frequently.

Shortcut menu A menu of context-appropriate commands for an object that opens when you right-click or press it.

Shut down To exit the operating system and turn off your computer.

Sign in To select a user account name and enter a password when a computer starts up, giving access to that user's files. Also called log in.

Single-click *See* Click.

Skype video A Microsoft program that lets you talk to another person in real time while viewing the other party using your device's video camera.

Slideshow A rotating display of pictures; the Personalization settings in the Settings app lets you set your desktop background to a slideshow using pictures you choose.

Snap Assist feature The Windows 10 feature that lets you drag a window to the left or right side of the screen, where it "snaps" to fill that half of the screen and displays remaining open windows as thumbnails you click or tap to fill the other half.

Sort Change the order of, such as the order of files or folders in a window, based on criteria such as date, file size, or alphabetical by filename.

Spam Unsolicited mass email messages.

Spin box A text box with up and down arrows; you can type a setting in the text box or click or tap the arrows to increase or decrease the setting.

Spooling *See* Background printing.

Spyware Software that tries to collect personal information or change computer settings without your consent.

Start button A button in the lower left corner of the Windows 10 screen that you click or tap to open the Start menu.

Start menu Appears after you click or tap the Start button; provides access to all programs, documents, and settings on the computer.

Steps Recorder A Windows accessory that lets you record computer actions to document a task; can be useful when communicating with technical support personnel.

Streaming media A technique for transferring media so that it can be processed as a steady and continuous stream. The Windows Media Player delivers streaming video, live broadcasts, sound, and music playback over the Internet.

Streaming music Music that you can listen to as it is being downloaded from the web.

Subfolder A folder within another folder.

Swipe A gesture that involves dragging your finger with a flicking motion at the end of a movement.

Sync *See* File syncing

System icons Images you can set to appear on the taskbar, such as clock, volume, and power settings; choose which icons appear at Settings > System > Notifications & actions > Select which icons appear on the taskbar.

System settings In the Settings app, the category of settings that let you control your screen display, notifications, apps, power, and storage.

Tab A page on an application program's Ribbon, or in a dialog box, that contains a group of related commands and settings.

Tablet mode A Windows 10 view in which tiles fill the screen; a Windows device without a keyboard will open in tablet mode by default.

Tapping The act of touching and removing your finger on an item, such as a tile or icon, to select it.

Task view A new Windows 10 area, accessible from the Task view button on the taskbar, that lets you switch applications and create multiple desktops (also called virtual desktops).

Taskbar The horizontal bar at the bottom of the Windows 10 desktop; displays icons representing apps, folders, and/or files on the left, and the Notification area, containing the date and time and special program messages, on the right.

Text box An area in a Windows program that you click or tap to enter text.

Theme A customized user interface that includes a desktop background, screen saver, pointers, sounds, icons, and fonts.

Third-party cookie A file created by a website you are not currently viewing, such as a banner ad on the current website you are viewing, that stores information on your computer, such as your preferences and history.

Thread An instant message conversation that consists of text exchanges.

Thumbnails Small images of open windows; appear when using Snap Assist, where the main window occupies half the screen and thumbnails occupy the other half, ready for you to select one to fill the other half of the screen.

Tile A shaded rectangle on the Windows 10 Start menu that represents an app. *See also* App *and* Application program.

Time & Language settings A category in the Settings app that lets you set your computer's time zone, region, and language.

Title bar The shaded top border of a window that displays the name of the window, folder, or file and the app name. Darker shading indicates the active window.

Toolbar In an application program, a set of buttons, lists, and menus you can use to issue program commands.

Trojan Horse A program that appears to be useful and to come from a legitimate source, but actually causes problems, such as gathering personal information or deleting files.

Uniform Resource Locator (URL) A webpage's address.

Universal apps *See* Windows 10 apps.

Unpin To remove a pinned item from the taskbar or Start menu.

URL *See* Uniform Resource Locator.

USB flash drive A removable storage device for folders and files that you plug into a USB port on your computer; makes it easy to transport folders and files to other computers. Also called a pen drive, flash drive, jump drive, keychain drive, or thumb drive.

USB port An external hardware interface that enables you to connect to a USB device as a plug and play device.

User account A special area in a computer's operating system where users can store their own files and preferences.

User interface The controls that let you interact with an operating system or an application program (app).

User profile In the Xbox app, the information that identifies you to other game players and tracks your gaming achievements.

View In a window, a set of appearance choices for folder contents, such as Large Icons view or Details view.

Virtual desktop An additional desktop that you can create in Windows 10, with its own taskbar; created using the Task View button on the taskbar.

Web Consists of websites located on computers around the world connected through the Internet.

Web address A unique address on the Internet where a webpage resides. *See also* URL.

Web browsers Software applications that you use to "surf the web," or display, navigate, and interact with webpages.

Web Notes In Microsoft Edge, page annotations that you can make using a on-screen pen, highlighter, or typed notes tool; annotated pages can then be sent to your Reading list or shared with others.

Webpages Specially formatted documents that contain highlighted words, phrases, and graphics that open other webpages when you click or tap them.

Website A location on the World Wide Web that contains webpages linked together.

Window A rectangular-shaped work area that displays an app or a collection of files, folders, and Windows tools.

Window control buttons The set of three buttons on the right side of a window's title bar that let you control the window's state, such as minimized, maximized, restored to its previous open size, or closed.

Windows 10 apps Apps (application programs) for Windows 10 that often have a single purpose, such as Photos, News, or OneDrive.

Windows 10 desktop An electronic work area that lets you organize and manage your information, much like your own physical desktop.

Windows 10 UI The Windows 10 user interface. *See also* User interface.

Windows accessories Application programs (apps), such as Paint or WordPad, that come with the Windows 10 operating system.

Windows Action Center A pane that appears in the lower right corner of the Windows 10 screen that lets you quickly view system notifications and selected settings; also has Quick Action buttons to perform common actions in one click or tap.

Windows app Small program available for free or for purchase in the Windows Store; can run on Windows desktops, laptops, tablets, and phones.

Windows Defender Software included in Windows 10 that protects your computer against viruses and spyware.

Windows Fax and Scan A Windows accessory that lets you send and receive faxed documents without having a fax machine.

Windows Firewall A Windows feature that monitors all communication between your computer and the Internet and prevents unsolicited inbound traffic from the Internet from entering your computer.

Windows Journal A Windows accessory that lets you handwrite notes and drawings with a graphics tablet or a tablet PC.

Windows Media Player A Windows program that allows you to play video, sound, and mixed-media files.

Windows Search The Windows feature that lets you look for files and folders on your computer storage devices; to search, type text in the Search text box in the title bar of any open window, or click or tap the Start button and type text in the search text box.

Windows SmartScreen Filter A Windows 10 feature that blocks malicious websites and downloads; useful against phishing, a realistic-looking email, pop-up, or website that asks for personal information in order to defraud you.

Wireless connection A type of connection that uses radio waves or microwaves, instead of cables, to maintain communications.

Wireless printer A type of printer that is connected to either a wired or wireless network to which you have access.

Wizard A series of questions that appears in selected Control Panel areas that sets your preferences for that area.

World Wide Web (WWW) *See* Web.

Worm A computer virus that can spread without human action across networks.

Xbox One A Microsoft gaming system consisting of a console and wireless handheld controller, featuring sophisticated electronics, graphics, and controls.

Xbox Live A Microsoft gaming community and media delivery service.

XML Paper Specification (XPS) A secure fixed-layout format—similar to an Adobe PDF file—developed by Microsoft that retains the format you intended on a monitor or printer.

XPS *See* XML Paper Specification.

XPS Viewer A Windows accessory that comes with Windows 10, which lets you open and view XPS (XML Paper Specification) documents.

Index